I0482627

U.S. COMMISSION ON CIVIL RIGHTS

The U.S. Commission on Civil Rights is an independent, bipartisan agency established by Congress in 1957. It is directed to:

- Investigate complaints alleging that citizens are being deprived of their right to vote by reason of their race, color, religion, sex, age, disability, or national origin, or by reason of fraudulent practices.

- Study and collect information relating to discrimination or a denial of equal protection of the laws under the Constitution because of race, color, religion, sex, age, disability, or national origin, or in the administration of justice.

- Appraise federal laws and policies with respect to discrimination or denial of equal protection of the laws because of race, color, religion, sex, age, disability, or national origin, or in the administration of justice.

- Serve as a national clearinghouse for information in respect to discrimination or denial of equal protection of the laws because of race, color, religion, sex, age, disability, or national origin.

- Submit reports, findings, and recommendations to the President and Congress.

- Issue public service announcements to discourage discrimination or denial of equal protection of the laws.

MEMBERS OF THE COMMISSION

Martin Castro, Chairman

Abigail Thernstrom, Vice Chair

Roberta Achtenberg

Todd Gaziano

Gail Heriot

Peter Kirsanow

David Kladney

Michael Yaki

Marlene Sallo, Staff Director

U.S. Commission on Civil Rights
1331 Pennsylvania Ave NW
Washington, DC 20425

(202) 376-8128

www.usccr.gov

This report is available on CD/DVD in ASCII Text, Adobe PDF, and Microsoft Word 2010. Please call (202) 376-8110.

Sexual Assault in the Military

U.S. Commission on Civil Rights

2013 Statutory Enforcement Report

UNITED STATES COMMISSION ON CIVIL RIGHTS

1331 PENNSYLVANIA AVENUE, NW, WASHINGTON, DC 20425
www. usccr.gov

President Barack Obama
Vice President Joe Biden
Speaker of the House John Boehner

On behalf of the U.S. Commission on Civil Rights, and pursuant to Public Law 103-419, I am pleased to transmit our 2013 Statutory Enforcement Report, *Sexual Assault in the Military*. The report is also available, in full, on the Commission's website. The purpose of the report is to examine how the Department of Defense and its Armed Services—the Army, Navy, Marine Corps, and Air Force—respond to Service members who report having been sexually assaulted and how they investigate and discipline Service members accused of perpetrating sexual assault.

The Commission staff conducted extensive research on the topic and, thereafter, the Commission held a briefing to hear the testimony of military officials, scholars, advocacy groups, and practitioners on the topic of sexual assault in the military. This data included responses from the Department of Defense and branches of the Armed Services, as well as interviews and statements from attorneys and advocates uniquely aware of the challenges sexual assault reports pose in the military setting. The Commission also received input and communication from members of the public affected by the topic.

The report revealed the need for greater data collection to better evaluate the efforts of the Department of Defense in addressing the issue of sexual assault in its ranks. The report also revealed the importance of commander accountability and standardized training. On July 12, 2013, the Commission approved this report. The vote was as follows: Commissioners Achtenberg, Castro, Kladney, Thernstrom, and Yaki supported the approval of the report; Commissioners Heriot and Kirsanow opposed the approval of the report; and Commissioner Gaziano abstained from voting on the report.

After extensive research conducted by the Commission and the testimony of the panelists involved in the briefing, we believe the report is both constructive and insightful and we hope it contributes to your addressing and resolving the challenges faced by those involved in the issue of sexual assault in our armed forces. We owe at least this much to protect the rights of those men and women in uniform who place themselves in harm's way to protect our rights and liberties.

For the Commission,

Martin R. Castro
Chairman

TABLE OF CONTENTS

EXECUTIVE SUMMARY

The U.S. Commission on Civil Rights chose to focus on sexual assault in the U.S. military for its annual 2013 Statutory Enforcement Report. This report examines how the Department of Defense and its Armed Services—the Army, Navy, Marine Corps, and Air Force (the Services)—respond to Service members who report having been sexually assaulted ("victims") and how it investigates and disciplines Service members accused of perpetrating sexual assault ("perpetrators"). This report also reviews how the military educates Service members and trains military criminal investigators and military lawyers about sexual assault offenses. The topic is both relevant and timely, as Congress is currently considering ways to address this issue.

The Commission has authority to examine questions related to sexual assault in the military because the issues involve both sex discrimination and the denial of equal protection in the administration of justice. The issue of sex discrimination involves female Service members, who represent 14 percent of the military population, but are disproportionately likely to be victims at a rate five times that of their male counterparts. The questions related to a possible denial of equal protection in the administration of justice led the Commission to examine cases in which sexual assault victims, as well as Service members accused of sexual assault, claim unfair treatment in the military justice system.

Through this report, the Commission sheds light on the scope, response, investigation, and discipline of sexual assault in the U.S. military. The Commission held a briefing on January 11, 2013 to hear the testimony of military officials, scholars, advocacy groups, and practitioners on the topic of sexual assault in the military. In response to written questions from the Commission, the Department of Defense and its Armed Services provided documents and other materials, including data on investigated sexual assault allegations, which the Commission analyzed. The results of these efforts are memorialized in this report.

The report reveals that the Department of Defense may benefit from greater data collection to better understand trends in sexual assault cases and to implement improvements in future initiatives. Although the Department of Defense has already implemented policies to reduce sexual and sexist material from the military workplace in an effort to reduce sexual harassment, the effects of such recent efforts have yet to be measured. The Department of Defense also has a plan to standardize sexual assault response and prevention training across the Services to promote best practices. There will be a need to track the success of such policies over time. Greater commander accountability for leadership failures to implement such policies, especially in cases where victims claim sexual assault at the hands of superiors within the chain of command, should also be considered. Without increased data collection, however, it is difficult to measure the effects of any new changes the military chooses to implement.

CHAPTER 1:   INTRODUCTION AND SCOPE OF THE PROBLEM

This report examines how the Department of Defense (DoD) and its Armed Services—the Army, Navy, Marine Corps, and Air Force (the Services)—respond to Service members who report having been sexually assaulted ("victims") and investigate and discipline Service members accused of perpetrating sexual assault ("perpetrators"). It also reviews how the military educates Service members and trains military criminal investigators and military lawyers about sexual assault offenses.[1]

It has been 50 years since the Commission has examined civil rights in the military.[2] The Commission has authority to examine questions related to sexual assault in the military because the issues involve both sex discrimination and the denial of equal protection in the administration of justice.[3] The issue of sex discrimination involves female Service members, who represent 14 percent of the military population, and the likelihood that they are over five times more likely to experience some form of sexual assault, as defined by the DoD, than their male counterparts.[4] The questions related to a possible denial of equal protection in the administration of justice led the Commission to examine reports of many cases in which sexual assault victims, as well as Service members accused of sexual assault, claim that they are not treated fairly in the military justice system.

This chapter addresses the scope of the problem of sexual assault in the military and how it compares to sexual assault in other populations. Chapter Two discusses the DoD's on-going efforts to prevent sexual assault. Chapter Three addresses military response to victims and barriers to reporting. Chapter Four describes the consequences for victims who report. Chapter Five addresses military investigations of sexual assaults, specialized training for criminal investigators and judge advocates, and trends in investigations revealed by DoD's data. Chapter

---

[1] For purposes of this report, the term "military" refers to the Armed Services.

[2] *See* U.S. COMM'N ON CIVIL RIGHTS, FAMILY HOUSING AND THE NEGRO SERVICEMAN (1963).

[3] *See* 42 U.S.C. § 1975a(2)(A) (2013) (The Commission has a duty to "study and collect[] information" concerning "discrimination or denials of equal protection of the laws under the Constitution of the United States because of . . . sex . . . or in the administration of justice."). *See also* 110 CONG. REC. 12714 (1964) (statement of Sen. Hubert H. Humphrey) (explaining that the Commission has jurisdiction over, among other things, "denials of equal protection in the administration of justice, whether or not related to [a protected class].").

[4] *See* DEP'T OF DEFENSE SEXUAL ASSAULT PREVENTION AND RESPONSE, DEPARTMENT OF DEFENSE ANNUAL REPORT ON SEXUAL ASSAULT IN THE MILITARY FISCAL YEAR 2012, VOLUME I, 81 (2013) [hereinafter *DoD FY12 Annual Report on Sexual Assault, Vol. 1*], *available at* http://www.sapr.mil/public/docs/reports/FY12_DoD_SAPRO_Annual_Report_on_Sexual_Assault-VOLUME_ONE.pdf (6.1 percent of female and 1.2 percent of male Service members indicate that they experienced some form of sexual assault, as defined by DoD policy, while on active duty within the past year).

Six examines how perpetrators are disciplined and reviews the broad discretion afforded to commanders.[5]

Background

The issue of sexual assault among Service members first garnered national attention during the Navy Tailhook scandal in 1991. Ninety Service members alleged that they were sexually assaulted or harassed by 119 Naval officers and 21 Marine Corps officers during a convention in Las Vegas.[6] Reports of sexual assault at Aberdeen Proving Ground in 1996 and the Air Force Academy in 2003 created more public awareness of the issue.[7] Most recently, the scandal at Lackland Air Force Base resulted in six drill sergeants being convicted of sexual misconduct, two others receiving administrative punishment, and nine trials still pending as of February 2013.[8] Efforts to address this issue by the military are being investigated by Congress.

Sexual assault in the military imposes significant costs and impairs mission readiness as a whole. According to a U.S. Department of Justice (DOJ) report, rape has the highest annual

---

[5] Throughout this report, the term "commander" refers to a commander with disposition authority for sexual assault allegations. While the term usually refers to the commanding officer of a unit (such as a company commander, battalion commander, or brigade commander), in April 2012, the Secretary of Defense withheld disposition authority for allegations of completed or attempted rape, sexual assault, and forcible sodomy from all commanders who do not possess at least Special court-martial convening authority and who are not in the grade of O-6 (i.e., colonel or Navy captain) or higher. Memorandum from the Secretary of Defense, Withholding Initial Disposition Authority Under the Uniform Code of Military Justice in Certain Sexual Assault Cases (Apr. 20, 2012), *available at* http://www.dod.gov/dodgc/images/withhold_authority.pdf, *effective by* June 28, 2012.

[6] *See* OFF. OF THE INSPECTOR GEN., THE TAILHOOK REPORT: THE OFFICIAL INQUIRY INTO THE EVENTS OF TAILHOOK '91 (1993). The website for the1996 PBS Frontline special, *The Navy Blues*, available at http://www.pbs.org/wgbh/pages/frontline/shows/navy/tailhook/, details the experience of 83 women and 7 men who were found to have been sexually harassed and/or assaulted by their peers at a Las Vegas convention in 1991. A total of 119 Navy and 21 Marine Corps officers were cited for incidents of indecent assault, indecent exposure, conduct unbecoming an officer, or failure to act in a proper leadership capacity while at the 35th Annual Tailhook Symposium in 1991. Critics of the handling of Tailhook, including former Navy Secretary James Webb, argued that members of Congress and the Navy overreacted, resulting in mismanaged investigations and violations of due process. *See* James Webb, *Witch Hunt in the Navy*, N.Y. TIMES, Oct. 6, 1992, at A23.

[7] *See* Art Pine, *Army Reacts Quickly to Sex Harassment Charges*, L.A. TIMES, Nov. 8, 1996, *available at* http://articles.latimes.com/1996-11-08/news/mn-62470_1_sexual-harassment (describing charges of sexual harassment and rape of over a dozen female recruits at an Army training base by superiors); *see also* Cathy Booth Thomas/Tucson, *Conduct Unbecoming*, TIME, Mar. 6, 2003, *available at* http://www.time.com/time/magazine/article/0,9171,428045,00.html (stating over 20 women, who were either former cadets or enrolled in the Air Force Academy, charged officials with failing to investigate sexual assaults, discouraging reporting, and retaliating against those who reported assaults).

[8] Molly Hennessy-Fiske, *Air Force Defends Handling of Sex Scandal*, L.A. TIMES, Jan. 23, 2013, *available at* http://articles.latimes.com/2013/jan/23/nation/la-na-lackland-hearing-20130124.

victim cost of any non-fatal crime.[9] The costs include short-term medical care, long-term and short-term mental health services, lost productivity, and pain and suffering.

Military sexual assault also impairs military readiness and disrupts unit cohesion. Data indicates that 55 percent of female victims and 38 percent of male victims are sexually harassed and stalked by the perpetrator who sexually assaults them.[10] When a victim is sexually assaulted at a military installation, the victim's job performance is impaired and mission readiness is hurt.[11]

Definition of "Sexual Assault"

The Uniform Code of Military Justice (UCMJ) criminalizes various forms of unwanted sexual contact and includes a broader range of conduct than is generally understood in common usage of the term "sexual assault" or as typically used in civilian criminal statutes.[12] The term "sexual assault," as defined by the DoD, incorporates sexual contact offenses, as well as sexual penetration offenses. Current DoD policy defines "Sexual Assault" as:

> Intentional sexual contact characterized by use of force, threats, intimidation, or abuse of authority or when the victim does not or cannot consent. The term includes a broad category of sexual offenses consisting of the following specific UCMJ offenses: rape, sexual assault, aggravated sexual contact, abusive sexual

---

[9] TED R. MILLER ET AL., U.S. DEP'T OF JUST., OFF. OF JUST. PROGRAMS, NAT'L INST. OF JUST., VICTIM COSTS AND CONSEQUENCES: A NEW LOOK 1, 9 (Jan. 1996), *available at* www.ncjrs.gov/pdffiles/victcost.pdf (noting that the majority of these costs are related to medical and mental healthcare, and "if rape's effect on the victim's quality of life is quantified, the average rape costs $87,000—many times greater than the cost of prison . . . ."); *see* Christine Hansen & Kate B. Summers, *A Considerable Sacrifice: The Costs of Sexual Violence in the U.S. Armed Forces*, Yale Manifesta 1, 38, 42 (2005).

[10] *See* LINDSAY M. ROCK ET AL., DEF. MANPOWER DATA CTR. (DMDC), 2010 WORKPLACE AND GENDER RELATIONS SURVEY OF ACTIVE DUTY MEMBERS: OVERVIEW REPORT ON SEXUAL ASSAULT 30 (2011) [hereinafter *2010 DoD Gender Relations Survey*], *available at* http://servicewomen.org/SAPRO_Reports/DMDC_2010_WGRA_Overview_Report_of_Sexual_Assault.pdf .

[11] Sixty-seven percent of female and 73 percent of male Service members who experienced unwanted sexual contact said the most serious incident occurred at a military installation; 41 percent of females and 49 percent of males said it occurred during duty hours; and 58 percent of females and 35 percent of males thought that, as a result, their work performance decreased. DMDC, 2012 WORKPLACE AND GENDER RELATIONS SURVEY OF ACTIVE DUTY MEMBERS: OVERVIEW REPORT ON SEXUAL ASSAULT 21-22, 67 (2013) [hereinafter *2012 DoD Gender Relations Survey*], *available at* http://www.sapr.mil/public/docs/research/2012_Workplace_and_Gender_Relations_Survey_of_Active_Duty_Members-Survey_Note_and_Briefing.pdf. *See also* Capt. Megan N. Schmid, U.S. Air Force, *Combating a Different Enemy: Proposals to Change the Culture of Sexual Assault in the Military*, 55 VILL. L. REV. 475, 503-4 (2010).

[12] UCMJ Arts. 120 & 125; 10 U.S.C. §§ 920, 925 (2012). These statutes and others relevant to sexual assault in the military are listed in Appendix A to this report.

contact, forcible sodomy (forced oral or anal sex), or attempts to commit these acts.[13]

"Sexual contact" is defined in Article 120 of the UCMJ as:

> (A) touching, or causing another person to touch, either directly or through the clothing, the genitalia, anus, groin, breast, inner thigh, or buttocks of any person, with an intent to abuse, humiliate, or degrade any person; or (B) any touching, or causing another person to touch, either directly or through the clothing, any body part of any person, if done with an intent to arouse or gratify the sexual desire of any person.[14]

Throughout this report, the term "sexual assault" will be used as defined by DoD, unless otherwise indicated.

DoD's sexual assault prevention and response (SAPR) policies do *not* address stalking, indecent exposure, and indecent conduct (which does not include physical contact), although the UCMJ criminalizes such actions.[15] DoD may consider these types of behaviors as sexual harassment and addresses them under separate policies.[16]

---

[13] DOD DIRECTIVE 6495.01, SEXUAL ASSAULT PREVENTION AND RESPONSE (SAPR) PROGRAM 18 (Jan. 23, 2012, Incorporating Change 1, Apr. 30, 2013), *available at* http://www.dtic.mil/whs/directives/corres/pdf/649501p.pdf. The legal definitions of the various forms of sexual offenses are found in Articles 120 and 125 of the UCMJ and are listed in Appendix A to this report. The DoD Directives are overseen directly by the Secretary of Defense and exclusively establish policy, assign responsibilities, and delegate authority to different defense components without addressing procedures. *See* OVERVIEW OF DEP'T OF DEF. ISSUANCES, DOD WASHINGTON HEADQUARTERS SERVICES, *available at* http://www.dtic.mil/whs/directives/corres/writing/DoD_Issuances.ppt. In comparison, DoD Instructions contain implementation of directives and can include overarching procedures. *See id.*

[14] UCMJ Art. 120; 10 U.S.C. §§ 920 (2012).

[15] Before June 2012, stalking, indecent exposure, and indecent conduct were included in UCMJ Article 120—the article that defines sexual assault—but such conduct was not included in the SAPR policies. *See* UCMJ Art. 120a; 10 U.S.C. § 920 (2012).

[16] *See* DOD DIRECTIVE 1350.2, DEPARTMENT OF DEFENSE MILITARY EQUAL OPPORTUNITY (MEO) PROGRAM (Aug. 18, 1995, Incorporating Change 1, May 7, 1997, Certified Current as of Nov. 21, 2003), *available at* http://www.uscg.mil/hq/cg00/cg00h/History_files/DOD_EO_Manual.pdf. *See also* Army Regulation (AR) 600-20, Army Command Policy (Sept. 20, 2012), Chapter 7, Prevention of Sexual Harassment, and Appendix D, Equal Opportunity/Sexual Harassment Complaint Processing System; SECRETARY OF THE NAVY INSTRUCTION (SECNAVINST) 5300.26D, DEPARTMENT OF THE NAVY (DON) POLICY ON SEXUAL HARASSMENT (Jan. 3, 2006); SECNAVINST 5354.1, POLICY ON MILITARY EQUAL OPPORTUNITY COMPLAINT PROCESSING (JAN. 2, 1997); MARINE CORPS ORDER (MCO) 1000.9A, SEXUAL HARASSMENT (MAY 30, 2006); MCO P5354.1D WITH CHANGE 1, MARINE CORPS EQUAL OPPORTUNITY (EO) MANUAL (Apr. 14, 2003); and AIR FORCE INSTRUCTION (AFI) 36-2706, MILITARY EQUAL OPPORTUNITY PROGRAM (Oct. 5, 2011).

Prevalence of Sexual Assault in the Military

The Department of Defense's Annual Reports

Since DoD began maintaining data on reported sexual assaults, the number of reported sexual assaults has increased from 1,700 in calendar year 2004 to 3,374 in fiscal year (FY) 2012.[17] Since sexual assault is an underreported crime, it is difficult to determine whether a variation in reports of sexual assault correlates to a variation in the actual number of incidents of sexual assault. That being said, the number of reports reflects how comfortable victims feel coming forward. According to some, "If the SAPRO is truly accomplishing its goals, one should see increased initial reporting as victims feel more comfortable and then a decrease in rates of reported victimization over time." [18]

In fiscal years 2011 and 2012, information was available on three-quarters of the sexual assault reports because these reports were unrestricted.[19] The vast majority of Service member and civilian victims who made an unrestricted report of sexual assault were women (88 percent).[20] The vast majority of those accused were men (90 percent in FY 2012; 89 percent in FY 2011).[21] It is worth noting that the military is approximately 86 percent male and 14 percent female.[22]

Approximately half of those accused of sexual assault were junior enlisted Service members (grades E-1 to E-4); approximately a quarter were enlisted members with supervisory duties (grades E-5 to E-9); and four percent were officers.[23] Service members were victims in 77 percent of the unrestricted reports investigated in 2012 and 76 percent of those investigated in

---

[17] *See DoD FY12 Annual Report on Sexual Assault, Vol.,* at 58-59. The number of reports has increased each year, except for a small decrease in 2007 and 2010. *Id.*

[18] Jessica A. Turchik & Susan M. Wilson, *Sexual Assault in the U.S. Military: A Review of the Literature and Recommendations for the Future,* 15:4 AGGRESSION AND VIOLENT BEHAV. 267, 274 (2010).

[19] *See* Chapter 3, *infra,* at 15 for a discussion about restricted versus unrestricted reporting options.

[20] *DoD FY12 Annual Report on Sexual Assault, Vol. 1* at 81; *See* DEP'T OF DEF., DEPARTMENT OF DEFENSE FISCAL YEAR 2011 ANNUAL REPORT ON SEXUAL ASSAULT IN THE MILITARY 53 (2012) [hereinafter *DoD FY11 Annual Report on Sexual Assault*], *available at* http://www.sapr.mil/public/docs/reports/Department_of_Defense_Fiscal_Year_2011_Annual_Report_on_Sexual_Assault_in_the_Military.pdf.

[21] *DoD FY12 Annual Report on Sexual Assault, Vol. 1* at 83; *DoD FY11 Annual Report on Sexual Assault* at 54.

[22] *See* DoD, ACTIVE DUTY MILITARY PERSONNEL BY RANK/GRADE (Sept. 30, 2012), *available at* http://siadapp.dmdc.osd.mil/personnel/MILITARY/rg1209.pdf; DoD, ACTIVE DUTY MILITARY PERSONNEL BY RANK/GRADE (Sept. 30, 2012) (Women Only), *available at* http://siadapp.dmdc.osd.mil/personnel/MILITARY/rg1209f.pdf.

[23] *DoD FY12 Annual Report on Sexual Assault, Vol. 1* at 84; *DoD FY11 Annual Report on Sexual Assault* at 53-55. The remaining 15 percent of perpetrators in FY 2012 and 23 percent in FY 2011 were either unidentified or not Service members.

2011.[24] The majority (61 percent in 2012, 68 percent in 2011) of the reported sexual offenses involved a completed, penetration-type offense—rape, aggravated sexual assault, and forcible sodomy. Over a third (39 percent in 2012, 32 percent in 2011) involved sexual contact offenses (i.e., non-penetration type sexual offenses).[25]

The remaining 816 reports in FY 2012 and 753 reports in FY 2011 were restricted, confidential, and not investigated, thus no additional information is known about these incidents.

The Department of Defense's Anonymous Surveys of Active-Duty Service Members

Since 1988, the DoD has conducted periodic anonymous surveys asking active-duty Service members about a variety of types of unwanted sexual contact and unwanted gender-related behaviors, such as sexual harassment.[26] It is difficult to compare earlier surveys to more current ones due to differences in survey methodology, changes in the military's mission and the surges in forces and military climate changes due to the wars in Afghanistan and Iraq. Beginning in 2006, the anonymous surveys asked about "unwanted sexual contact" while on active duty within the past year.[27] The 2006 survey marked the first time that male Service members were asked about sexual assault. The anonymous surveys captured data related to both reported and unreported sexual assaults.

The most recent survey, conducted in 2012, indicated that 6.1 percent of female Service members and 1.2 percent of male Service members reported being the victim of some form of unwanted sexual contact within the past year.[28] According to the DoD:

> For women, the rate was statistically significantly higher in 2012 than in 2010 (6.1% vs. 4.4%); there was no statistically significant difference between 2012 and 2006 (6.1% vs. 6.8%). There was no statistically significant difference for

---

[24] *DoD FY12 Annual Report on Sexual Assault, Vol. 1* at 82; *DoD FY11 Annual Report on Sexual Assault* at 38.

[25] *DoD FY12 Annual Report on Sexual Assault, Vol. 1* at 62; *DoD FY11 Annual Report on Sexual Assault* at 38. The remaining incidents (less than 1 percent) involved an attempt to commit a sexual offense.

[26] *See* DMDC, 1995 SEXUAL HARASSMENT SURVEY (1996), *available at* http://www.dtic.mil/cgi-bin/GetTRDoc?AD=ADA323942 (includes 1998 and 1995 survey results); DMDC, ARMED FORCES 2002 SEXUAL HARASSMENT SURVEY (2003), *available at* http://www.defense.gov/news/Feb2004/d20040227shs1.pdf. These earlier surveys indicate a decrease in the rate of sexual assault between 1988 and 2002.

[27] *2010 DoD Gender Relations Survey* at 1-2 ("Unwanted sexual contact refers to a range of activities that the Uniform Code of Military Justice (UCMJ) prohibits . . . .").

[28] *2012 DoD Gender Relations Survey* at 2

men in the overall rate between 2012 and 2010 and 2006 (1.2% vs. 0.9% and 1.8%).[29]

The 2012 survey also indicated that 23 percent of women and 4 percent of men reported experiencing unwanted sexual contact since enlistment.[30] Because approximately 85 percent of military personnel are male,[31] the total number of men who have experienced unwanted sexual contact is estimated to be equal to or greater than the number of women who have experienced such contact.[32] Based on this survey, the DoD estimates that approximately 26,000 Service members experienced some form of unwanted sexual contact, ranging from sexual contact crimes such as groping, to rape in 2012.[33]

The anonymous survey data from 2012 also revealed that many victims were being targeted by a Service member with superior rank and about half were targeted by a co-worker.[34] Ninety-four percent of the female victims stated their perpetrator was male.[35] In contrast, male victims indicated that their perpetrator was slightly more likely to be female (40 percent) than male (35 percent) in the 2010 survey, as results were not reportable for male victims in 2012.[36]

---

[29] *Id.*

[30] *Id.* at 137-38.

[31] The active-duty military population in the DoD (including cadets and midshipmen in the Service academies) is approximately 1.4 million members, 15 percent of whom are women. Of the approximately 237,000 military officers, 16 percent are women. *See* DEP'T OF DEF., ACTIVE DUTY MILITARY STRENGTH REPORT FOR FEB. 28, 2013, *available at* http://siadapp.dmdc.osd.mil/personnel/MILITARY/ms1_1302.pdf.

[32] *See* James Dao, *In Debate Over Military Sexual Assault, Men Are Overlooked Victims*, N.Y. TIMES, Jun. 23, 2013 (describing that although women are more likely to be sexually assaulted and file a formal complaint, the majority of victims are thought to be men), *available at* http://www.nytimes.com/2013/06/24/us/in-debate-over-military-sexual-assault-men-are-overlooked-victims.html?pagewanted=all&_r=0.

[33] *See* Courtney Kube and Jim Miklaszewski, *Pentagon's Annual Report on Sexual Assault Shows Alarming Rise*, NBC NEWS (May 6, 2013), *available at* http://usnews.nbcnews.com/_news/2013/05/06/18090415-pentagons-annual-report-on-sexual-assault-shows-alarming-rise?lite. The DoD estimated 19,000 incidents annually based on the 2010 survey data. *See also Panetta: Could be 19,000 military sex assaults each year*, NBC NEWS (Jan. 18, 2012), http://usnews.nbcnews.com/_news/2012/01/18/10184222-panetta-could-be-19000-military-sex-assaults-each-year?lite.

[34] *2012 DoD Gender Relations Survey* at 37-38 (In 2012, 25 percent of female victims and 27 percent of male victims who experienced unwanted sexual contact said they were victimized by someone in their chain of command; 38 percent of female victims and 17 percent of male victims said they were victimized by someone of a higher rank; and 57 percent of female victims and 52 percent of male victims said there were victimized by a military co-worker); *see also 2010 DoD Gender Relations Survey* at 21-22 (In 2010, 23 percent of female victims and 26 percent of male victims said they were victimized by someone in their chain of command; 39 percent of females and 25 percent of males said they were victimized by someone of a higher rank.).

[35] *2012 DoD Gender Relations Survey* at 32.

[36] *2010 DoD Gender Relations Survey* at 18. The 2012 DoD Gender Relations Survey did not provide this information as it was "not reportable." *See 2012 DoD Gender Relations Survey* at 32-35.

Of the active-duty Service members who stated that they had experienced unwanted sexual contact in the past year, 34 percent of women and 24 percent of men indicated they reported the incident to a military and/or civilian authority on the survey in 2012,[37] in contrast to the 2010 survey which revealed that only 29 percent of female victims and 14 percent of male victims reported.[38] In both surveys, over half of the female victims said they had been the victim of completed or attempted penetration (57 percent in 2012 and 58 percent in 2010).[39] In addition, 15 percent of the male victims in 2012 and 31 percent in 2010 stated they had been the victim of completed or attempted penetration.[40] Of those who stated they had experienced unwanted sexual contact, 34 percent of men and 10 percent of women declined to specify the form of unwanted sexual contact they experienced.[41] Compared this to the number of reported incidents, this data suggests that Service members are more likely to report penetration-type sexual offenses than sexual contact offenses.

Prevalence of Sexual Assault in the Military Compared to Other Populations

The Commission received testimony that 18- to 24-year-olds are at maximum risk for sexual assault.[42] Thus, any community or institution, like the military or any college, that brings together high concentrations of young people is arguably likely to have higher rates of sexual assault than the general population.[43]

----

[37] *2012 DoD Gender Relations Survey* at 79. There is no way to know how many unreported incidents would have been substantiated if they had been investigated.

[38] *2010 DoD Gender Relations Survey* at 35-36. In a 2010 Air Force Survey, 17 percent of women and 6 percent of men who had experienced sexual assault said they formally reported it. DARBY MILLER ET AL., GALLUP GOV'T, FINDINGS FROM THE 2010 PREVALENCE/INCIDENCE SURVEY OF SEXUAL ASSAULT IN THE AIR FORCE 34 (2010).

[39] *2012 DoD Gender Relations Survey* at 14; *2010 DoD Gender Relations Survey* at 13.

[40] *2012 DoD Gender Relations Survey* at 15; *2010 DoD Gender Relations Survey* at 13.

[41] *2012 DoD Gender Relations Survey* at 14-15; *2010 DoD Gender Relations Survey* at 13.

[42] David Lisak, Ph.D., testimony, *Briefing Before the U.S. Commission on Civil Rights*, Washington, D.C., Jan. 11, 2013 [hereinafter *Briefing Transcript*], at 102, *available at* http://www.eusccr.com/msa1.htm.

[43] *See* Statement of Dr. Nathan W. Galbreath, Senior Executive Advisor, Accountability and Assessment, DoD, Sexual Assault Prevention & Response Office (SAPRO), submitted to the U.S. Commission on Civil Rights 4 [hereinafter *Galbreath Statement*], *available at* http://www.eusccr.com/msa1.htm. *Cf.* Antonia Abbey, *Alcohol-Related Sexual Assault: A Common Problem Among College Students*, 14 J. STUD. ON ALCOHOL SUPPL.118, 119 (2002); Antonia Abbey et al., *The Relationship Between the Quantity of Alcohol Consumed and the Severity of Sexual Assaults Committed by College Men*, 18:7 J. INTERPERSONAL VIOLENCE 813 (2003); *see also* DARBY MILLER ET AL., GALLUP GOV'T, FINDINGS FROM THE 2010 PREVALENCE/INCIDENCE SURVEY OF SEXUAL ASSAULT IN THE AIR FORCE 4-7 (2010). Young adults attending military academies also cite alcohol as a significant factor in a majority of sexual assaults on campus. *See* DMDC, 2011 SERVICE ACADEMY GENDER RELATIONS FOCUS GROUPS 7-11, 44-47, 85-86, 138-39 (2011), *available at* http://www.dtic.mil/cgi-bin/GetTRDoc?AD=ADA551683. Recent studies have shown that military academy students' perceptions of the

(cont'd)

The military environment is unlike college/university settings and even other civilian settings for a variety of reasons. For example, Service members tend to live in an insular environment and are required to live and work with people not of their own choosing. Additionally, the military environment fosters an expectation of group cohesion and loyalty. As a result, these expectations and cultural norms can hamper the ability of military personnel to transfer out of their unit if they are feeling harassed or if they have been victims of assault. In contrast, college students may have greater ability to remove themselves from their environment, either temporarily or permanently. Also for Service members, attempts to transfer out of their unit may be denied and leaving their military unit without permission may lead to criminal penalties for being absent without leave (AWOL) or for insubordination.

Another challenge in comparing military sexual assault rates to those researched in other young populations, such as colleges or universities, lies in the fact that various available studies use different definitions for the term "sexual assault" and also implement different study methodologies.[44] Therefore, available data does not provide a meaningful comparison. For example, a large study of sexual assault on college campuses, conducted by the National Institute of Justice in 1997, estimated that the victimization rate was 4.9 percent for a one-year period.[45] However, there has not been a study focused on college and university women that would provide insight into whether sexual assault rates in that population have changed over the past 15 years. In addition, the DoD includes a wider range of sexual contact crimes, such as groping, in its definition of sexual assault.[46] Nationally, the DOJ reported a decline in the sexual assault rate against women in the general population from a peak of 5 per 1,000 women (0.5 percent) in 1995 to 2.1 per 1,000 women (0.21 percent) in 2005, and remained unchanged from 2005 to 2010.[47]

(cont'd from previous page)

rate of sexual assault have shifted. *See* DMDC, 2011 SERVICE ACADEMY GENDER RELATIONS FOCUS GROUPS 11, 49, 94, 141 (in comparison to the previous 2008 survey, fewer students in 2010 at West Point, the Naval Academy, the Air Force Academy, and the Coast Guard Academy perceived that the military academies had lower sexual assault incident rates than civilian colleges/universities or were safer in that respect).

[44] *See Galbreath Statement* at 8; *see also* Tim Hoyt et al., *Military Sexual Trauma in Men: A Review of Reported Rates*, 12:3 J. TRAUMA & DISSOCIATION 244 (2011) (noting inconsistencies in definition and assessment of military sexual assault in various studies).

[45] *See* BONNIE S. FISHER ET AL., U.S. DEP'T OF JUST., OFF. OF JUST. PROGRAMS, BUREAU OF JUST. STATISTICS, THE SEXUAL VICTIMIZATION OF COLLEGE WOMEN 3 (2000), *available at* http://www.ncjrs.gov/pdffiles1/nij/182369.pdf.

[46] *Id.*

[47] MICHAEL PLANTY ET AL., U.S. DEP'T OF JUST., OFF. OF JUST. PROGRAMS, BUREAU OF JUST. STATISTICS, FEMALE VICTIMS OF SEXUAL VIOLENCE, 1994-2010 at 1 (2013), *available at* http://bjs.gov/content/pub/pdf/fvsv9410.pdf.

While the military does a better job than many college campuses in educating its members about and responding to sexual assault, military leaders have said that more can be done. As Pentagon spokesman George Little stated, "[It is] not good enough to compare [the military] to the rest of society . . . We must hold [the military] to a higher standard, and that's what the American people demand."[48]

---

[48] Austin Wright & Tim Mak, *DoD's Top Spokesman Rebukes Air Force Chief*, POLITICO, May 16, 2013, *available at* http://www.politico.com/morningdefense/0513/morningdefense10695.html.

CHAPTER 2:   MILITARY EFFORTS TO PREVENT SEXUAL ASSAULT

For over two decades, the military has been trying to address the issue of sexual assault. When measured effectively, prevention efforts have increased significantly in recent years. However, it is too soon to evaluate fully and properly the long-term effects of these new efforts.

Sexual Harassment and Sexual Assault

DoD and its Services understand the connection between sexual harassment and sexual assault. In response to sexual assaults at the Naval Tailhook convention in 1991, and the investigation that followed, Acting Navy Secretary Sean O'Keefe said, "We get it. . . . We know that the larger issue is a cultural problem which has allowed demeaning behavior and attitudes towards women to exist . . . ."[1] In 2009, a Defense Task Force similarly stated that "culture change is essential for the Military Services to improve how they prevent and address sexual assault."[2] Chairman of the Joint Chiefs of Staff Martin Dempsey stated that the ban on women in combat created a two-tiered military culture that fostered tolerance of sexual harassment and sexual assault.[3] In a public speech on April 2, 2013, Defense Secretary Chuck Hagel stated that "[c]reating a culture free of the scourge of sexual assault requires establishing an environment where dignity and respect is afforded to all, and where diversity is celebrated as one of our greatest assets as a force."[4]

At the Commission's briefing, Psychologist David Lisak, a frequent consultant to the military on its sexual assault prevention efforts, testified: "Research has shown that a climate in which

---

[1] Melissa Healy, *Pentagon Blasts Tailhook Probe, Two Admirals Resign*, L.A. TIMES, *reprinted in* THE TECH (Sept. . 25, 1992), http://tech.mit.edu/V112/N44/tailhook.44w.html. Former Navy Secretary and later Senator James Webb took issue with O'Keefe's statement. *See* James Webb, *Witch Hunt in the Navy*, N.Y. TIMES, Oct. 6, 1992.

[2] DoD, REPORT OF THE DEFENSE TASK FORCE ON SEXUAL ASSAULT IN THE MILITARY SERVICES at ES-1 (2009) [hereinafter *Report of the Defense Task Force*], *available at* http://www.ncdsv.org/images/SAPR_DTFSAMS_Report_Dec_2009.pdf.

[3] J.K. Trotter, *Highest-ranking Military Officer Ties Ban on Women to Sexual Assault*, THE ATLANTIC WIRE, Jan. 24, 2013, http://www.theatlanticwire.com/politics/2013/01/highest-ranking-military-officer-says-combat-ban-women-tied-sexual-assault/61386/. *See also* HELEN BENEDICT, THE LONELY SOLDIER: THE PRIVATE WAR OF WOMEN SERVING IN IRAQ 227 (2009) ("Many women believe that such recognition [of their service in combat] will win them more respect and so reduce sexual violence."); *id.* at 4-5, 135-136, 172, 227-229 (describing how women have, in fact, been serving in combat situations during the wars in Iraq and Afghanistan).

[4] Secretary of Defense Chuck Hagel, Message on Sexual Assault Awareness and Prevention Month (Apr. 2, 2013), *available at* http://www.defense.gov/Speeches/Speech.aspx?SpeechID=1763.

sexual harassment is perceived to be permissible conduct is one in which sexual harassment is more likely to occur. Further, when sexual harassment is more common, sexual assault is more common."[5] Dr. Lisak explained to the Commission that the military has the power to create a "climate [that] can either help to curtail a rapist's behavior, or it can facilitate and camouflage his behavior . . . ."[6]

Bystander Intervention Training

In order to address climates that may facilitate or camouflage sexual assault, the military recently implemented a method of sexual assault prevention training known as "bystander intervention training." This method encourages people to intervene safely when they see situations at risk for sexual assault.[7] The training is based on the understanding that most sexual assaults occur between people who know each other, and that behavior leading to a sexual assault usually begins in a social setting. Every Service branch now incorporates this bystander intervention through SAPR training.[8] The goals of the program are to educate the military community about the reality of sexual violence, to identify the times and places where sexual assaults are occurring, and to equip members of the community with the skills they need to intervene in high-risk situations.

Psychologist David Lisak stated that the military's implementation of bystander intervention training is of a magnitude never seen before: "Bystander education programs have been

---

[5] Statement of David Lisak, Ph.D. submitted to the U.S. Commission on Civil Rights 3 [hereinafter *Lisak Statement*], *available at* http://www.euscr.com/msa1.htm. An internal study by the Department of Veterans Affairs reported that "officers who permitted sexual harassment saw four times the level of rapes in their units." Anne G. Sadler et al., *Factors Associated with Women's Risk of Rape in the Military Environment*, AMER. J. INDUS. MED., 43:3, 262–73 (2003) (finding that increased rates of reported rape were associated with environmental factors such as officers allowing others to make demeaning remarks or gestures about women); Melanie S. Harned et al., *Sexual Assault and Other Types of Sexual Harassment by Workplace Personnel: A Comparison of Antecedents and Consequences,* 7 J. OCCUPATIONAL HEALTH PSYCHOL. 174, 180 (2002) (finding that, of military women who had been sexually assaulted, 99.7 percent had also been sexually harassed within the last 12 months with the definition of sexual harassment, consistent with the majority of social science literature on the topic, being "used throughout [the] article in a behavioral rather than a legal sense.")

[6] *Lisak Statement* at 3.

[7] *Galbreath Statement* at 12-13. It also encourages Service members to express disapproval of language and jokes that demean women. *See* Training videos and materials produced by DoD and the Services to the U.S. Commission on Civil Rights (on file with Commission).

[8] The military also uses a variety of other prevention interventions, including those that focus on obtaining consent, having healthy adult relationships, and encouraging responsible alcohol use. *Galbreath Statement* at 12-13.

partially implemented in many universities, but nowhere with the commitment of the U.S. Air Force. Virtually every member of the Air Force is or will be trained in bystander intervention."[9]

Dr. Galbreath, a psychologist in the DoD's Sexual Assault Prevention and Response Office (SAPRO), told the Commission that bystander intervention training seems to be having a positive impact: "There are a number of interventions that demonstrate short and long term improvements in knowledge, skills, behavioral intention, confidence, and victim empathy." [10] He stated the military's perspective is that, by "reinforcing these initiatives," the military "can produce a shift in its culture" so that "sexual assault prevention is understood as being one more way of looking out for your comrades in arms."[11]

In the DoD's 2012 survey, nearly all Service members thought the sexual assault training they received provided a good understanding of what actions are considered sexual assault, explained how sexual assault is a mission readiness problem, and taught them how to intervene when they witness a situation that poses a risk for sexual assault involving a Service member.[12]

Command Training and Efforts to Address Sexual Assault

The military recognizes that commanders set the climate in their units and should be held accountable if they allow environments that foster sexual harassment or sexual assault.[13] Therefore, in addition to the bystander intervention training that all Service members will receive, the military provides commanders with additional training aimed at preventing and responding to sexual assault. Legislation passed in 2013 established mandatory SAPR training requirements for new and prospective commanders. Pursuant to the legislation, the Secretary of Defense is required to include SAPR training for new or prospective commanders at all levels, which is tailored to the command position's responsibilities and leadership.[14] The legislation

---

[9] *Lisak Statement* at 4.

[10] *Galbreath Statement* at 13-14.

[11] *Id.*

[12] *2012 DoD Gender Relations Survey* at 230-31.

[13] *See* Testimony of Gen. Raymond T. Odierno, Chief of Staff of the Army, Gen. James F. Amos, Commandant of the Marine Corp, Adm. Jonathan Greenert, Chief of Naval Operations, Adm. Robert J. Papp, Jr., Commandant of the Coast Guard, *Hearing of the Senate Armed Services Committee*, June 4, 2013, at time markers 1:33-1:39, 2:24-2:30, http://www.senate.gov/isvp/?type=live&comm=armed&filename=armed060413.

[14] National Defense Authorization Act for Fiscal Year 2013, Pub. L. No. 112-239, § 574. DoD policy provides that Commanders should meet with the unit's Sexual Assault Response Coordinator (SARC) for one-on-one training within 30 days of taking command. DoD INSTRUCTION 6495.02, SEXUAL ASSAULT PREVENTION AND RESPONSE (SAPR) PROGRAM PROCEDURES 32 (Mar. 28, 2013), *available at* http://www.dtic.mil/whs/directives/corres/pdf/649502p.pdf.

also requires annual unit climate assessment surveys to assist commanders with improving prevention and response to sexual assaults.[15] Commanders also are required to receive training to help guide their decisions related to the needs of a sexual assault victim and the rights of the accused.[16]

The DoD is also directing its leadership to remove sexual and sexist material from the military workplace. In December 2012, under the leadership of General Mark Welsh, the Air Force conducted a sweep of pornography, military song books with offensive lyrics, and other military paraphernalia with images demeaning to women.[17] In May 2013, Secretary of Defense Chuck Hagel directed the other Services to follow suit.[18] It is too soon to know what effect these efforts will have.[19]

Commanders also may help eliminate sexual harassment through the performance evaluation process. For example, the Army has a regulation that encourages commanders and supervisors to discuss, during performance evaluations, their objectives and expectations related to the Equal Opportunity Programs and to document deviations from those programs.[20] Military leaders testified to the Senate Armed Services Committee that commanders are evaluated for

---

[15] National Defense Authorization Act for Fiscal Year 2013, Pub. L. No. 112-239, § 572.

[16] *See, e.g.,* DoD INSTRUCTION 6495.02 at Enclosure 10; DOD. SAPRO, EVALUATION OF PRE-COMMAND SEXUAL ASSAULT PREVENTION AND RESPONSE TRAINING, *available at* http://www.sapr.mil/public/docs/news/PreCommand_Training_Evaluation_Final_Report.pdf.

[17] Kristin Davis, *Welsh Battles Culture of Disrespect for Women*, AIR FORCE TIMES, Dec. 10, 2012. A January 2013 inspection found 33,216 items offensive or inappropriate in Air Force installations, including items specific to military history such as patches, coins, log books, and song books. U.S. Air Force, *Air Force Releases Results of Health and Welfare Inspection*, Jan. 18, 1013, http://www.af.mil/News/ArticleDisplay/tabid/223/Article/109840/air-force-releases-results-of-health-and-welfare-inspection.aspx.

[18] Memorandum from the Secretary of Defense, Sexual Assault Prevention and Response, 2 (May 6, 2013), *available at* http://usarmy.vo.llnwd.net/e2/c/downloads/294405.pdf.

[19] Nancy J. Parrish, President of Protect Our Defenders, argued that Gen. Welsh's sweep of offensive material did not go far enough. Because the sweep was announced ahead of time, Parrish argues that it gave Service members the opportunity to hide offensive material. Furthermore, the sweep did not extend to individual desks, cabinets, lockers, or military-issued computer hard drives, where much of the offensive content is located. *See* Statement of Nancy J. Parrish submitted to the U.S. Commission on Civil Rights 2 [hereinafter *Parrish Statement*], *available at* http://www.euscer.com/msa1.htm. *See also* Jennifer Hlad, *Does Social Media Add Fuel to Degrading Actions?*, STARS AND STRIPES, May 20, 2013, *available at* http://www.military.com/daily-news/2013/05/20/does-social-media-add-fuel-to-degrading-actions.html?comp=7000024213943&rank=1, (describing cyber-sexual harassment perpetrated by Service members and social media websites popular with Service members that contain jokes about rape and domestic violence).

[20] AR 600-20, Army Command Policy, Ch. 6-11a (Mar. 18, 2008).

their "command climate," which would include a tolerance of sexual harassment, but sexual harassment in the unit is not an explicit factor in their evaluations.[21]

Critiques of the Military's Efforts

Even in light of the military's recently-increased efforts to prevent sexual assault, some critics argue that more needs to be done to curtail sexual assault.[22] Victim advocacy groups argue that the issue needs to be addressed in the same way that integration of African Americans in the military was addressed, with stiff rules against sex-based bias and requirements that commanders uphold those rules or face dismissal.[23]

Professor and former military attorney, Victor Hansen, argues that the military is not going far enough:

> There exists within the military a culture against fully investigating and clearly identifying the command failings which may have contributed to the under-detection of these sexual assault crimes. The failure to fully investigate and identify these command failings sends a mixed message both to the Service members and to other commanders. They are left to wonder what further actions could or should be taken to detect, prevent, and suppress these crimes. . . . If, as the military claims, the solution to these problems rests with the military leadership, then that leadership must be much clearer in addressing command failings. The leadership culture must change.[24]

Other critics argue that sexual harassment and sexual assault would decrease if there were more women in key leadership positions.[25] The DoD's January 2013 decision to lift the ban on

---

[21] *See Hearing of the Senate Armed Services Committee*, June 4, 2013, at time markers 1:33 to 1:39, http://www.senate.gov/isvp/?type=live&comm=armed&filename=armed060413.

[22] *See* HELEN BENEDICT, THE LONELY SOLDIER: THE PRIVATE WAR OF WOMEN SERVING IN IRAQ 50 (2009) (comparing rules that now prohibit drill instructors from using racial epithets, but they may still denigrate recruits by using words like "girl" or "fairy"); *see also* MIC HUNTER, HONOR BETRAYED: SEXUAL ABUSE IN AMERICA'S MILITARY 40-41 (2007) (describing the inherent misogyny of comparing weak male performers to a "bunch of girls" or "lady boys", which must be battled at an institutional level similar to the earlier battles against racism).

[23] *Parrish Statement* at 11.

[24] Statement of Victor Hansen, Professor, New England School of Law, submitted to the U.S. Commission on Civil Rights 2 [hereinafter *Hansen Statement*], *available at* http://www.eusccr.com/msa1.htm.

[25] Capt. Megan N. Schmid, U.S. Air Force, *Combating a Different Enemy: Proposals to Change the Culture of Sexual Assault in the Military*, 55 VILL. L. REV. 475, 498-99 (2010) (recommending that women's token presence in the military needs to change, including increasing the number of women in key leadership positions, to transform the culture and end sexual assault).

women serving in combat may allow this theory to be tested in coming years by opening new paths for women to achieve positions at higher levels of authority.[26]

In sum, the DoD and the Services recognize that sexual harassment and negative views of women correlate with an increased rate of sexual assault.[27] They have attempted to remedy the problem by training commanders, beginning to purge sexually offensive material from the workplace, and educating Service members to become more active in protecting their colleagues through bystander intervention. While some critics argue this is still insufficient, the existing efforts have not been in place long enough to evaluate their effectiveness.

---

[26] *See* Martha McSally, *Women in Combat: Is the Current Policy Obsolete?*, 14 DUKE J. OF GENDER L. & POL'Y 1011, 1053 (2007) ("America needs a policy that assigns both men and women to positions for which they are qualified, with no limiting exclusions—based on physical and intellectual capabilities—leadership skills, and aptitude.").

[27] *See* Anne G. Sadler et al., *Factors Associated with Women's Risk of Rape in the Military Environment*, AMER. J. INDUS. MED., 43:3, 262–73 (2003) (finding that increased rates of reported rape were associated with environmental factors such as officers allowing others to make demeaning remarks or gestures about women); Melanie S. Harned et al., *Sexual Assault and Other Types of Sexual Harassment by Workplace Personnel: A Comparison of Antecedents and Consequences,* 7 J. OCCUPATIONAL HEALTH PSYCHOL. 174, 180 (2002) (finding that, of military women who had been sexually assaulted, 99.7 percent had also been sexually harassed within the last 12 months with the definition of sexual harassment, consistent with the majority of social science literature on the topic, being "used throughout [the] article in a behavioral rather than a legal sense."); *see also* HELEN BENEDICT, THE LONELY SOLDIER: THE PRIVATE WAR OF WOMEN SERVING IN IRAQ 50 (2009).

CHAPTER 3:   MILITARY RESPONSE TO VICTIMS

T he DoD has established a sexual assault response system that requires a wide variety of military personnel to respond to victims, including Victim Advocates, Sexual Assault Response Coordinators (SARCs), physicians, nurses, mental healthcare providers, and chaplains.

The Department of Defense's Sexual Assault Prevention and Response Office

The DoD established a Victim and Witness Assistance Program in 1994 to address victims of all crimes.[1] In October 2005, the DoD established the Sexual Assault Prevention and Response Office (SAPRO). In the FY11 National Defense Authorization Act, SAPRO's mission was codified to "serve[] as the single point of authority, accountability, and oversight for the sexual assault prevention and response (SAPR) program; and provide[] oversight to ensure that the military departments comply with SAPR program policy."[2] SAPRO's mission is limited to policy and data collection. It does not provide services to victims or hold offenders accountable. It does not have authority to intervene or advocate on behalf of a victim in any sexual assault investigation or case.[3] The Services are responsible for providing training, investigating incidents of sexual assault, holding offenders accountable, and providing victim services.[4]

Reporting Options

According to DoD's 2012 Workplace and Gender Relations survey, of the 67 percent of female Service members who did not report unwanted sexual contact to a military authority, 48 percent indicated that they did not report the unwanted sexual contact because the incidents were not

---

[1] DOD INSTRUCTION 1030.2, VICTIM AND WITNESS ASSISTANCE PROCEDURES (Dec. 23, 1994, superceded by revised DoD Instruction 1030.2 on June 4, 2004), *available at* http://www.dtic.mil/whs/directives/corres/pdf/103002p.pdf.

[2] Statement of Major General Gary S. Patton submitted to the U.S. Commission on Civil Rights 3 [hereinafter *Patton Statement*], *available at* http://www.eusccr.com/msa1.htm. However, medical care, legal processes, and criminal investigations remained the responsibility of other offices. *DoD FY11 Annual Report on Sexual Assault* at 68. SAPRO Headquarters currently consists of 11 civilian personnel and seven uniformed personnel: the Director, the Deputy Director, a Training Officer, and a Victim Assistance Officer.

[3] DoD Response to the U.S. Commission on Civil Rights' Interrogatory No. 50.

[4] DoD Inspector General comments to U.S. Commission on Civil Rights 3, June 14, 2013, in response to affected agency review.

serious enough to report.[5] Service member victims of sexual assault have two reporting options: unrestricted or restricted.[6] The unrestricted reporting option initiates a criminal investigation in which command and law enforcement are provided details of the incident.[7] A Service member who makes an unrestricted report of sexual assault may access healthcare and may request a protective order or transfer to avoid ongoing contact with the accused.

The restricted reporting option allows Service members, and their dependents 18 years of age and older who are victims of sexual assault,[8] to access medical and mental healthcare through the military confidentially and without triggering an investigation or revealing the identity of the perpetrator.[9] The purpose behind restricted reporting is to allow and encourage victims to report and seek services and medical treatment without making an official complaint for investigation. However, there are limitations to this option: victims cannot obtain an expedited transfer or protective order;[10] commanders receive limited information about the incident, and they are not informed of the victim's identity.[11] Only healthcare providers, Victim Advocates,

---

[5] *2012 DoD Gender Relations Survey* at 106.

[6] DoD DIRECTIVE 6495.01, SEXUAL ASSAULT PREVENTION AND RESPONSE (SAPR) PROGRAM 4 (Jan. 23, 2012, Incorporating Change 1, Apr. 30, 2013), *available at* http://www.dtic.mil/whs/directives/corres/pdf/649501p.pdf. With the assistance of the SARC or Victim Advocate, the victim completes Defense Department (DD) Form 2910, *Victim Reporting Preference Statement*, which explains the benefits and limitations of each reporting option. *See DoD FY11 Annual Report on Sexual Assault* at 71. Before 2005, the restricted reporting option was not available to sexual assault victims; victims had no way to obtain military-sponsored medical or psychological treatment without triggering a criminal investigation. *See Report of the Defense Task Force* at 2.

[7] DoD DIRECTIVE 6495.01, *supra* note 6, at 18.

[8] The restricted reporting option is only available to active duty Service members, not to military dependents or to civilian DoD employees even though they, like Service members, may have to access medical and psychological care through the military, in general. Lt. Commander Ann M. Vallandingham JAGC, USN, *Department of Defense's Sexual Assault Policy: Recommendations for a More Comprehensive and Uniform Policy*, 54 NAVAL L. REV. 205, 228-232 (2007) (arguing that the restricted reporting option should be available to civilian DoD employees and military dependents).

[9] Sexual assault victims who seek medical care or sexual assault forensic exams in the state of California, however, cannot make a restricted report because state law mandates reporting by healthcare providers. *See* Cal. Penal Code § 11160. Victims in Arizona also may be subject to California's reporting law if the nearest military treatment facility is in California. *DoD FY11 Annual Report* at 70.

[10] *See* DoD INSTRUCTION 6495.02, SEXUAL ASSAULT PREVENTION AND RESPONSE (SAPR) PROGRAM PROCEDURES 25 (Mar. 28, 2013), *available at* http://www.dtic.mil/whs/directives/corres/pdf/649502p.pdf; DoD, SAPRO, Reporting Options – Restricted Reporting, http://www.myduty.mil/index.php/reporting-options/restricted-reporting; DoD DIRECTIVE TYPE MEMORANDUM 11-063, *infra* note 18, at page 19.

[11] *DoD FY11 Annual Report on Sexual Assault* at 70. SARCs are required to give non-identifying information of a restricted report to a "senior commander," but each of the Services defines this differently. *See* Lt. Commander Ann M. Vallandingham, JAGC, USN, *Department of Defense's Sexual Assault Policy: Recommendations for a More Comprehensive and Uniform Policy*, 54 NAVAL L. REV. 205-206 (2007).

and SARCs are authorized to receive restricted reports.[12] Victims are eligible for legal assistance whether they file restricted or unrestricted reports.[13]

It is important to note that if a victim tells an officer or non-commissioned officer in his or her chain of command, or DoD law enforcement about the assault s/he loses the restricted reporting option,[14] but if a victim tells a roommate, friend, or family member, this does not in and of itself, prevent the victim from later electing to make a restricted report.[15] Victims may voluntarily convert a report from restricted to unrestricted and initiate an investigation at any time.[16] If a commander or law enforcement officer learns of a sexual assault, independent of a victim's restricted report, DoD policy mandates an investigation be initiated.[17]

Expedited Transfers and Protective Orders

For unrestricted reports, the DoD implemented an expedited transfer policy in 2011 to allow victims to request an immediate transfer from a unit or base.[18] The request must be decided

---

[12] DoD DIRECTIVE 6495.01, *supra* note 6, at 5; DoD, SAPRO, Reporting Options – Restricted Reporting, http://www.myduty.mil/index.php/reporting-options/restricted-reporting.

[13] U.S. Air Force Office of The Judge Advocate General comments to U.S. Commission on Civil Rights at 1, June 7, 2013, in response to affected agency review.

[14] DoD INSTRUCTION 6495.02, *supra* note 10, at 27.

[15] *Id.* At the outset, however, these communications are "NOT confidential and do not receive the protections of restricted reporting."

[16] *DoD FY11 Annual Report on Sexual Assault* at 70.

[17] DoD INSTRUCTION 6495.02, *supra* note 10 at 27; *DoD FY11 Annual Report on Sexual Assault* at 70-71.

[18] DoD DIRECTIVE TYPE MEMORANDUM 11-063, EXPEDITED TRANSFER OF MILITARY SERVICE MEMBERS WHO FILE UNRESTRICTED REPORTS OF SEXUAL ASSAULT (Dec. 16, 2011, Incorporating Change, 2 Dec. 7, 2012), *available at* http://www.afpc.af.mil/shared/media/document/AFD-130416-051.pdf (Note: Directive-Type Memorandum 11-063 was incorporated into reissued DoDI 6495.02 published on March 28, 2013). The need for an expedited transfer policy was illustrated by the tragic situation of Marine Corps Lance Corporal Maria Lauterbach. Although a verbal protective order was imposed on the Marine whom Lauterbach reported for raping her, Lauterbach was physically attacked, her car was vandalized after she reported, and the Marine she accused of rape ultimately murdered her. *See* DoD, OIG, REVIEW OF MATTERS RELATED TO THE SEXUAL ASSAULT OF LANCE CORPORAL MARIA LAUTERBACH, U.S. MARINE CORPS 2-3, 22 (Oct. 18, 2011), *available at* http://www.dodig.mil/Inspections/IPO/reports/LauterbachFR_(redacted).pdf. The need for expedited transfer also was demonstrated by Army Specialist Suzanne Swift who was court-martialed in 2006 for desertion, demoted, and incarcerated for a month for refusing to redeploy under the command of a sergeant whom she had reported for repeatedly raping her. *See* Donna St. George, *From Victim To Accused Army Deserter*, WASH. POST, Sept. 19, 2006, http://www.washingtonpost.com/wp-dyn/content/article/2006/09/18/AR2006091801506.html. Similarly, Marine Corps Corporal Sarah Albertson alleged that her Command forced her to interact repeatedly with her rapist for two years and eventually required her to report to him after his promotion. Cioca v. Rumsfeld, Case No. 1:11-cv-00151(LO/TCB) (E.D. Va.), Compl. filed Feb. 15, 2011, para. 61-66, *available at* http://www.plainsite.org/flashlight/case.html?id=1758304.

upon within 72 hours, and, if it is denied, the victim may appeal to the first general or flag officer in his or her chain of command.[19]

According to the testimony of one advocate, this transfer policy was not always followed.[20] It is not possible to say with any accuracy how often transfer requests were granted, delayed, or denied in the past because data was not maintained. Federal law now requires DoD to collect data on transfer requests.[21] According to data from FY 2012, nearly all requests for expedited transfers were granted.[22]

Additionally, commanders may issue a military protective order to prohibit an alleged perpetrator from having contact with the victim.[23] While military protective orders are enforceable on military installations, these orders are not enforceable by civilian courts and law enforcement. As a result, victims are advised to seek a civilian protective order.[24]

---

[19] *Patton Statement* at 5; DoD Directive-Type Memorandum 11-063, *supra* note 18.

[20] "Frequently victims are told that their [transfer] papers are lost, they don't qualify [for a transfer], or are placed on 'med[ical]-hold' under false pretenses." *Parrish Statement* at 8; *see also* Karisa King, *Assault Victims Struggle to Transfer to Other Posts*, SAN ANTONIO EXPRESS-NEWS, May 20, 2013, *available at* http://www.mysanantonio.com/twice-betrayed/article/Assault-victims-struggle-to-transfer-to-other-4532717.php#ixzz2U2VBcvEO.

[21] National Defense Authorization Act for Fiscal Year 2012, Pub. L. No. 112-81, 125 Stat. 1298, § 582.

[22] In their 2012 Annual Reports on Sexual assault (attached to *DoD FY12 Annual Report on Sexual Assault, Vol. 1*), the Army stated that it granted 86 and denied three requests for expedited transfers in FY 2012; the Navy granted 43 and denied none; the Marine Corps granted 34 and denied none; and the Air Force granted 48 and denied none.

[23] *See* DoD INSTRUCTION 6495.02, SEXUAL ASSAULT PREVENTION AND RESPONSE (SAPR) PROGRAM PROCEDURES 40-41 (Mar. 28, 2013), *available at* http://www.dtic.mil/whs/directives/corres/pdf/649502p.pdf; DD FORM 2873, MILITARY PROTECTIVE ORDER (July 2004); AR 600-20, Army Command Policy 73 (Sept. 20, 2012). Federal law requires the military to maintain data on these protective orders. National Defense Authorization Act for Fiscal Year 2010, Pub. L. No. 111-84, 123 Stat. 2190 § 567(c), 10 U.S.C. § 1561 (Historical and Statutory Notes). In their 2012 Annual Report on Sexual assault, the Army stated that it issued 201 military protective orders in FY 2012, none of which were violated; the Navy issued none; the Marine Corps issued 248, nine of which were violated by the accused; and the Air Force issued 127, two of which were violated by the accused and seven by the victim. *DoD FY12 Annual Report on Sexual Assault, Vol. 1.*

[24] U.S. Air Force Office of The Judge Advocate General comments to U.S. Commission on Civil Rights at 1, June 7, 2013, in response to affected agency review.

Victim Assistance

Sexual Assault Response Coordinators and Victim Advocates

Every military installation has a Sexual Assault Response Coordinator (SARC) and at least one Victim Advocate.[25] SARCs and Victim Advocates are responsible for connecting victims with appropriate resources and services, assisting them with the reporting process, and addressing concerns of physical safety and retaliation.[26] If a victim obtains a transfer, s/he is assigned a new SARC and Victim Advocate at the new installation.[27]

SARCs manage an installation's SAPR program. They serve as the single point of contact to coordinate victim care and track services provided to each victim.[28] In an unrestricted report case, the SARC is required to keep the victim updated on the status of the investigation and whether charges are referred to court-martial.[29] In non-deployed settings, the SARC can be a Service member, DoD civilian employee, or National Guard Technician.[30] In deployed settings, a certified SARC is provided according to each Service's guidelines and operational commitments.[31]

Victim Advocates provide direct assistance to victims and help them navigate the military's response system.[32] They are trained to be attentive listeners and to support victims.[33] Both

---

[25] National Defense Authorization Act for Fiscal Year 2013, Pub. L. No. 112-239, 126 Stat. 1632 § 572; *DoD FY11 Annual Report on Sexual Assault* at 71.

[26] *DoD FY11 Annual Report on Sexual Assault* at 71-72.

[27] U.S. Marine Corps SAPRO Response to Interrogatory No. 57; DoD SAPRO Response to Interrogatory 143.

[28] *DoD FY11 Annual Report on Sexual Assault* at 72. Commanders also are required to provide victims with monthly updates on the status of their case. *See* DoD INSTRUCTION 6495.02, *supra* note 23 at 33.

[29] *DoD FY11 Annual Report on Sexual Assault* at 71-72.

[30] DoD DIRECTIVE 6495.01, SEXUAL ASSAULT PREVENTION AND RESPONSE (SAPR) PROGRAM 10 (Jan. 23, 2012, Incorporating Change 1, Apr. 30, 2013), *available at* http://www.dtic.mil/whs/directives/corres/pdf/649501p.pdf. For the Army, a SARC is a full-time position. Dep't of the Army Response to Interrogatory No. 79. In the Navy, it is predominantly a full-time permanent position, but it also may be a collateral duty based on the needs of the command and the installation. Chief of Naval Operations' Response to Interrogatory No. 79. The Marine Corps has both full-time, permanent position and collateral duty SARCs, who may be uniformed or civilian. U.S. Marine Corps Response to Interrogatory No. 79. *See also* Nonappropriated Fund Position Description, Job Title: Sexual Assault Response Coordinator, Job Code: 093134. The victim advocacy group, Protect Our Defenders, argues that it is preferable for trained civilians, rather than Service members, to be SARCs because they are less susceptible to being influenced by the victim's or the accused's commander. *See Parrish Statement* at 9.

[31] DoD SAPRO comments to the U.S. Commission on Civil Rights at 8, June 12, 2013, in response to affected agency review. *See, e.g.,* AR 600-20, Army Command Policy 75 (Mar. 18, 2008) (SARC position is assumed by military personnel as a collateral duty).

[32] Victims of all crimes in the military are assigned a victim liaison to support them through the Victim and Witness Assistance Program, but "Victim Advocates" are specific to the SAPR program. In the Army's SAPR

(cont'd)

uniformed and civilian employees serve as Victim Advocates. In the past, unit Service members served as Victim Advocates as a collateral duty to their other responsibilities.[34] Current law requires all locations (installations and deployed areas) to have a Victim Advocate available 24 hours, seven days per week.[35] For some civilians, it is a full-time duty; for others, it is a voluntary collateral duty, depending on the Service.[36]

Victim Advocates are not "advocates" in the manner of an attorney. Nonetheless, communications they have with victims, such as providing advice or support, are privileged from disclosure.[37] Thus, a Victim Advocate cannot be compelled in court-martial proceedings to disclose communications with a victim.

(cont'd from previous page)

program, in addition to the Installation (military base) SARC, there are (1) installation Victim Advocates who work directly with the installation SARC, victims of sexual assault, unit Victim Advocates, and other installation response agencies, and (2) unit Victim Advocates who are soldiers trained to provide limited victim advocacy as a collateral duty. In a deployed environment, there is one deployable SARC at each brigade (ranging from 2,500 to 4,000 personnel) or unit of action who is a soldier trained and responsible for coordinating the SAPR Program as a collateral duty, and two unit Victim Advocates for each battalion-sized unit who are soldiers trained to provide victim advocacy as a collateral duty. AR 600–20, para. 8-3a and 8-3b.

[33] *DoD FY11 Annual Report on Sexual Assault* at 71-72.

[34] DD FORM 2909, VICTIM ADVOCATE AND SUPERVISOR STATEMENT OF UNDERSTANDING (June 2006). Victim advocates and their supervisors sign a Statement of Understanding in which the Victim Advocate agrees, among other things, to maintain victim confidentiality, report directly to the SARC for all Victim Advocate duties, and attend monthly case management meetings. Notably, the Statement of Understanding does not indicate any duties of the Victim Advocate's regular supervisor or provide any guidance as to how to resolve situations where Victim Advocate duties may compete for time, energy, or an otherwise conflict with his/her regular duties. The unit commander is supposed to consult with the SARC to resolve conflicts between a Victim Advocate's primary duty and advocacy responsibilities. *See* DOD INSTRUCTION 6495.02, SEXUAL ASSAULT PREVENTION AND RESPONSE (SAPR) PROGRAM PROCEDURES at Enclosure 5 (Mar. 28, 2013), *available at* http://www.dtic.mil/whs/directives/corres/pdf/649502p.pdf. The Marine Corps has an order providing that, once a victim is assigned to a uniformed Victim Advocate, the victim is the Victim Advocate's primary responsibility. MCO 1752.5A, SEXUAL ASSAULT PREVENTION AND RESPONSE (SAPR) PROGRAM 5-2 (Feb. 5, 2008); U.S. Marine Corps Response to Interrogatory No. 66.

[35] *See* DOD INSTRUCTION 6495.02, *supra* note 34 at 4; National Defense Authorization Act for Fiscal Year 2012, Pub. L. No. 112-81, 125 Stat. 1298 § 581, 584.

[36] The Army reports that it is currently hiring over 300 civilian Victim Advocates. The Marine Corps has 42 full-time civilian Victim Advocates, but they support the Family Advocacy Program, not the SAPR program. In FY 2013, the Marine Corps plans to hire 22 full-time civilian Victim Advocates whose duties are entirely dedicated to the SAPR program. Both civilian and uniformed Victim Advocates in the Navy and Air Force are volunteers. DoD SAPRO Response to Interrogatory No. 146; U.S. Marine Corps Response to Interrogatory No. 75. *See also* Nonappropriated Fund Position Description, Job Title: Victim Advocate Program Specialist, Job Code: 090159. Until recently, the Navy only utilized uniformed Victim Advocates, but it hired civilians for the job pursuant to requirements of recent legislation. Chief of Naval Operations' Response to Interrogatory No. 68-69.

[37] Military Rule of Evidence 514. Generally, information communicated to chaplains during spiritual counseling is also privileged and, therefore, kept confidential. *See* Military Rule of Evidence 503.

Selection and Training of Victim Advocates

DoD's policy requires each Service to "establish standardized criteria for selection and training" of Victim Advocates.[38] There has been considerable variation in how Victim Advocates are selected among the Services.

Army policy requires that Victim Advocates be recommended by their chain of command and, among other things, have outstanding duty performance, demonstrate stability in their personal affairs, and have no history of domestic violence, significant indebtedness, excessive use of alcohol, or use of illegal drugs.[39] They also must have at least one year of military service left to complete.[40]

The Marine Corps has requirements similar to the Army's, but the Marine Corps discourages executive officers, the lowest-level supervisors, legal officers, equal opportunity representatives, and law enforcement personnel from being Victim Advocates, as those positions might pose a conflict of interest.[41]

In contrast, the Navy and Air Force have no expressed guidelines for selecting Victim Advocates. The Navy simply requires SARCs to screen Victim Advocates.[42] The Air Force relies on volunteers who are recruited, screened, and selected by SARCs.[43]

Currently, all Victim Advocates must obtain certification through the DoD Sexual Assault Advocate Certification Program by October 2013.[44]

---

[38] DoD INSTRUCTION 6495.02, SEXUAL ASSAULT PREVENTION AND RESPONSE PROGRAM PROCEDURES 16 (June 23, 2006, Incorporating Change 1, Nov. 13, 2008) (on file with the Commission). This policy was reissued on March 28, 2013. The new version states, "standardized criteria for the selection and training of SARCs and [Victim Advocates] shall comply with specific Military Service guidelines and certification requirements, when implemented by SAPRO," and "all DoD sexual assault responders shall receive the same baseline training." DoD INSTRUCTION 6495.02, *supra* note 34, at 33, 66.

[39] AR 600–20, Army Command Policy 77 (Sept. 20, 2012).

[40] *Id.*

[41] MCO 1752.5A, SEXUAL ASSAULT PREVENTION AND RESPONSE (SAPR) PROGRAM 4-1 (Feb. 5, 2008). The Marine Corps policy also expressly states that Victim Advocates should be approachable, non-judgmental, good communicators, comfortable with sensitive topics, and have the ability to listen to all persons regardless of rank or position. *Id.* at M-1.

[42] DoD SAPRO and the Services' Consolidated Response to Interrogatory No. 139.

[43] *Id.*; AFI 36-6001, SEXUAL ASSAULT PREVENTION AND RESPONSE (SAPR) POLICY 13 (Sept. 29, 2008, Incorporating Change 1, Sept. 30, 2009, Certified Current Oct. 14, 2010).

[44] DoD INSTRUCTION 6495.02, *supra* note 38 at 65; *Patton Statement* at 6.

Victim Witness Assistance Programs and Special Victims Capabilities

Many installations have a Victim Witness Assistance Program separate from the SAPR program.[45] While a case is being investigated and prosecuted, personnel in the Victim Witness Assistance Program may help victims to understand their legal rights, to understand and participate in the military criminal justice process, and to obtain resources.[46] Such duties partially overlap those of a Victim Advocate.[47]

In 2012, Secretary of Defense Leon Panetta mandated the creation of Special Victims Capabilities in each Service, which is comprised of investigators and prosecutors specially trained to handle sexual assault cases.[48] Prosecutors in these Special Victims Capabilities also may provide some of the same services that Victim Advocates provide, such as educating victims about the court-martial process and referring victims to resources for physical and emotional support.[49]

Prosecutors and investigators in Special Victims Capabilities may have specialized training but, as some advocacy groups note, their priorities and interests may not necessarily align with those of victims.[50]

Safe Helpline

In 2011, DoD contracted with the non-profit organization Rape, Abuse & Incest National Network (RAINN) to operate a Safe Helpline, which is an anonymous and confidential crisis support service.[51] It is available 24 hours a day, seven days a week, worldwide via telephone,

---

[45] *See* DOD DIRECTIVE 1030.01, VICTIM AND WITNESS ASSISTANCE (Certified Current as of Apr. 23, 2007); DOD INSTRUCTION 1030.2, VICTIM AND WITNESS ASSISTANCE PROCEDURES (June 4, 2004), *available at* http://www.dtic.mil/whs/directives/corres/pdf/103002p.pdf.

[46] *DoD FY11 Annual Report on Sexual Assault* at 72.

[47] Victim liaisons in the Victim Witness Assistance Programs provide information about where the victim can obtain medical care and social services, arrange for the victim to receive "reasonable protection" from an accused, and keep the victim informed of the status of the investigation and any court-martial proceedings or plea bargain negotiations. AFI 51-201, ADMINISTRATIVE MILITARY JUSTICE 102-104 (Oct. 25, 2012).

[48] *DoD FY11 Annual Report on Sexual Assault* at 72.

[49] Dep't of the Army Response to Interrogatory No. 60.

[50] *See* Statement of Rachel Natelson to the U.S. Commission on Civil Rights 1, [hereinafter *Natelson Statement*] *available at* http://www.eusccr.com/msa1.htm. Prosecutors and investigators in the Special Victims Capabilities represent the government, not the victim; their ethical duty is to the government. DoD SAPRO comments to the U.S. Commission on Civil Rights at 10, June 12, 2013, in response to affected agency review.

[51] *DoD FY11 Report on Sexual Assault* at 12.

text, or online.[52] There is now a Safe Helpline Mobile Application for smartphones, as well as a Safe HelpRoom (a moderated and secure chat room for survivors of sexual assault).[53]

Healthcare for Victims

Military physicians, physician assistants, and nurses are responsible for treating the physical injuries of Service members who are sexually assaulted. Service members may receive treatment for sexually transmitted diseases as well as emergency contraception.[54] Military psychiatrists, psychologists, social workers, and other professionals assist victims with their mental healthcare needs.

DoD has made efforts to improve mental healthcare for sexual assault victims. The Office of the Assistant Secretary of Defense for Health Affairs established the Health Affairs Sexual Assault Integrated Product Team in October 2009 to facilitate effective and efficient coordination of sexual assault response in the DoD medical community.[55] The Center for Deployment Psychology at the Uniformed Services University of Health Sciences includes sexual assault and SAPR Program information in its training program for deploying mental health providers, nurses, and chaplains. This information includes instruction on working with the SAPR Program in a deployed clinical setting with the intent to improve access to quality mental healthcare for sexual assault victims in deployed environments.[56] The DoD also coordinates and collaborates with civilian medical facilities for DoD-reimbursable healthcare, including psychological care, through Memoranda of Understanding (MOU) and Memoranda of Agreement (MOA) to ensure adequate victim care is available.[57]

Despite these efforts, some victims have criticized the available psychological care as inadequate.[58] The Government Accountability Office (GAO) recently found that medical and

---

[52] *DoD FY12 Report on Sexual Assault, Vol. 1* at 30. In June 2012, the Safe Helpline was expanded to help the transition of victims separated from military service to begin care with the Department of Veterans Affairs. *Patton Statement* at 8.

[53] *DoD FY11 Report on Sexual Assault* at 30, 37. *See* https://www.safehelpline.org/.

[54] Military women have access to comprehensive healthcare through the TRICARE program (https://www.tricare.mil/), which covers emergency contraception. Kelsey Holt, et al., *Unintended Pregnancy and Contraceptive Use Among Women in the U.S. Military: A Systematic Literature Review*, 176 MILITARY MED. 8 (Sept. 1, 2011).

[55] *DoD FY 2011 Annual Report on Sexual Assault* at 14.

[56] *Id.*

[57] DoD INSTRUCTION 6495.02, SEXUAL ASSAULT PREVENTION AND RESPONSE (SAPR) PROGRAM PROCEDURES 14 (Mar. 28, 2013), *available at* http://www.dtic.mil/whs/directives/corres/pdf/649502p.pdf.

[58] One veteran explained that the psychiatrists "basically throw you sleeping pills [and] anti-depressants, and send you back to continue what you were doing." Irina Sadovich Gillett, et al., *Female Veterans and Military Sexual*

(cont'd)

mental healthcare services for victims are not always available in deployed environments.[59] It further found that victims did not always receive adequate or consistent medical care, healthcare providers did not have a consistent understanding of their responsibilities in caring for victims who made restricted reports, and SARCs and Victim Advocates were not always aware of the healthcare services available to victims at their respective locations.[60]

Legal Assistance for Victims

All Service members have access to some types of *general* legal counsel provided by the military.[61] Legislation passed in 2012 mandated that sexual assault victims be provided legal counsel, but the law did not explain how it was intended to expand the existing legal services.[62] As a result, application of the law may be inconsistent.[63]

(cont'd from previous page)

Trauma, 3 J. DIVERSE SOCIAL WORK 50 (Spring 2012). Some male victims only had the option for treatment at a women's health clinic. *Report of the Defense Task Force* at 73; *see also* DEP'T OF VETERANS AFFAIRS, MILITARY SEXUAL TRAUMA/SEXUAL TRAUMA RESIDENTIAL TREATMENT RESOURCES, http://www.ncdsv.org/images/VAMHS_MST-SexualTraumaResidentialTreatmentResources_10-2010.pdf (noting that there is only one all-male facility for military sexual assault victims).

[59] GAO, MILITARY PERSONNEL: DoD HAS TAKEN STEPS TO MEET THE HEALTH NEEDS OF DEPLOYED SERVICEWOMEN, BUT ACTIONS ARE NEEDED TO ENHANCE CARE FOR SEXUAL ASSAULT VICTIMS 17 (2013), *available at* http://www.gao.gov/assets/660/651624.pdf.

[60] *Id.* at 9-22. Additionally, often DoD rules on Restricted reporting are in apparent conflict with instructions issued by each Service for labeling forensic evidence and keeping the victim's chain of command informed, as meetings between GAO and senior medical personnel from the command "confirmed that provisions in their medical policy conflicted with other command policy and had created confusion for healthcare providers regarding the extent of their responsibility to maintain the confidentiality of victims who choose to make a restricted report of sexual assault." *Id.* at 21.

[61] For example, legal assistance attorneys help Service members with civil matters such as will preparation, taxes, family law, and consumer finance issues. *See, e.g.,* 10 U.S.C. § 1044; DEP'T OF NAVY, JUDGE ADVOCATE GENERAL (JAG) INSTRUCTION 5800.7E, THE MANUAL OF THE JUDGE ADVOCATE GENERAL 7-1 – 7-11 (June 26, 2012), *available at* http://www.jag.navy.mil/library/instructions/JAGMAN2012.pdf. Military defense counsel are appointed when a Service member is investigated and/or charged with a violation of the UCMJ. UCMJ, Art. 38(b)(1), 10 U.S.C. § 838(b)(1) (2000); MANUAL FOR COURTS-MARTIAL, R. 506, at II-50 (Joint Service Committee on Military Justice 2012) [hereinafter *MCM*], *available at* http://www.loc.gov/rr/frd/Military_Law/pdf/MCM-2012.pdf. The DoD took the position that legal services to sexual assault victims could be provided within the parameters of pre-existing legislation. *See* Memorandum from the Under Secretary of Defense for Personnel and Readiness, Legal Assistance for Victims of Crime (Oct. 17, 2011).

[62] National Defense Authorization Act for Fiscal Year 2012, Pub. L. No. 112-81, 125 Stat. 1298 § 581.

[63] For example, the victim advocacy group, Protect Our Defenders, reported that some victims in the Air Force had been unable to get legal assistance to protect their privacy rights when their confidential communications with psychotherapists or other medical personnel had been inappropriately disclosed. *Parrish Statement* at 8.

Prior to 2012 legislation, victims had access to legal assistance attorneys within Victim and Witness Assistance Programs.[64] But, depending on the Service, different types of military attorneys (judge advocates) assisted victims with the various negative consequences of reporting. Army legal assistance attorneys assisted victims with rebuttals to adverse evaluations or reprimands.[65] In the Navy, personal representation attorneys assisted victims with the professional or administrative consequences of reporting.[66] In the Air Force, area defense counsel and special victims' counsel assisted victims with disciplinary action that may have resulted from collateral misconduct and associated adverse evaluations or reprimands.[67] If an enlisted Service member was being separated involuntarily from the Service, such as via an administrative discharge based on a psychological diagnosis[68] or for unsatisfactory performance, a defense attorney provided representation.[69] Also, victims who were involved in collateral misconduct at the time they were sexually assaulted had the right to defense counsel.[70]

In January 2013, the Air Force began a new initiative called the Special Victims' Counsel Program to provide Air Force victims with a personal attorney.[71] The Air Force Judge Advocate General, Lieutenant General Richard C. Harding, testified to the Commission that providing victims with this additional legal counsel may encourage more victims to participate in the military justice system and, therefore, increase the likelihood that more perpetrators are

---

[64] The Victim and Witness Assistance Program provides support to all crime victims and witnesses. *See* 10 U.S.C. § 1044; JAG INSTRUCTION 5800.7E, the MANUAL OF THE JUDGE ADVOCATE GENERAL; MARINE CORPS, LEGAL ASSISTANCE PRACTICE ADVISORY 7-11 (July 26, 2011); DoD INSTRUCTION 1030.2, VICTIM AND WITNESS ASSISTANCE PROCEDURES 45, (June 4, 2004), *available at* http://www.dtic.mil/whs/directives/corres/pdf/103002p.pdf. *See also* NAVAL OPERATIONS (OPNAV) INSTRUCTION 5800.7A, VICTIM AND WITNESS ASSISTANCE PROGRAM (VWAP) (Mar. 4, 2008); MCO P5800.16A, MARINE CORPS MANUAL FOR LEGAL ADMINISTRATION, Chapter 6; Navy Memorandum from James W. Houck, Notification to Crime Victims of Available Legal Assistance Services (Sept. 9, 2011).

[65] DoD SAPRO Response to the U.S. Commission on Civil Rights' Interrogatory No. 144.

[66] DoD SAPRO Response to the U.S. Commission on Civil Rights' Interrogatory No. 145. The Marine Corps presumably follows the same policies as the Navy.

[67] U.S. Air Force Office of The Judge Advocate General comments to U.S. Commission on Civil Rights at 2, June 7, 2013, in response to affected agency review.

[68] For a discussion on victims' administrative discharges based on psychological diagnoses, *see* Chapter 4.

[69] DoD SAPRO Response to the U.S. Commission on Civil Rights' Interrogatory No. 144; AR 635-200, Active Duty Enlisted Administrative Separations 55-56 (July 6, 2005 and revised on Sept. 6, 2011).

[70] Uniform Code of Military Justice, Art. 27, 10 U.S.C. § 827.

[71] Harding testimony, *Briefing Transcript,* at 168-69.

punished.[72] As discussed in Chapter 5, investigation and prosecution of some of the sexual assault cases in all the Services in FY 2011 ended when the victim declined to continue participating in the criminal justice process.

Confidentiality Concerns

Although confidential restricted reporting has been available since 2005, victims are still wary of using this option. In the DoD's 2010 anonymous survey of active-duty Service members, 60 percent of women and 36 percent of men who experienced unwanted sexual contact and did not report to a military authority, stated they did not report because they believed the report would not be kept confidential.[73]

After a Service member makes either a restricted or an unrestricted report, Commanders are required to keep information regarding reports on a need-to-know basis.[74] Maintaining confidentiality, even with a restricted report, may be difficult in deployed environments and on smaller installations.[75] Also, there are concerns that commanders may try to breach the confidentiality of a restricted report because they prefer to know the details of criminal offenses that occurred in their units.[76]

When applying for updated security clearances, seeking either re-enlistment or a promotion, Service members must disclose whether they have received psychological counseling.[77]

---

[72] *Id.* Gen. Harding informed the Commission that, in FY 2011, 96 Air Force sexual assault victims (29 percent) made an unrestricted report, and originally agreed to participate in the prosecution of their alleged offender but later changed their minds. *Id.*

[73] *2010 DoD Gender Relations Survey* at 43. In the DoD's 2012 anonymous survey, 51 percent of women stated they did not report their sexual assault for fear their information would not remain confidential; the relatively small number of male Service members who participated in the 2012 survey may have contributed to a lack of statistically significant response numbers for this question on the survey questionnaire. *See DoD 2012 Gender Relations Survey* at 106-7; *DoD FY12 Annual Report on Sexual Assault, Vol. 1* at 18.

[74] DOD INSTRUCTION 6495.02, SEXUAL ASSAULT PREVENTION AND RESPONSE (SAPR) PROGRAM PROCEDURES 4 (Mar. 28, 2013), *available at* http://www.dtic.mil/whs/directives/corres/pdf/649502p.pdf; *see, e.g.*, AR 600-20, Army Command Policy 72 (Mar. 18, 2008).

[75] *See Report of the Defense Task Force* at 35 ("[R]estricted reporting is more challenging in deployed environments…Commanders may . . . want a detailed justification for airlifting Service Members out of the area [for a forensic examination or for medical care] because doing so creates risks and constrains resources. Military personnel have limited privacy on smaller bases: people may make assumptions when they see someone meeting with the [deployed Victim Advocate or SARC].")

[76] *Id.* at 23; Emily Hansen, *Carry that Weight: Victim Privacy within the Military Sexual Assault Reporting Methods*, 28 J. MARSHALL J. COMPUTER & INFO. L. 551, 579 (2011).

[77] *See* OFFICE OF PERSONNEL MANAGEMENT, STANDARD FORM 86, QUESTIONNAIRE FOR NATIONAL SECURITY POSITIONS, at 84, *available at* http://www.opm.gov/forms/pdf_fill/sf86.pdf.

Although an exception for disclosing combat-related mental health counseling existed previously, victims of sexual assault who sought counseling were not afforded a similar exception until April 2013.[78] Prior to that date, some victims may have avoided seeking treatment for fear that psychological counseling could affect their abilities to receive a security clearance or job promotion.[79]

Additional Barriers to Reporting

Even with the option of restricted reporting, only a fraction of victims report.[80] Fear of negative consequences is a significant factor in many victims' decision not to report.[81] Lack of confidence in the military justice system also may contribute to victims' reluctance to report sexual assault. Participants in focus groups conducted by the Defense Task Force on Sexual Assault expressed the view that it was "difficult to report sexual assault if the perpetrator was of higher rank and/or in the victim's chain of command…[P]articipants felt they would face reprisal for reporting or that senior leaders would protect the accused."[82]

---

[78] Office of the Director of National Intelligence, Press Briefing, New Interim Guidance Question 21 on the Standard Form 86, Questionnaire for National Security Positions, 4 (Apr. 5, 2013), *available at* http://www.fas.org/irp/news/2013/04/dni-clearance.pdf.

[79] *See* Service Women's Action Network, Director of National Intelligence Issues Security Clearance Change for Military Sexual Assault Survivors Seeking Counseling (Apr. 5, 2013), available at http://servicewomen.org/wp-content/uploads/2013/04/4.5.2013-Victory-for-Survivors.pdf ("From numerous calls we receive on our Helpline, we know that Question 21 has kept survivors from seeking the critical mental health services they have needed to heal in the aftermath of sexual assault."). Air Force Technical Sergeant Jennifer Norris contends that her military career ended because she refused to release to a security clearance investigator records of her psychological counseling for PTSD due to military sexual assault. James Kitfield, *The Enemy Within*, NATIONAL JOURNAL, Sept. 13, 2012, http://www.nationaljournal.com/magazine/the-military-s-rape-problem-20120913?mrefid=site_search&page=1.

[80] *See 2012 DoD Gender Relations Survey* at 106-9 (67 percent of women and 81 percent of men who had experienced unwanted sexual contact in the past year stated they did not report it); *see also 2010 DoD Gender Relations Survey* at 35-36 (71 percent of women and 85 percent of men who had experienced unwanted sexual contact in the past year stated they did not report it).

[81] *2010 DoD Gender Relations Survey* at 43 (54 percent of women and 27 percent of men did not report because they feared retaliation; 47 percent of women and 20 percent of men did not report because they had heard other victims had a negative experience after reporting). *See also* Technical Sergeant Jennifer Norris, USAF (Ret.), written testimony, *Hearing of the U.S. House Armed Services Committee*, Jan. 23, 2012, http://armedservices.house.gov/index.cfm/files/serve?File_id=f1febb51-8d17-4148-8146-e5df227d4a50 (explaining that she did not initially report being raped because she witnessed the negativity against another Service member after reporting sexual harassment).

[82] *Report of the Defense Task Force* at 31.

CHAPTER 4:   CONSEQUENCES OF REPORTING

The DoD's Whistleblower Protection policy prohibits retaliation or "reprisal" against those who report sexual assault.[1] The Services also have similar policies prohibiting retaliation.[2] The DoD Office of the Inspector General (OIG) and the Services' Inspector General offices investigate allegations of reprisal for reporting sexual assault.

Nevertheless, 60 percent of women who reported unwanted sexual contact believed they experienced negative social, professional, or administrative consequences.[3] A witness at the Commission's briefing testified to the significant, long-term effect such negative consequences may cause, including limiting or precluding access to veterans' benefits.[4]

Types of Consequences

The testimony of Rachel Natelson, Legal Director of Service Women's Advocacy Network, before the Commission indicated that many victims are retaliated against after they report, but many commanders also assist in alleviating such retaliation.[5] Because the DoD does not track victims, the Commission cannot determine how many victims have experienced retaliation.[6]

---

[1] DoD DIRECTIVE 7050.06, MILITARY WHISTLEBLOWER PROTECTION (July 23, 2007), *available at* http://www.dtic.mil/whs/directives/corres/pdf/705006p.pdf. "Reprisal" is defined as "[t]aking or threatening to take an unfavorable personnel action, or withholding or threatening to withhold a favorable personnel action, for making or preparing a protected communication." *Id.* at 12. Title 10 United States Code section 1034, "Protected Communication; prohibition of retaliatory personnel actions," prohibits reprisal against a member of the armed forces for communicating a violation of law or regulation to, among other things, a member of a DoD law enforcement organization or any organization designated for receiving such communications. Because sexual assault is clearly a violation of law or regulation, reporting alleged sexual assaults to law enforcement or to a SARC is a protected communication under 10 U.S.C. 1034, as well as DoD Directive 7050.06, "Military Whistleblower Protection."

[2] *See, e.g.* SECNAINST 5370.7C, MILITARY WHISTLEBLOWER REPRISAL PROTECTION (May 18, 2008); AR 600-20, Army Command Policy 46 (Mar. 18, 2008) ("Commanders and supervisors are prohibited from initiating any type of disciplinary or adverse action against any Soldier or civilian employee because the individual registered a complaint."); *id.* at 48-49 (implementing the DoD's Whistleblower Protection policy); *id.* at 64 ("Do not allow Soldiers to be retaliated against for filing complaints."). *See also* 10 USC § 1034 (defining protected communications).

[3] *2010 DoD Gender Relations Survey* at 42.

[4] Natelson testimony, *Briefing Transcript,* at 59-60.

[5] *See Natelson Statement* at 4. For example, one victim told DoD researchers, "The Marines in my office and in my chain of command took great care of me. . . . [M]y chain of command and the surrounding units were very adamant about getting me the help and assistance I needed, while punishing the [accused] Marine for his individual actions." Nevertheless, she also told researchers, "After my incident, many of my peers and the peers of my assaulter looked at me . . . like I wore the scarlet letter, when in fact I was the victim. No Marine wants to accept that one of their own would do something like that to another person. So I think, they all just assumed I was

(cont'd)

According to victim advocacy groups, the process of appealing professional or administrative retaliation is "daunting."[7] To allege reprisal for reporting sexual assault, a Service member must first file a complaint petition with the DoD Inspector General's Office.[8] Only if the Inspector General's Office substantiates the petition may the Service member petition his/her Service's Board for the Correction of Military Records (Board) for redress.[9] If the Board makes an unfavorable outcome that is accepted by the Military Service Secretary, the Service member may appeal the decision to the Secretary of Defense.[10]

Statistically, a majority of appeals are not investigated fully, and most that are investigated are not substantiated. According to a recent study by the GAO, the Inspector General's Office fully investigated an average of 29 percent of all reprisal complaints between fiscal years 2006 and 2011, and it substantiated 25 of those investigated complaints.[11] Thus, six percent of all complaints between fiscal years 2006 and 2011were substantiated and could be considered by a Board.[12]

(cont'd from previous page)

lying, making it up, wanted attention, or I was mad at him." Afterwards, however, the victim's Battalion began bi-annual classes on sexual harassment and sexual assault. *Report of the Defense Task Force* at F-10.

[6] The only statistics available are from the DoD's anonymous surveys of the military population as a whole.

[7] *Natelson Statement* at 3. The National Defense Authorization Act for FY 2013, Public Law No. 112-239, §572, contains a requirement for a general education campaign to notify Service members of the right to seek the correction of military records when a Service member experiences any retaliatory personnel action for making a report of sexual assault or sexual harassment.

[8] A Service member is instructed to submit a complaint to the DoD's OIG or to an Inspector General within a Military Department for investigation within 60 days of the date the member became aware of the alleged reprisal. DoD DIRECTIVE 7050.06, MILITARY WHISTLEBLOWER PROTECTION 14 (July 23, 2007), *available at* http://www.dtic.mil/whs/directives/corres/pdf/705006p.pdf. If more than 60 days have passed since the Service member became aware of the personnel action that is the subject of the alleged reprisal, the Inspector General may nevertheless consider the complaint for investigation "based on compelling reasons for the delay in submission or the strength of the evidence submitted." *Id*. The DoD's Inspector General should conduct an investigation within 180 days. *Id.* at 6.

[9] *Natelson Statement* at 3. *See also* DoD DIRECTIVE 7050.06, *supra* note 8 at 6-7 (the Board is supposed to review the Inspector General's report; gather additional evidence, if necessary; receive oral arguments; examine and cross-examine witnesses; take depositions as necessary; and, if appropriate, conduct a hearing). If the Board "determines that a personnel action was in reprisal . . . , it may recommend to the Secretary of the Military Department concerned that disciplinary action be taken against the individual(s) responsible for such personnel action." *Id.* at 7.

[10] DoD DIRECTIVE 7050.06, *supra* note 8 at 15-16.

[11] GAO, ACTIONS NEEDED TO IMPROVE DOD'S MILITARY WHISTLEBLOWER REPRISAL PROGRAM 64 (Jan. 2012), *available at* http://www.gao.gov/assets/590/588784.pdf.

[12] *Id.*

The Boards are not staffed by judges or attorneys, but rather, civilian DoD employees who convene on an *ad hoc* basis in addition to other full-time duties.[13] Board members need not undergo extensive or specialized training in military law, nor are they bound by the judicial doctrine of precedent, but their decisions are reviewed by an attorney prior to a recommendation being submitted to the Secretary of the Military Service.[14] Data indicates that the Army and Navy Board members devote an average of 3.72 and 6.73 minutes, respectively, to deciding each case.[15]

Professional and Administrative Consequences

Professional and administrative consequences include adverse actions by commanders in the victim's chain of command such as "plac[ing the victim] on a medical or legal hold, denial of promotion, job assignments that are not career enhancing, [and] denial of requests for training."[16] It also includes efforts to remove the victim from military service. Service members may be removed from the military through an involuntary administrative discharge initiated by their command.[17] The basis of such an administrative discharge may be a psychological diagnosis.

Psychological Diagnoses

The diagnosis of an "adjustment disorder" or "personality disorder" based on psychological symptoms after a sexual assault, if incorrect, may be the most troubling consequence of reporting.[18] Military criminal defense attorney, Major Bridget Wilson, testified that a

---

[13] *Natelson Statement* at 4.

[14] DoD SAPRO comments to the U.S. Commission on Civil Rights at 14, June 12, 2013, in response to affected agency review.

[15] *See* Raymond J. Toney, Remarks at State Bar of Texas Annual Meeting: Military Record Correction Boards and Their Judicial Review 3 (June 11, 2010), *available at* http://www.texasbar.com/flashdrive/materials/military_law/militarylaw_toney_militaryrecord_finalarticle.pdf.

[16] *2010 DoD Gender Relations Survey* at 41. Veteran BriGette McCoy testified to the Senate Armed Services Committee that she was "put on extra duties that conflicted with [her] medical profiles" after she reported sexual harassment. BriGette McCoy, written testimony, *Hearing Before the U.S. Senate Armed Services Committee*, Mar. 13, 2013, *available at* http://www.armed-services.senate.gov/statemnt/2013/03_March/McCoy_03-13-13.pdf.

[17] DoD INSTRUCTION 1332.14, ENLISTED ADMINISTRATIVE SEPARATIONS 12 (Aug. 28, 2008, Incorporating Change 3, Sept. 30, 2011), *available at* http://www.dtic.mil/whs/directives/corres/pdf/133214p.pdf.

[18] *See* Karisa King, *In the Military, Sex Assault Victims Labeled as Mentally Ill and Forced Out*, SAN ANTONIO EXPRESS-NEWS, May 18, 2013, *available at* http://www.mysanantonio.com/news/military/article/In-the-military-sex-assault-victims-labeled-as-4526251.php#ixzz2U2R7EDvk; David S. Martin, *Rape Victims Say Military Labels Them 'Crazy'*, CNN.com, Apr. 14, 2012, http://www.cnn.com/2012/04/14/health/military-sexual-assaults-

"personality disorder" or "adjustment disorder" is "the fastest and easiest way to get rid of someone" in the military.[19]

Post-traumatic stress disorder (PTSD) is a mental health condition that is triggered by a traumatic or stressful event.[20] PTSD justifies a service-related medical discharge if the traumatic event occurred during military service.[21] A service-related medical discharge entitles a veteran to disability benefits and access to ongoing healthcare. According to victim advocacy groups, although PTSD is a likely consequence of sexual assault, "commanders can and do dismiss victims as merely presenting an attitude problem."[22]

Unlike PTSD, which is a response to a traumatic event, an "adjustment disorder" is a response to a distressing life event (such as sudden job loss) or a life challenge (such as leaving home for the first time) which typically lasts no longer than six months after the stressful situation or life event has been resolved;[23] and a "personality disorder" is a pre-existing condition originating during the early developmental years.[24] Neither an "adjustment disorder" nor a "personality

---

personality-disorder/index.html. According to Major Wilson, she handled a case where a woman was diagnosed with a "personality disorder" and the Navy sought to discharge her on that basis after she complained that her supervisor was viewing pornography on his computer all day. Wilson testimony, *Briefing Transcript,* at 57.

[19] Wilson testimony, *Briefing Transcript,* at 57.

[20] AM. PSYCHIATRIC ASS'N, DIAGNOSTIC AND STATISTICAL MANUAL OF MENTAL DISORDERS (Am. Psychiatric Ass'n 5th ed. 2013)(defining PTSD as a trauma- and stressor-related disorder resulting from exposure to actual or threatened death, serious injury or sexual violation, and causes impairment, is not a consequence of another mental disorder or the physiological effect of a substance, and includes symptoms divided into four clusters: intrusion, avoidance, negative alterations in cognitions and mood, and alterations in arousal and reactivity) (Prior to May 2013, the Manual's definition of PTSD did not include sexual assault specifically.).

[21] *See* DEP'T OF VETERANS AFFAIRS, NEW REGULATIONS ON PTSD CLAIMS (July 12, 2010), *available at* http://www.va.gov/ptsd_qa.pdf; Combat-Related Special Compensation, 10 U.S.C. § 1413a (2013).

[22] *Natelson Statement* at 5.

[23] AM. PSYCHIATRIC ASS'N, DIAGNOSTIC AND STATISTICAL MANUAL OF MENTAL DISORDERS 286-87 (Am. Psychiatric Ass'n 5th ed. 2013)(Chronic adjustment disorder may persist for longer than six months.). The current definition of an adjustment disorder does not reflect the definition used by DoD to diagnose adjustment disorders for administrative discharges prior to May of 2013, although both definitions are similar and share most criteria. *See* AM. PSYCHIATRIC ASS'N, DIAGNOSTIC AND STATISTICAL MANUAL OF MENTAL DISORDERS TR 679-80 (Am. Psychiatric Ass'n 4th ed. 2000)(defining an adjustment disorder as the development of emotional or behavioral symptoms in response to an identifiable stressor, occurring within three months of the stressful event, persisting no longer than six months, and reflecting marked distress in excess of what would be expected from exposure to the stressor or significant impairment in either social or occupational functioning); *see also* DOD INSTRUCTION 1332.14, ENLISTED ADMINISTRATIVE SEPARATIONS 6 (Aug. 28, 2008, Incorporating Change 3, Sept. 30, 2011), *available at* http://www.dtic.mil/whs/directives/corres/pdf/133214p.pdf (instructing DoD components to use the current edition of the Diagnostic and Statistical Manual of Mental Disorders).

[24] "A *personality disorder* is an enduring pattern of inner experience and behavior that deviates markedly from the expectations of the individual's culture, is pervasive and inflexible, has an onset in adolescence or early adulthood, is stable over time, and leads to distress or impairment." AM. PSYCHIATRIC ASS'N, DIAGNOSTIC AND STATISTICAL

disorder" qualifies for a service-related medical discharge but instead may be the basis for an administrative discharge.[25] An administrative discharge may limit a Service member's access to disability benefits and ongoing treatment for the sexual trauma after discharge if the symptoms are labeled as not service-related or the result of a pre-existing condition.[26] A Service member should not be administratively discharged based on a "personality disorder" or "adjustment disorder" if a service-related PTSD is also diagnosed, as the PTSD would qualify for a disability discharge—not an administrative discharge.[27] Service members recommended for an administrative discharge with a behavioral condition and who served in an imminent danger pay area are now screened for PTSD and Traumatic Brain Injury as a precautionary measure.[28]

The Armed Forces Health Surveillance Center found "adjustment disorder" diagnoses to be disproportionately applied to women and 10 times more prevalent than PTSD diagnoses among

---

(cont'd from previous page)

MANUAL OF MENTAL DISORDERS 645 (Am. Psychiatric Ass'n 5th ed. 2013)(emphasis in original). DoD considers personality disorders a preexisting condition, and Service members discharged on that basis cannot receive disability benefits or other benefits, including healthcare, for symptoms that are considered part of their personality disorder. DoD INSTRUCTION 1332.14,*supra* note 23 at 13. The current definition of a personality disorder does not reflect the definition used by DoD to diagnose personality disorders for administrative discharges prior to May of 2013, although both definitions are similar and share most criteria. *See* AM. PSYCHIATRIC ASS'N, DIAGNOSTIC AND STATISTICAL MANUAL OF MENTAL DISORDERS TR 685-86 (Am. Psychiatric Ass'n 4th ed. 2000)(defining a personality disorder as an enduring pattern of inner experience and behavior that deviates markedly from the expectations of the individual's culture that is pervasive and inflexible, leads to impairment, has an onset in adolescence or early adulthood, is stable over time, is not a consequence of another mental disorder or the physiological effect of a substance, and is manifested in at least two of the following areas: cognition, affectivity, interpersonal functioning, or impulse control).

[25] DoD Office of Clinical & Program Policy Response to Request for Documents No. 5 (on file with the U.S. Commission on Civil Rights). *See also* AR 635-200, Active Duty Enlisted Administrative Separations 58 (July 6, 2005 and revised on Sept. 6, 2011) (A "personality disorder" is a "deeply ingrained maladaptive pattern of behavior of long duration."); James Kitfield, *The Enemy Within*, NATIONAL JOURNAL, Sept. 13, 2012, at 3, http://www.nationaljournal.com/magazine/the-military-s-rape-problem-20120913?mrefid=site_search&page=1 ("[A] personality disorder is a long-standing pattern of maladaptive behavior, not something caused by a recent . . . condition such as sexual trauma."). In the Diagnostic and Statistical Manual of Mental Disorders, personality disorder is characterized as an Axis II disorder, whereas PTSD is an Axis I disorder. *See also* VIETNAM VETERANS OF AM., CASTING TROOPS ASIDE: THE UNITED STATES MILITARY'S ILLEGAL PERSONALITY DISORDER DISCHARGE PROBLEM (2012), *available at* http://www.vva.org/PPD-Documents/WhitePaper.pdf.

[26] Veterans' benefits are available only for a pre-existing condition if the condition was aggravated by military service and there is no finding that the aggravation is due to the natural progress of the disease or disability. 38 C.F.R. § 3.303(a) 38 C.F.R. § 3.306.

[27] DoD INSTRUCTION 1332.14, *supra* note 23 at 13. *See also id.* at para. 3(a)8.3, p. 12; AR 635-200, Active Duty Enlisted Administrative Separations 58 (July 6, 2005 and revised on Sept. 6, 2011) ("A Soldier will not be processed for administrative separation [based on a personality disorder diagnosis] if PTSD, [traumatic brain injury], and/or other comorbid mental illness are significant factors to a diagnosis of personality disorder, but will be evaluated under the physical disability system.").

[28] DoD INSTRUCTION 1332.14, *supra* note 23, at 8-9.

female Service members.[29] On the other hand, women in the general U.S. population are diagnosed for adjustment disorders twice as often as men.[30] Without specific data indicating how many sexual assault victims are discharged for personality or adjustment disorders in the military, the Commission cannot assess whether these female Service members are discharged as a result of experiencing or reporting a sexual assault.

Although the issue of personality disorder discharges received public attention in recent years,[31] which led to a reduction in such diagnoses and related discharges,[32] some military healthcare providers simply may have substituted the use of "adjustment disorders" as an alternative to a medical discharge of PTSD for military sexual assault victims.[33] The long-term effect is the same—such diagnoses limit or precludes veterans from receiving disability benefits because the psychological symptoms are deemed not to be service-related.

Health benefits through the Veterans Health Administration also are affected by the character of a Service member's discharge. Any discharge that is not under honorable conditions precludes access to healthcare with the Veterans Health Administration, unless a Service member obtains an administrative ruling by the Veterans Benefits Administration. [34] Some

---

[29] Armed Forces Health Surveillance Ctr., *Mental Disorders and Mental Health Problems, Active Component, U.S. Armed Forces, 2000-2011*, MED. SURVEILLANCE MONTHLY REPORT 11 (June 2012), *available at* http://www.afhsc.mil/viewMSMR?file=2012/v19_n06.pdf. "Figures . . . indicate that the armed services are disproportionately applying [personality disorder] diagnoses to women. Women make up 21 percent of the Air Force but account for 35 percent of the personality-disorder discharges; they're 16 percent of the Army but 24 percent of such discharges; they're 17 percent of the Navy but 26 percent of discharges for personality disorder; and they're 7 percent of the Marines but 14 percent of such discharges." James Kitfield, *The Enemy Within*, NATIONAL JOURNAL, Sept. 13, 2012, http://www.nationaljournal.com/magazine/the-military-s-rape-problem-20120913.

[30] MAYO CLINIC, ADJUSTMENT DISORDERS: CAUSES (Mar. 2011), *available at* http://www.mayoclinic.com/health/adjustment-disorders/DS00584/DSECTION=causes. Conversely, men are three times more likely to be diagnosed with antisocial personality disorder than women across the globe. WORLD HEALTH ORG., GENDER AND WOMEN'S MENTAL HEALTH, *available at* http://www.who.int/mental_health/prevention/genderwomen/en/.

[31] *See* GAO, DEFENSE HEALTH CARE, ADDITIONAL EFFORTS NEEDED TO ENSURE COMPLIANCE WITH PERSONALITY DISORDER SEPARATION REQUIREMENTS (Oct. 2008), *available at* http://www.gao.gov/assets/290/283014.pdf.

[32] In 2008, the GAO found that the Services were not fully compliant with DoD's personality disorder separation guidance in DoD Instruction 1332.14. *See Id. See also* GAO, DEFENSE HEALTHCARE STATUS OF EFFORTS TO ADDRESS LACK OF COMPLIANCE WITH PERSONALITY DISORDER SEPARATION REQUIREMENTS (Sept. 15, 2010). Since then, DoD has required the Services to audit personality disorder separation files annually. *See* Memorandum of the Under Secretary of Defense for Personnel and Readiness, Continued Compliance Reporting on Personality Disorder Separations (Sept. 10, 2010).

[33] *Natelson Statement* at 4. Major Bridget Wilson agreed that "adjustment disorder has become the substitute for personality disorder." Wilson testimony, *Briefing Transcript,* at 57.

[34] If discharged under a category that is not honorable, Service members are precluded from all healthcare benefits, but may appeal to the Veterans Benefits Administration. Veterans Health Administration's Response to U.S.

(cont'd)

victims diagnosed with a "personality disorder" or "adjustment disorder" and discharged without honorable conditions have claimed that that diagnosis and discharge operate hand in hand to deny them treatment.[35]

Procedural Safeguards for Service Members Facing Administrative Discharges Based on Psychological Diagnoses

The DoD's Whistleblower Protection policy prohibits commanders from using mental health evaluations as a means of retaliation.[36] The fact that a Service member experienced a sexual assault does not, in and of itself, mean that the Service member automatically meets the threshold criteria for a command-directed mental health evaluation.[37]

On August 28, 1997, the DoD issued a policy stating the requirements for mental health evaluations.[38] Under that policy, before a commander could refer a Service member for a

---

(cont'd from previous page)

Commission on Civil Rights Report: "Sexual Assault in the Military" at 1-2, June 3, 2013, in response to affected agency review.

[35] Several of the military sexual assault victims who brought civil lawsuits were separated from the military "under Other Than Honorable Conditions" or with a bad-conduct discharge, which they allege was retaliatory. Cioca v. Rumsfeld, Case No. 1:11-cv-00151 (LO/TCB) (E.D. Va.), Compl. filed Feb. 15, 2011, para. 26, 74, 125, 148; Klay v. Panetta, Case No. No. 12–0350 (ABJ) (D.DC), Compl. filed Mar. 6, 2012, para. 37; Marquet v. Gates, Case No. 12 cv 3117 (S.D.N.Y.), Compl. filed Apr. 20, 2012, at para. 34. The complaints in all three cases are available at http://www.protectourdefenders.com/military-sexual-assault-litigations. *See also Natelson Statement* at 5. Moreover, a "personality disorder" or "adjustment disorder" diagnosis may limit a veteran's civilian employment opportunities. *Id.*

[36] DoD DIRECTIVE 7050.06, MILITARY WHISTLEBLOWER PROTECTION 12 (July 23, 2007), *available at* http://www.dtic.mil/whs/directives/corres/pdf/705006p.pdf ("Personnel action," includes "referral for mental health evaluations."). DoD DIRECTIVE 6490.1, MENTAL HEALTH EVALUATIONS OF MEMBERS OF THE ARMED FORCES 4 (Oct. 1, 1997), *available at* http://biotech.law.lsu.edu/blaw/dodd/corres/pdf2/d64901p.pdf ("No person may refer a Service member for mental health evaluation as a reprisal for making or preparing a lawful communication to a Member of Congress, any appropriate authority in the chain of command of the Service member, an IG or a member of a DoD audit, inspection, investigation or law enforcement organization."). *See also* Army Medical Command Regulation 40-38, Command-Directed Behavior Health Evaluations 5-7; AR 600-8-24, Officer Transfers and Discharges 9; AR 635-200, Active Duty Enlisted Administrative Separations 22, 23 (July 6, 2005 and revised on Sept. 6, 2011); SECNAVINST 6320.24A, MENTAL HEALTH EVALUATIONS OF MEMBERS OF THE ARMED FORCES 16 (Feb. 16, 1999); SECNAVINST 5370.7C, MILITARY WHISTLEBLOWER REPRISAL PROTECTION 3-5 (Oct. 14, 2005); AFI 44-109, MENTAL HEALTH, CONFIDENTIALITY, AND MILITARY LAW para. 4.9.3 (Mar. 1, 2000).

[37] DoD Office of Clinical & Program Policy Response to the U.S. Commission on Civil Rights' Interrogatory No. 42. Proper criteria for a mental health evaluation include situation where the Service member is likely to cause serious injury to him or herself or to others, or when the commanding officer believes that the Service member may be suffering from a severe mental disorder. DoD Office of Clinical & Program Policy Response to the U.S. Commission on Civil Rights' Interrogatory No. 42.

[38] DoD INSTRUCTION 6490.4, MENTAL HEALTH EVALUATIONS OF MEMBERS OF THE ARMED FORCES 5 (Aug. 28, 1997) (on file with the U.S. Commission on Civil Rights).

mental health evaluation, s/he had to consult with a mental healthcare provider,[39] submit a formal written request, and provide the Service member with written justification.[40] If the mental healthcare provider discovered a procedural violation or an indication of retaliation, s/he was required to report it.[41]

This policy was subsequently updated and reissued on March 4, 2013.[42] The previous procedural safeguards were removed from the 2013 updated version of the policy, in accordance with a statutory change removing these requirements.[43] The 2013 policy simply states that if a Service member believes a command-directed psychological evaluation is retaliatory, s/he may file a complaint with the Inspector General.[44] Nevertheless, if a psychiatrist or Ph.D.-level psychologist makes a requisite diagnosis for a personality disorder and recommends administrative discharge for a Service member serving in an imminent danger pay area, the Military Service's Surgeon General must approve it before a commander can initiate discharge.[45] The diagnosis must address PTSD, and a majority of cases are referred to a medical evaluation board for PTSD before discharge.[46] Further, Service members may not be discharged based on a "personality disorder" if personnel records indicate misconduct or unsatisfactory performance, even if a "personality disorder" exists.[47]

Since the National Defense Authorization Act of 2013, victims of sexual assault who are involuntarily discharged (including those with a "personality disorder" or "adjustment disorder" diagnosis) may seek another level of review to determine whether a discharge was

---

[39] A "mental health provider" is a "psychiatrist, doctoral-level clinical psychologist or doctoral-level clinical social worker with necessary and appropriate professional credentials who is privileged to conduct mental health evaluations for DoD Components." DOD DIRECTIVE 6490.1, *supra* note 36 at 12.

[40] DOD INSTRUCTION 6490.4, *supra* note 38 at 4. *See also id.* at 23.

[41] *Id.* at 7.

[42] *Id.* at 6.

[43] 10 U.S.C. § 1090a, National Defense Authorization Act for Fiscal Year 2012, Public Law 112-81 § 711(b); DOD INSTRUCTION 6490.4, *supra* note 38 at 9-10.

[44] DOD INSTRUCTION 6490.4, *supra* note 38 at 14.

[45] DOD INSTRUCTION 1332, ENLISTED ADMINISTRATIVE SEPARATIONS 13 (Aug. 28, 2008, Incorporating Change 3, Sept. 30, 2011); DOD DIRECTIVE 6490.1, MENTAL HEALTH EVALUATIONS OF MEMBERS OF THE ARMED FORCES 6 (Oct. 1, 1997, Certified Current as of Nov. 24, 2003), *available at* http://biotech.law.lsu.edu/blaw/dodd/corres/pdf2/d64901p.pdf.

[46] DoD SAPRO comments to the U.S. Commission on Civil Rights at 18, June 12, 2013, in response to affected agency review (Additionally, in the Army, a Service member may choose to go before the Army Board for Corrections of Military Records without going to the Inspector General to challenge a personality disorder administrative discharge.); DOD INSTRUCTION 1332, *supra* note 45 at 13.

[47] *Id.*; DOD INSTRUCTION 1332, *supra* note 45 at 13.

retaliation for reporting sexual assault.[48] Prior to this Act, the DoD Inspector General's Office would first investigate and recommend action *before* a Service member could seek a hearing before a Board for Correction of Military Records.[49]

Victims' Inability to Seek Recovery in Civil Proceedings

Victims of sexual assault perpetrated by a Service member have no recourse against the U.S. government in civil proceedings.[50] The *Feres* doctrine, first articulated in *Feres v. United States*,[51] bars tort claims brought "for injuries to servicemen where the injuries arise out of or are in the course of activity incident to service."[52] The doctrine rests on three grounds: "(1) the distinctly federal nature of the relationship between the government and members of its armed forces; (2) the availability of alternative compensation systems; and (3) the fear of damaging the military disciplinary structure."[53]

In *Shearer v. United States*, the Supreme Court confirmed that the most important rationale for upholding the *Feres* doctrine was the potential disruption of military discipline by civil suits.[54] Thus, in addition to the three rationales outlined in the original *Feres* holding, the doctrine bars suits where (1) a civilian court may second-guess military decisions or (2) the plaintiff's activities directly implicate the need to safeguard military discipline.[55] Military leadership remains supportive of the current doctrine.[56] Even those who would prefer limits to the broader

---

[48] Legislation enacted in 2013 requires DoD to create a policy that a general officer or flag officer must review the circumstances of, and grounds for, the proposed involuntary separation of any member of the Armed Forces who (1) made an Unrestricted Report of a sexual assault; (2) within one year after making the Unrestricted Report of a sexual assault, is recommended for involuntary separation from the Armed Forces; and (3) requests review on the grounds that the member believes the recommendation for involuntary separation from the Armed Forces was initiated as reprisal for making the report. The general officer or flag officer must concur in the proposed involuntary separation of the member in order to separate the member. National Defense Authorization Act for Fiscal Year 2013, Pub. L. No. 112-239, 126 Stat. 1632 § 578.

[49] DoD DIRECTIVE 7050.06, MILITARY WHISTLEBLOWER PROTECTION 7 (July 23, 2007), *available at* http://www.dtic.mil/whs/directives/corres/pdf/705006p.pdf (emphasis added).

[50] This does not preclude criminal proceedings against perpetrators in civilian court. *See* Chapter 5, *infra*, at 46-47 for a discussion about civilian law enforcement action and prosecution.

[51] 340 U.S. 135, 71 S.Ct. 153 (1950).

[52] Feres v. U.S., 340 U.S. 135, 146 (1950).

[53] Madsen v. U.S. ex rel. U.S. Army Corps of Engineers, 841 F.2d 1011, 1013 (10th Cir.1987) (quotation omitted).

[54] United States v. Shearer, 473 U.S. 52 (1985).

[55] Jeffrey R. Simmons, *Military Medical Malpractice*, ARIZ. B.J., Feb. /Mar. 1988, at 22, 25.

[56] The Feres Doctrine: An Examination of This Military Exception to the Federal Tort Claims Act, 107th Cong., S. Hrg. 107-977, 43 (2002) (response to written questions by RADM Christopher Weaver, Commandant, Naval

(cont'd)

application of the *Feres* doctrine acknowledge that military decision making often requires leaders to make decisions based on a limited amount of information and time. Civil suits could open the door to Service members second-guessing the decisions of their leaders and threaten the military command structure.[57]

The Commission heard testimony from Attorney Rachel Natelson criticizing the *Feres* doctrine as applied to sexual assault victims.[58] Attorney Bridget Wilson testified that the tradeoff for Service members is the "alternative compensation system,"[59] i.e., the "ability to have military disability and veterans' disability [benefits] related to their injuries" through the Veterans Administration.[60] Wilson acknowledged, however, that it may not be a fair trade-off and that "there may be some overriding policy issues that would merit change."[61]

Broad application of the *Feres* doctrine continues to be debated. Arguably, Congress did not intend access to veterans' benefits to be a tradeoff or the exclusive remedy for Service members. In a dissenting opinion of a subsequent Supreme Court case, *United States v. Johnson*, Justice Scalia criticized the Court's reliance on the existence of veterans' benefits, arguing that the Court had held in the past that veterans' benefits were not an exclusive remedy.[62] Furthermore, because veterans' benefits are generally less extensive and more easily terminable than typical worker's compensation benefits, Justice Scalia stated that the presence of veterans' benefits as an alternative compensation system did not justify broad application of the *Feres* doctrine.[63] To date, however, Congress has not clarified its intentions with respect to whether Service members can bring civil claims against the military, and the *Feres* doctrine remains binding authority.

(cont'd from previous page)

District Washington) *available at* http://www.gpo.gov/fdsys/pkg/CHRG-107shrg88833/pdf/CHRG-107shrg88833.pdf.

[57] Major Deirdre G. Brou, *Alternatives to the Judicially Promulgated Feres Doctrine*, 192 MIL. L. REV. 1, 55 (2007); *see also* Robert Cooley, *Method to This Madness: Acknowledging the Legitimate Rationale Behind the Feres Doctrine*, 68 B.U. L. REV. 981, 991 (1988).

[58] *Natelson Statement* at 2-3.

[59] Madsen v. United States ex rel. United States Army Corps of Engineers, 841 F.2d 1011, 1013 (10th Cir.1987).

[60] Wilson testimony, *Briefing Transcript*, at 77-78.

[61] *Id.*

[62] United States v. Johnson, 481 U.S. 681, 697-98 (1987) (Scalia, J., dissenting). *See also* Pringle v. U.S., 208 F.3d 1220, 1223-24 (10th Cir. 2000) (noting that courts have broadened *Feres* to bar any claim even slightly related to a plaintiff's status as a military member, even if the claim does not appear to relate to military decisions). Joining Justice Scalia in dissent were Justices Brennan, Marshall, and Stevens.

[63] *Id.* at 698.

Impact on Victims' Access to Veterans' Benefits

Because veterans' benefits are currently the exclusive remedy available to victims of military sexual assault, access to benefits is crucial. However, for some victims the negative consequence of reporting has resulted in a loss of benefits.

Veterans Health Administration facilities are required to screen all patients for military-related sexual trauma.[64] According to the officials within the Veterans Health Administration, all Service members who were discharged under Honorable conditions are entitled to treatment for military sexual trauma.[65] However, as discussed above, victims who are discharged under conditions that are not Honorable may be ineligible for care through the Veterans Health Administration.[66]

Officials within the Veterans Health Administration also state a victim's testimony is sufficient to obtain care for military sexual trauma.[67] Legislation has been proposed to loosen the evidentiary requirements so that victims who did not report may prove that their symptoms are due to military sexual assault.[68] Prior to FY 2013, Service members who did report also

---

[64] VETERANS HEALTH ADMINISTRATION DIRECTIVE 2010-033, MILITARY SEXUAL TRAUMA (MST) PROGRAMMING 3 (July 14, 2010), *available at* http://www.va.gov/vhapublications/ViewPublication.asp?pub_ID=2272. *See also* Rachel Kimerling, Ph.D., et al., *The Veterans Health Administration and Military Sexual Trauma*, 97:12 AM. JOURNAL OF PUB. HEALTH, 2160, 2161 (2007).

[65] Susan McCutcheon, National Mental Health Director, Family Svc/Women's MH/MST, VA Central Office, Washington, DC; Margret Bell, VA Mental Health Services, national MST Support Team; Rachel E. Kimerling, VA Mental Health Services, national MST Support Team and the National Center for Posttraumatic Stress Disorder, telephone interview [hereinafter *VHA Officials Interviews*], Nov. 26, 2012.

[66] Discharges under Other Than Honorable Conditions are not unusual among military sexual assault victims for a variety of reasons. Symptoms of PTSD and of sexual trauma, as well as psychotropic medications prescribed by military doctors to victims, may interfere with a Service member's ability to do his or her job, resulting in poor performance evaluations and even disciplinary action. Nancy J. Parrish, President, Protect Our Defenders, telephone interview, Nov. 28, 2012. *See also* Galbreath testimony, *Briefing Transcript,* at 185-86 (DoD Psychologist Nate Galbreath testified that some victims' performance level falls when they are recovering from a sexual assault).

[67] *VHA Officials Interviews.* This is especially important for female veterans who live below the poverty line or are homeless and previously experienced military sexual trauma, as the Veterans Health Administration may be their primary access to healthcare. The GAO has noted that "Military sexual trauma (MST) has been linked to homelessness among women veterans." GAO, HOMELESS WOMEN VETERANS, ACTIONS NEEDED TO ENSURE SAFE AND APPROPRIATE HOUSING 1 (2011), *available at* http://www.gao.gov/assets/590/587334.pdf.

[68] H.R. 671, 113th Cong. (2013); S. 294, 113th Cong. (2013); H.R. 930, 112th Cong. (2012); S. 1391, 112th Cong. (2012).

encountered difficulty due to the military's destruction of evidence of assault after one year.[69] New legislation now requires evidence of sexual assault to be maintained for 50 years.[70]

Access to Discharge Upgrades

Each Service branch permits veterans who receive discharges with any designation other than "Honorable" to seek upgrades in their discharge classification by appealing to a Discharge Review Board.[71] Any veteran may request a discharge upgrade within 15 years of his or her discharge by completing the very brief DD Form 293, *Application for the Review of Discharge or Dismissal from the Armed Forces of the United States.* This form allows filers to choose to appear at their hearings if they wish to do so "at no expense to the government."[72] Veterans who seek upgrades more than 15 years after discharge must file instead for Correction of Military Records.[73]

Veterans who request discharge upgrades or corrections of their military records do not obtain relief a majority of the time:

> In the last several years, overall success rates in discharge upgrade cases at the Navy Discharge Review Board have run around 4%. The Army DRB success rate in upgrades is 41%. The Air Force rate is 19%; (that breaks down to 15% for upgrade applicants who don't have a personal appearance and 45% for those who have an appearance). The Coast Guard DRB has a success rate of only 1%.
>
> The Board for Correction of Naval Records upgrades approximately 15-20% of cases, while the Army Board for Correction of Military Records (BCMR) upgrades 10-15% and the Air Force BCMR upgrades 20%. Coast Guard BCMR rates are 15-20%.[74]

---

[69] *FY11 DoD Annual Report on Sexual Assault* at 70 ("[M]ilitary law enforcement holds the evidence under an anonymous alphanumeric identifier for one year" in the context of a restricted report.).

[70] National Defense Authorization Act for Fiscal Year 2013, Pub. L. No. 112-239, 126 Stat. 1632 § 577.

[71] 10 U.S.C. § 1553.

[72] DD FORM 293, APPLICATION FOR THE REVIEW OF DISCHARGE FROM THE ARMED FORCES OF THE UNITED STATES (Nov. 2012), *available at* http://www.dtic.mil/whs/directives/infomgt/forms/eforms/dd0293.pdf.

[73] *See, e.g.,* United States Army Trial Defense Service Region V, Fort Lewis Field Office, *What You Should Know About How to Upgrade Your Military Discharge, available at* http://www.monterey.army.mil/legal/trial_defense/how_to_upgrade_your_discharge.pdf (last updated May 9, 2011)

[74] Kathleen Gilberd, *Upgrading Less-Than-Fully-Honorable Discharges*, THE AMERICAN VETERANS AND SERVICEMEMBERS SURVIVAL GUIDE 324 (2008), *available at* http://www.veteransforamerica.org/wp-content/uploads/2008/11/15-Discharge-Upgrades.pdf.

Veterans who seek discharge upgrades bear the burden of all costs involved, such as attorneys' fees. The costs associated with seeking discharge upgrades, especially when understood in the context of the low success rates, may serve as a barrier to relief for veterans who were sexually assaulted while in the military and discharged without honorable conditions.

The federal Servicemember Mental Health Review Act, currently under bicameral consideration as H.R. 975 and S. 628, seeks to expand review of disability determinations of veterans discharged with a personality disorder or adjustment disorder. If enacted, this legislation will require that an expanded Physical Disability Board of Review include at least one psychologist and one psychiatrist independent from the military. Further, the Board would have the authority to review discharges of veterans who did not request review, upon the veterans' consent.[75]

Command Accountability

DoD Policy states that commanders and others engaged in retaliation are subject to punishment.[76] Some military personnel and researchers have called for the Services to go further by punishing commanders who impede the goals of the SAPR programs or interfere with those who report sexual harassment or sexual assault.[77] Professor Victor Hansen advocates for holding commanders criminally liable for failing to respond appropriately to sexual assault in their ranks.[78]

DoD psychologist Nate Galbreath testified that, in his experience as an Air Force clinical psychologist, he has tried to educate commanders about how persons suffering from sexual trauma and other mental health problems might comport themselves, and how he encourages commanders not to simply discipline a victim for performance problems.[79]

---

[75] *See, e.g.,* http://www.govtrack.us/congress/bills/113/hr975, http://www.govtrack.us/congress/bills/113/s628.

[76] 10 U.S.C. § 892; DoD DIRECTIVE 6490.1, MENTAL HEALTH EVALUATIONS OF MEMBERS OF THE ARMED FORCES 3-4 (Oct. 1, 1997), *available at* http://biotech.law.lsu.edu/blaw/dodd/corres/pdf2/d64901p.pdf.

[77] *See, e.g.,* Capt. Megan N. Schmid, U.S. Air Force, *Combating a Different Enemy: Proposals to Change the Culture of Sexual Assault in the Military,* 55 VILL. L. REV. 475, 505 (2010); HELEN BENEDICT, THE LONELY SOLDIER: THE PRIVATE WAR OF WOMEN SERVING IN IRAQ 227 (2009) (recommending increased command accountability).

[78] *Hansen Statement* at 3.

[79] Galbreath testimony, *Briefing Transcript,* at 186.

CHAPTER 5:   INVESTIGATIONS — TRAINING AND PROCEDURES

The DoD has dedicated resources to the training of investigators and judge advocates to properly handle sexual assault cases. New procedures have been implemented to address the growing concern of protecting the rights of both victims and alleged perpetrators. Congress passed legislation in 2013 requiring the Secretary of Defense to establish a panel to conduct an independent review and assessment of the systems used to investigate, prosecute, and adjudicate crimes involving adult sexual assault for the purpose of developing recommendations regarding how to improve them.[1]

Training – Investigators and Judge Advocates

Dr. David Lisak, a guest instructor at the Army's advance sexual assault training course, testified about the need to train investigators and judge advocates because of the unique nature of sexual offenses:

> [T]he men and women in the military's investigative agencies in the JAG Corps, must receive the specialized training that is required to competently handle non-stranger rape cases. These cases are marked by complexities and challenges unseen in any other type of violent crime, and these challenges can and very often still do derail these cases and prevent them from being successfully prosecuted. The specialized training should include interviewing skills that increase trust and disclosure in victims and that do not intimidate and shut down victims, skills that incorporate neuroscience research on the impact of trauma on memory formation and memory retrieval, recognition of the unique evidence needed to effectively prosecute sexual assault cases in which the issue of consent will be central, in-depth training on victim privacy issues and ways to safeguard victims from undue trampling of their privacy rights. Some of this advanced training is already under way, but it must become more widespread and crucially, it must be sustained.[2]

Investigator Training and Coordination

Although all Services operate under the common standard of the UCMJ, historically each Service developed its own training for investigators for all categories of crime, including sexual assaults.[3] Due to the growing awareness in recent years of the pervasive problem of sexual

---

[1] National Defense Authorization Act for FY 2013, Pub. L. No. 112-239, 126 Stat. 1632 § 576.

[2] Lisak testimony, *Briefing Transcript,* at 105-6.

[3] GAO, MILITARY JUSTICE: OVERSIGHT AND BETTER COLLABORATION NEEDED FOR SEXUAL ASSAULT INVESTIGATIONS AND ADJUDICATIONS 18 (2011), *available at* http://www.gao.gov/new.items/d11579.pdf

(cont'd)

assaults attempted or perpetrated on military installations, DoD has established a common policy objective to achieve consistency across the Services, including training for investigators.[4]

In 2012, an evaluation by the DoD's Inspector General revealed that the Services' Military Criminal Investigation Organizations (MCIOs)[5] did not have common, minimum standards for improved basic, refresher, or advanced sexual assault investigative training.[6] Although the MCIOs addressed the required topics, the evaluation found that the number of hours varied, and refresher training could be improved by measurement guidelines.

Judge Advocate Training

Every Service's Judge Advocate General (JAG) Corps includes attorneys responsible for both prosecuting and defending military Service members. While Service members may be represented by private defense counsel instead of a judge advocate, the prosecutor must be a member of the JAG Corps.

The Army's Military Police School administers a course for Criminal Investigators and for judge advocates from all the Services, as well as the Coast Guard.[7] In the Navy, the JAG Corps

---

(cont'd from previous page)

(providing examples of different military divisions' training such as the Naval Criminal Investigative Service (NCIS) sending 42 investigators to an advanced family and sexual violence training course in FY 2010, the Naval Justice School offering courses for prosecutors handling complex sexual assault cases, and the Army JAG conducting seven conferences led by experts who trained prosecutors on litigation of sexual assault cases).

[4] *See* DoD INSTRUCTION 5505.18, INVESTIGATION OF ADULT SEXUAL ASSAULT IN THE DEPARTMENT OF DEFENSE (Jan. 25, 2013, Incorporating Change 1, May 1, 2013), *available at* http://www.dtic.mil/whs/directives/corres/pdf/550518p.pdf; GAO, MILITARY JUSTICE: OVERSIGHT AND BETTER COLLABORATION NEEDED FOR SEXUAL ASSAULT INVESTIGATIONS AND ADJUDICATIONS, *supra* note 3, at 17-18. As early as 2008, the DoD identified investigator training and resourcing, trial counsel training and resourcing, and commander training as priorities in SAPR programming. *See* DEP'T OF DEFENSE FISCAL YEAR 2009 ANNUAL REPORT ON SEXUAL ASSAULT IN THE MILITARY 13 (2010) [hereinafter *DoD FY09 Annual Report on Sexual Assault*], *available at* http://www.sapr.mil/public/docs/reports/fy09_annual_report.pdf.

[5] The MCIOs consist of the U.S. Army Criminal Investigation Command (CID), the NCIS, and the Air Force Office of Special Investigations (AFOSI). DoD INSTRUCTION 5505.3, INITIATION OF INVESTIGATIONS BY DEFENSE CRIMINAL INVESTIGATIVE ORGANIZATIONS (June 21, 2002, replaced by DoD Instruction 5505.03 on Mar. 24, 2011), *available at* http://www.dtic.mil/whs/directives/corres/pdf/550503p.pdf.

[6] DoD OIG Response to the U.S. Commission on Civil Rights' Interrogatory 137. The Inspector General recommended a working group be tasked with developing such minimum guidelines, but the Army Commander of CID opposed the recommendation for a working group to review periodic refresher sexual assault investigation training to establish common criteria and minimum requirements to refine methods for measuring effectiveness. DoD, OIG, EVALUATION OF THE MILITARY CRIMINAL INVESTIGATIVE ORGANIZATIONS' SEXUAL ASSAULT INVESTIGATION TRAINING i (2013), *available at* http://www.dodig.mil/pubs/documents/DODIG-2013-043.pdf.pdf.

[7] In addition, Army CID sends its senior sexual assault investigators to an annual conference to receive continuing training and expertise in sexual assault investigations. *See* Dep't of the Army Response to the U.S. Commission on

(cont'd)

trains judge advocates through a Military Justice Litigation Career Track.[8] By creating a specialized group of litigators who are assigned to "progressive . . . litigation billets," Navy JAG Corps ensured this group of attorneys would remain sharp in developing and maintaining military justice litigation skills.[9] In January of 2012, the Marine Corps held two training events for JAG Corps prosecutors at Marine Corps bases in the Pacific region.[10]

Investigative Procedures

General Investigations

Victims may initiate an investigation by reporting a sexual assault directly to law enforcement or to an MCIO.[11] A victim also may report a sexual assault to a commander, who is required to refer the matter to an MCIO. It is DoD policy that all sexual assaults reported to an MCIO be investigated and that no approval from the victim's or the accused's commander is necessary.[12] Further, it is DoD policy that "investigations are conducted entirely independent from the military chain of command."[13] Once an MCIO begins an investigation after a victim reports, only the Secretary of a military department may direct an MCIO to delay, suspend, or terminate the investigation, and such a decision must then be promptly reported to the DoD IG.[14] Commanders are not permitted to impede or limit an investigation.[15]

In the past, the accused's commander may have conducted a preliminary investigation into a sexual assault allegation. However, since the issuance of DoD Instruction 6495.02 in 2006 (and re-issued in March 2013), DoD policy requires that commanders immediately refer all sexual

---

(cont'd from previous page)

Civil Rights' Interrogatory Nos. 59 & 87. The Coast Guard reports to the Department of Homeland Security during peacetime and to the DoD (by way of the Navy) during wartime. *See* DoD, *Military Service Branches*, http://www.todaysmilitary.com/service-branches.

[8] U.S. Navy, Navy JAG Corps' Military Justice Litigation Career Track (document produced by the Navy, on file with the U.S. Commission on Civil Rights) at 1.

[9] *Id.* at 2.

[10] U.S. Marine Corps Response to the U.S. Commission on Civil Rights' Interrogatory No. 87.

[11] Nate Galbreath, during in-person meeting with DoD officials, Alexandria, VA, Nov. 29, 2012.

[12] DOD INSTRUCTION 5505.3, INITIATION OF INVESTIGATIONS BY DEFENSE CRIMINAL INVESTIGATIVE ORGANIZATIONS 1 (June 21, 2002, replaced by DoD Instruction 5505.03 on Mar. 24, 2011), *available at* http://www.dtic.mil/whs/directives/corres/pdf/550503p.pdf.

[13] *Patton Statement* at 11.

[14] DOD INSTRUCTION 5505.3, *supra* note 12 at 5.

[15] *Id.* at 6.

assault reports to an MCIO for investigation.[16] When a sexual assault perpetrated by a Service member occurs off base within the United States, local law enforcement agencies "may defer prosecution to the [military] or they may not."[17] Regardless of civilian law enforcement action, an MCIO conducts an investigation. For sexual assaults that occur off base in a foreign country, the MCIO "normally conducts joint or collateral investigations with local foreign law enforcement agencies."[18] Even if civilian or foreign law enforcement takes responsibility for conducting the investigation but then fails to complete it, the MCIO may make an independent decision to conduct further investigation.[19]

MCIO investigators are required to track and report developments in each case.[20] Supervisory agents review investigative case files for approval,[21] and criminal investigators also coordinate with the prosecutor handling the case.[22] While a Service member is under investigation for a criminal offense, his/her records are supposed to be flagged and all favorable actions suspended.[23]

A victim who is sexually assaulted within the United States[24] also has the option to initiate a criminal investigation with civilian authorities. Professor Dwight Sullivan testified:

---

[16] Telephonic meeting with Nathan Galbreath, Ph.D., DoD SAPRO, June 10, 2013; DOD INSTRUCTION 6495.02, SEXUAL ASSAULT PREVENTION AND RESPONSE (SAPR) PROGRAM PROCEDURES 17 (Mar. 28, 2013), *available at* http://www.dtic.mil/whs/directives/corres/pdf/649502p.pdf; *MCM*, R. 303, at II-19.

[17] Dep't of the Army Response to the U.S. Commission on Civil Rights' Interrogatory No.105.

[18] *Id.*

[19] Dep't of the Army Response to the U.S. Commission on Civil Rights' Interrogatory No.105 (referencing AR 195-2, Criminal Investigation Activities 8 (May 15, 2009), *available at* http://www.fas.org/irp/doddir/army/ar195-2.pdf. *See also* DOD INSTRUCTION 5525.07, IMPLEMENTATION OF THE MEMORANDUM OF UNDERSTANDING (MOU) BETWEEN THE DEPARTMENTS OF JUSTICE (DOJ) AND DEFENSE RELATING TO THE INVESTIGATION AND PROSECUTION OF CERTAIN CRIMES 5-12 (June 18, 2007), *available at* http://www.dtic.mil/whs/directives/corres/pdf/552507p.pdf.

[20] DOD OIG, REVIEW OF MATTERS RELATED TO THE SEXUAL ASSAULT OF LANCE CORPORAL MARIA LAUTERBACH, U.S. MARINE CORPS 10 (Oct. 18, 2011), *available at* http://www.dodig.mil/Inspections/IPO/reports/LauterbachFR_(redacted).pdf (describing Marine Corps tracking procedures).

[21] *Id.* at 11.

[22] *See, e.g.,* Criminal Investigative Division Regulation 195-1, Section 15-1 at 5 (on file with the U.S. Commission on Civil Rights).

[23] *See, e.g.,* AR 600-8-2, Suspension of Favorable Personnel Actions (Flag) 2-3 (Oct. 23, 2012), *available at* http://www.apd.army.mil/pdffiles/r600_8_2.pdf.

[24] On the other hand, according to DoD's Annual Report, there were 239 reported sexual assaults in combat areas (i.e., outside the United States) in FY 2012 and 261 such reports in FY 2011. This represents 8.1 percent of the total reports in FY 2012 and 9.6 percent of reports in FY 2011. These numbers do not include reports made in non-combat areas outside the United States. *DoD FY12 Annual Report on Sexual Assault, Vol. 1* at 85.

[A]ny sex offense committed by a military member in the United States can be prosecuted either by the . . . military criminal justice system, or by a state court or in federal district court, and in the case of state courts, the same case can actually be prosecuted in both the military justice system and the state court because you don't have the double jeopardy bar there with different sovereigns.

…

[I]f we allow military commanders to exercise their prosecutorial discretion while also allowing civilian authorities to exercise their prosecutorial discretion, we end up with a combination of more convictions than we would have if either one of those was the sole prosecutorial discretion authority.[25]

If a sexual assault victim is dissatisfied with how the investigation into his/her allegations is being conducted, the victim may file a complaint with DoD's OIG.[26] In 2011, the GAO found that DoD's OIG had not been performing its responsibilities of overseeing sexual assault investigations and was "not monitoring or evaluating the [S]ervice [branches'] investigations of sexual assault."[27] However, in 2012, the OIG evaluated closed cases of MCIOs' sexual assault investigations, as in prior years, and released a comprehensive report in July 2013.[28] The report investigated 501 closed sexual assault investigations from 2010 and found that 56 (or 11 percent) of these closed cases had significant deficiencies, and that 31 of the 56 closed investigations were reopened by the respective Service.[29]

Forensic Examinations

If a victim makes either a restricted or an unrestricted sexual assault report within one week of the assault (or longer if circumstances dictate), s/he has the opportunity to undergo a forensic examination during which a healthcare provider collects evidence from the victim's body.[30] In

---

[25] Sullivan testimony, *Briefing Transcript,* at 86-87. *See also id.* at 134-35.

[26] DoD Instruction 6495.02 specifies that the DoD Inspector General's Office shall oversee sexual assault investigations. DoD INSTRUCTION 6495.02, SEXUAL ASSAULT PREVENTION AND RESPONSE (SAPR) PROGRAM PROCEDURES 15 (Mar. 28, 2013), *available at* http://www.dtic.mil/whs/directives/corres/pdf/649502p.pdf.

[27] GAO, MILITARY JUSTICE: OVERSIGHT AND BETTER COLLABORATION NEEDED FOR SEXUAL ASSAULT INVESTIGATIONS AND ADJUDICATIONS 9, 13 (2011), *available at* http://www.gao.gov/new.items/d11579.pdf. The GAO found no evidence of Inspector General oversight at the service level for any of the 2,594 sexual assault investigations that DoD reported completed by the services in FY 2010. *Id.* at 13-14.

[28] DoD OIG Response to the U.S. Commission on Civil Rights' Interrogatory 137.

[29] DoD OIG, EVALUATION OF THE MILITARY CRIMINAL INVESTIGATIVE ORGANIZATIONS SEXUAL ASSAULT INVESTIGATIONS 5 (2013), *available at* http://www.dodig.mil/pubs/documents/DODIG-2013-091.pdf.

[30] *See* DoD DIRECTIVE 6495.01, SEXUAL ASSAULT PREVENTION AND RESPONSE (SAPR) PROGRAM 3-5 (Jan. 23, 2012, Incorporating Change 1, Apr. 30, 2013), *available at* http://www.dtic.mil/whs/directives/corres/pdf/649501p.pdf; DoD INSTRUCTION 6495.02, *supra* note 26 at 54.

the civilian context, this is called a "rape kit."[31] The DoD refers to it as a Sexual Assault Forensic Examination or "SAFE."[32]

In FY 2011, DoD's Sexual Assault Prevention and Response Office (SAPRO) revised and reissued its policy on SAFE[33] and its accompanying instructions for victims and subjects.[34] The revised policy clarified procedures, provided detailed instructions for evidence collection, and improved procedures for the examination of victims.[35] The DoD's goals were to provide comprehensive guidance to military healthcare practitioners conducting the exam,[36] and to emphasize military-wide best practices for the collection and maintenance of forensic evidence.[37]

If the victim's military installation does not have the capability to perform this forensic exam, DoD policy requires that the victim be transported to a military facility or a local, non-military facility that has the capability.[38] Additionally, the Navy has been selected to participate in a Sexual Assault Forensic Examination (SAFE) Telemedicine Center Pilot Project with the DOJ, Office of Crimes of Violence, Department of Navy Sexual Assault and Response Office, Navy Bureau of Medicine and Surgery, and Massachusetts Department of Health. This project allows Naval healthcare providers performing a forensic medical exam to get remote assistance from experts via audiovisual technology.[39]

---

[31] *See* Rape, Abuse & Incest National Network, *What is a Rape Kit?*, http://www.rainn.org/get-information/sexual-assault-recovery/rape-kit.

[32] DoD DIRECTIVE 6495.01, *supra* note 30, at 14.

[33] DD FORM 2911, DoD SEXUAL ASSAULT FORENSIC EXAMINATION REPORT (Sept. 2011), *available at* http://www.sapr.mil/public/docs/miscellaneous/toolkit/DD_Form_2911.pdf.

[34] *DoD FY11 Annual Report on Sexual Assault* at 13.

[35] *Id.*

[36] *Id.*

[37] DoD OIG Response to the U.S. Commission on Civil Rights' Interrogatory 103. Forensic evidence is of special significance, as it is often the most concrete, scientific evidence that a sexual assault occurred, and it is essential to keep such evidence safe to facilitate prosecution. *See* GAO, MILITARY PERSONNEL: DoD HAS TAKEN STEPS TO MEET THE HEALTH NEEDS OF DEPLOYED SERVICEWOMEN, BUT ACTIONS ARE NEEDED TO ENHANCE CARE FOR SEXUAL ASSAULT VICTIMS 21-22 (2013), *available at* http://www.gao.gov/assets/660/651624.pdf.

[38] DoD INSTRUCTION 6495.02, SEXUAL ASSAULT PREVENTION AND RESPONSE PROGRAM PROCEDURES 51, 54 (Mar. 28, 2013), *available at* http://www.dtic.mil/whs/directives/corres/pdf/649502p.pdf. (In cases where the military facility lacks capability, DoD has signed memoranda of understanding/agreements with local non-military facilities to perform the exams.)

[39] Navy SAPRO Response to the U.S. Commission on Civil Rights' Interrogatory No. 85, p. 7.

A recent study by the GAO found that military sexual assault victims did not always receive timely and confidential forensic exams,[40] but in 2012, DoD's OIG began evaluating DNA collection requirements for criminal investigations. The findings and accompanying report have yet to be released.[41]

Analysis of Investigation Outcomes in FY 2011

The DoD provided data to the U.S. Commission on Civil Rights covering unrestricted sexual assault reports with completed investigations for FY 2011 (the most recent year for which data was available).[42]

Sufficient Evidence to Support Command Action

In the civilian context, a prosecutor determines whether a charge is "substantiated" by determining if the allegations are supported sufficiently or verified by corroborating information to justify further action. However, in the military justice system, the decision of whether to proceed to trial rests in the accused's chain of command. Authority for initial disposition was recently raised from the subject's immediate commander to the first commander in the chain of command who is an O-6 *and* who is a Special Court-Martial Convening Authority.[43]

For the initial disposition of any alleged crime, including sexual assault charges, the discussion portion of the Rule for Courts-Martial 306 states that in deciding how an offense should be disposed of, factors the command should consider, to the extent they are known, include the

---

[40] GAO, MILITARY PERSONNEL: DOD HAS TAKEN STEPS TO MEET THE HEALTH NEEDS OF DEPLOYED SERVICEWOMEN, BUT ACTIONS ARE NEEDED TO ENHANCE CARE FOR SEXUAL ASSAULT VICTIMS, *supra* note 37 at 19-22 (finding that "Sexual Assault Response Coordinators, Victim Advocates, and healthcare personnel differed in their understanding as to where to take a sexual assault victim for a forensic examination—a potentially problematic issue, given that the quality of forensic evidence diminishes the later it is collected following a sexual assault."). *See also Report of the Defense Task Force* at 74 ("Most military medical clinics and hospitals do not perform SAFEs because their staffs are not trained in performing these exams or do not perform these exams frequently enough to maintain their proficiency."); *Id.* at 77 ("The Task Force found DOD's procedures for collecting and documenting data about military sexual assault incidents lacking in accuracy, reliability, and validity.") For example, Navy Petty Officer 3rd Class Jenny McClendon contends she was unable to get a SAFE aboard the ship where she was raped, and, therefore, never received one. James Kitfield, *The Enemy Within*, NATIONAL JOURNAL, Sept. 13, 2012, http://www.nationaljournal.com/magazine/the-military-s-rape-problem-20120913?mrefid=site_search&page=1.

[41] DoD OIG Response to the U.S. Commission on Civil Rights' Interrogatory No. 137.

[42] For a description of the data DoD produced, *see* Appendix B.

[43] DOD, OFF. OF THE SEC'Y OF DEF., INITIATIVES TO COMBAT SEXUAL ASSAULT IN THE MILITARY (2012), *available at* http://www.defense.gov/news/DoDSexualAssault.pdf (emphasis added).

availability and admissibility of evidence, and the character and military service of the accused.[44] Thus, commanders working with their judge advocate advisor may make disposition decisions that appear to be inconsistent for similar charges across commands.

As reflected in <u>Figure 5.1</u> below, among the 941 known Service member investigations for penetration offenses (rape, aggravated sexual assault, and forcible sodomy) in FY 2011,[45] 412 (or 43.8 percent) had sufficient evidence to support command action for a sexual assault charge.[46] <u>Figure 5.1</u> also shows that of the 577 Service member subjects investigated for sexual contact offenses and attempts to commit a sexual offense (including attempted penetration offenses), 378 (or 65.5 percent) had sufficient evidence to support command action for a sexual assault charge.

---

[44] *MCM* 306(b). Actions available to the commander include: no action; administrative action; nonjudicial punishment; disposition (preferral) of charges; or forwarding for disposition (to a higher command level with greater authority for a more severe disposition). *Id.*

[45] This figure does not include investigations where the identity of the perpetrator was unknown or where the perpetrator was a civilian or foreign national. It also excludes 110 Service members who were investigated and prosecuted by civilian authorities and seven who deserted or were deceased. Also, this figure does not include perpetrators identified as civilians or foreign nationals who had a military pay-grade.

[46] The subject records indicate the most serious sexual offense investigated. They do not indicate the offense for which there was insufficient evidence to support command action.

Figure 5.1
Subjects with sexual assault investigations the command reviewed for possible action by penetration offenses versus sexual contact and attempted sexual offenses, FY 2011

Case Disposition	Penetration Offenses	Sexual Contact and Attempts	Total
Command Action Precluded	**368**	**115**	**483**
Victim declined to participate in military justice action	153	31	184
Insufficient evidence of any offense	213	82	295
Statute of limitations has expired	2	2	4
Victim died	0	0	0
Action Declined by Commander	**40**	**7**	**47**
Case unfounded by Command	40	7	47
Evidence for commander action for sexual assault charge	**412**	**378**	**790**
Court-Martial Charge Preferred	362	126	488
Nonjudicial punishments (Article 15 UCMJ)	22	165	187
Administrative discharge	17	31	48
Adverse administrative action	11	56	67
Evidence for commander action for other criminal offenses	**121**	**77**	**198**
Probable cause for only non-sexual assault offense	121	77	198
Total	**941**	**577**	**1518**

Source: Compiled by USCCR from DOD FY 2011 sexual assault data.

As seen above, for FY 2011, victims declined to continue participating in the investigation or the prosecution against 153 of the 941 Service members investigated for penetration offenses (16.3 percent). For Service members investigated for sexual contact offenses and attempted sexual offenses, victims discontinued participation in 31 of 577 investigations (5.4 percent).

Depicted in Figure 5.2 below, among those cases that were sufficiently supported to merit command action for a sexual offense (although not necessarily for the most serious sexual offense investigated), 52 percent included investigations for penetration-type offenses.[47] The remaining 48 percent were investigated for a sexual contact offense or an attempted sexual offense.

---

[47] Figure 5.2 includes 10 subjects who were not designated as Service members but nevertheless received adverse administrative action for a sexual offense. It also includes four subjects, also not designated as Service members, who were deemed to have enough evidence against them to support command action for a non-sexual offense.

Figure 5.2
Offenses investigated with evidence for commander action, FY 2011

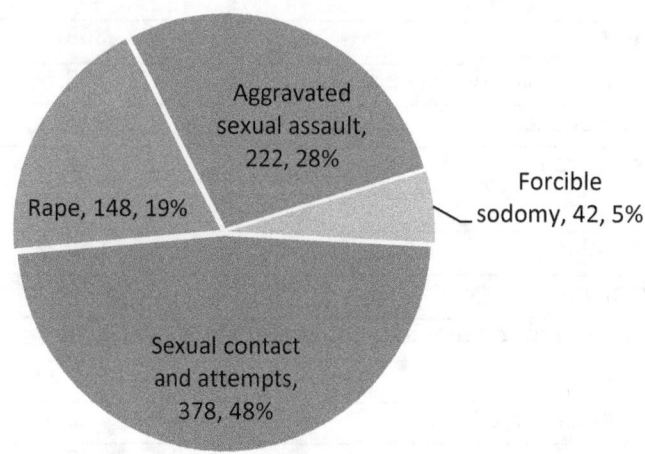

Subject records with evidence for Commander action, sexual offense

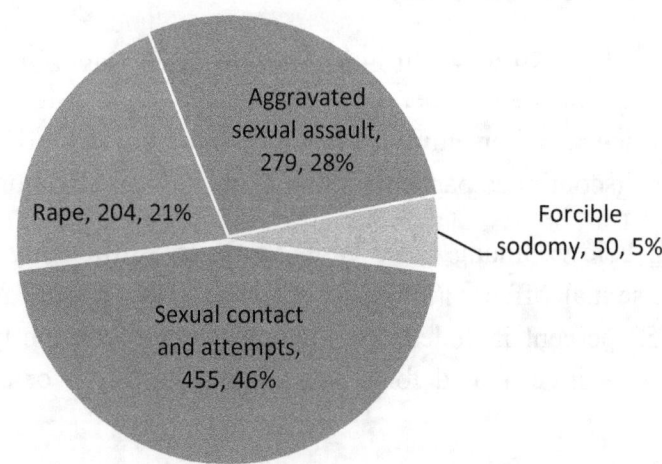

Subject records with evidence for Commander action, any offense

Source: Compiled by USCCR from DOD FY 2011 sexual assault data.

Because a commander has a broader range of options for disposition than a civilian prosecutor, any comparisons between the disposition of sexual assault allegations in the military and those handled in the civilian justice system is inherently unreliable.[48]

Victims' Decisions to Cease Prosecution

The willingness of the victim to maintain his or her participation in the judicial process until a final disposition of the case is another category of relevant data.

As is also true in a civilian criminal proceeding, if at any point the victim decides to stop cooperating with military investigators and prosecutors, the continued investigation or prosecution may end based on lack of evidence to support continued efforts. Nevertheless, even though the DoD's 2011 Annual Report on Sexual Assault categorized cases where the victim declined to participate as "Command Action Precluded,"[49] it is still within the Services' discretion to continue even without victim participation. According to the Navy,

> In most situations, the commanders will not move forward with the case if the victim does not want to participate because there will not be enough evidence with[out] the victim's statement to proceed. [But] if there is enough evidence to proceed and that evidence is admissible under the Military Rules of Evidence, then the determination to proceed will be made on a case-by-case basis and with the advice of a judge advocate.[50]

Likewise, according to the Army, "Commanders can and do take actions in some cases against offenders [even] when the victim declines to cooperate in the military justice proceeding."[51] In FY 2011, 184 subjects accused of perpetrating sexual assault did not receive any form of corrective action or discipline because their alleged victims declined to participate in the military justice process. However, in other cases where the victim refused to cooperate with a military justice proceeding, 10 subjects were administratively discharged, and two were given non-judicial punishment. Moreover, in four cases where the victim's lack of cooperation

[48] To provide some context, however, it has been estimated that in the civilian system "14% to 18% of all reported sexual assaults are prosecuted." Rebecca Campbell et al., *Systems Change Analysis of SANE Programs: Identifying the Mediating Mechanisms of Criminal Justice System Impact, Research Report Submitted to the U.S. Department of Justice*, Jan. 23, 2009, at 1 (citing Campbell, R. (2008), *The psychological impact of rape victims' experiences with the legal, medical, and mental health systems*, AMERICAN PSYCHOLOGIST, 68, 702-717; Spohn, C. (2008), *The criminal justice system's response to sexual violence*, Paper presented at the National Institute of Justice Sexual Violence Research Workshop, Washington, DC.), av*ailable at* www.ncjrs.gov/pdffiles1/nij/grants/226497.pdf.

[49] *DoD FY11 Annual Report on Sexual Assault* at 32, Exhibit 1, Point O.

[50] Dep't of the Navy, Chief of Naval Operations Response to the U.S. Commission on Civil Rights' Interrogatory No. 101.

[51] Dep't of the Army Response to the U.S. Commission on Civil Rights' Interrogatory No. 101.

resulted in findings of insufficient probable cause for the sexual offense, the subjects received other adverse administrative actions based on a concurrent non-sexual assault charge.[52]

Further, as depicted in Figure 5.3, female victims were more than twice as likely as male victims to cease participating in an ongoing investigation. Among the records with a sole female victim, where there was not enough evidence to support commander action, the victim ceased cooperating in 39 percent of the cases. For records with a sole male victim that ended with insufficient evidence to support commander action, the victim ceased participating in 16 percent of cases.[53] The motives of those victims who ceased participating in the investigation are unknown.

Figure 5.3
Reasons command action was precluded, by victim gender—subject records with disposition indicating that command action was precluded, FY 2011

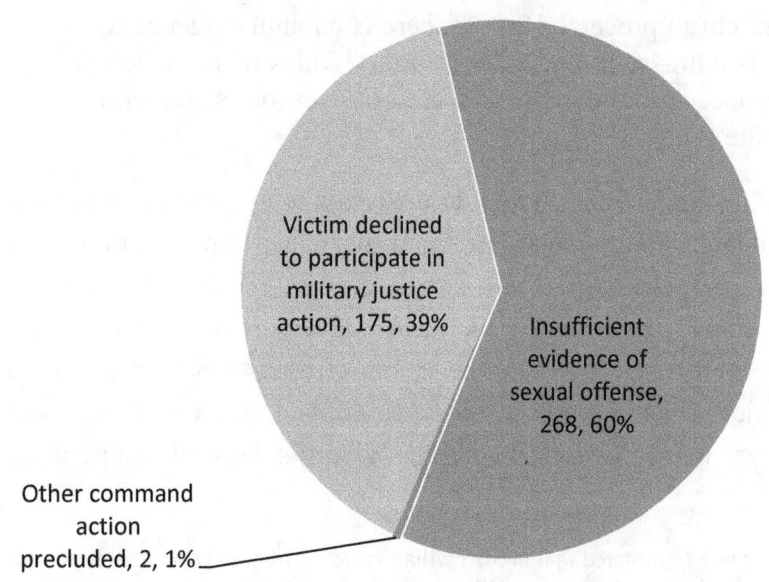

Subject records when command action was precluded for sole female victims

Victim declined to participate in military justice action, 175, 39%

Insufficient evidence of sexual offense, 268, 60%

Other command action precluded, 2, 1%

---

[52] *DoD FY11 Annual Report on Sexual Assault* at 35-36, Enclosure 1 (Army Annual Report on Sexual Assault).

[53] It should be noted, however, that sole male victims constituted only 25 disposition records, and therefore this statistic may not be reflective of a trend over time.

Subject records when command action was precluded for sole male victims

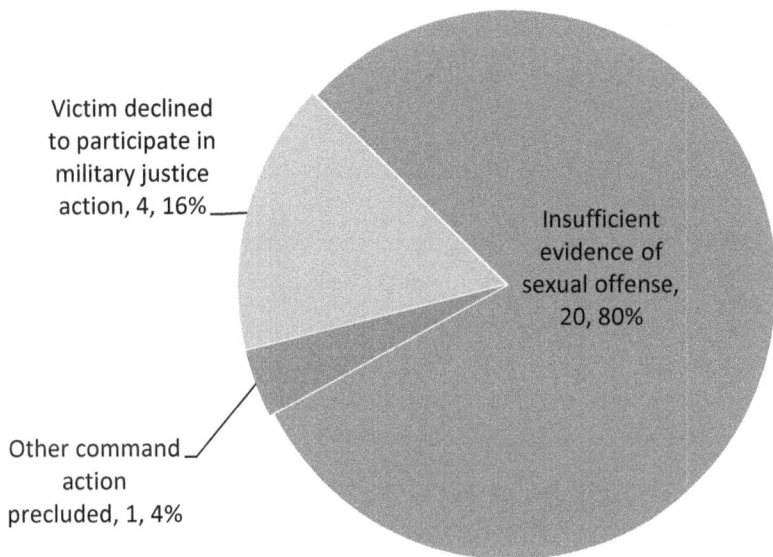

Source: Compiled by USCCR from DOD FY 2011 sexual assault data.

In recent years, DoD and the Services have focused on improving training for investigators and judge advocates, and have recognized the benefits of standardized training and processes. The Secretary of Defense has issued an updated strategic plan to continue with these efforts, and pledged to devote the necessary resources.[54] Thus, DoD now has a proposal to implement best practices across Services; to expand, improve, and standardize training; and to ensure oversight by the DoD OIG. The efficacy of such renewed efforts is yet to be determined.

---

[54] SEC'Y OF DEF., 2013 DEPARTMENT OF DEFENSE SEXUAL ASSAULT PREVENTION AND RESPONSE (SAPR) STRATEGIC PLAN (2013), *available at* http://www.sapr.mil/public/docs/reports/SecDef_SAPR_Memo_Strategy_Atch_06052013.pdf.

CHAPTER 6:   DISCIPLINE AND COMMANDER DISCRETION

The prosecution and imposition of discipline must be seen as fair by military personnel in order to protect the credibility of the military command structure. In addition, uniform and equitable standards safeguard the interests of both victims and alleged perpetrators.

Disciplinary Procedures

After an investigation is complete, the accused's commander[1] consults with legal counsel and decides the "initial case disposition" of alleged criminal offenses.[2] The disposition options available to a commander are: (1) taking no action, (2) taking administrative action, (3) imposing a nonjudicial punishment (known as "Article 15"[3]), or (4) referring the case to court-martial. Administrative action includes corrective measures such as admonition or reprimand. Adverse administrative actions and nonjudicial punishment are more severe and may include fines, forfeitures, reduction in grade, and even administrative discharge.[4] If the commander

---

[1] As explained in the Introduction, the term "commander," as used in this report, refers to a commander with disposition authority for sexual assault allegations. In April 2012, the Secretary of Defense withheld disposition authority for allegations of completed or attempted rape, sexual assault, and forcible sodomy from all commanders who do not possess at least Special court-martial convening authority and who are not in the grade of O-6 (i.e., colonel or Navy captain) or higher. Memorandum of Secretary of Defense, Withholding Initial Disposition Authority Under the Uniform Code of Military Justice in Certain Sexual Assault Cases (Apr. 20, 2012), *available at* http://www.dod.gov/dodgc/images/withhold_authority.pdf, *effective by* June 28, 2012.

[2] *MCM*, R. 306, at II-25. Navy commanders are required to send a Special Incident Report or Operations Report upon receiving an unrestricted sexual assault report and to file monthly updates until final resolution of the case. *See* NAVY OPERATIONS INSTRUCTION (NAVINST) F3100.6J, SPECIAL INCIDENT REPORTING (OPREP-3 PINNACLE, OPREP-3 NAVY BLUE, AND OPREP-3 NAVY UNIT SITREP) PROCEDURES (Oct. 4, 2011); OPNAVINST 1752.1B, SEXUAL ASSAULT VICTIM INTERVENTION (SAVI) PROGRAM (Dec. 29, 2006), *available at* http://doni.daps.dla.mil/Directives/01000_Military_Personnel_Support/01-700_Morale,_Community_and_Religious_Services/1752.1B.PDF.

[3] A commander's authority to impose nonjudicial punishment arises from Article 15 of the UCMJ.

[4] *See DoD FY11 Annual Report on Sexual Assault* at 47. The severity of nonjudicial punishment that a commander may impose is based on the rank of an accused and the rank of a commander. *MCM* PART V, at V-4 – V-5; JAG INSTRUCTION 5800.7F, MANUAL OF THE JUDGE ADVOCATE GENERAL Section 0111 (June 26, 2012), *available at* http://www.jag.navy.mil/library/instructions/JAGMAN2012.pdf. "Conditions that subject soldiers to discharge" include a pattern of minor disciplinary infractions as well as commission of a serious military or civil offense. *See, e.g.,* AR 635-200, Active Duty Enlisted Separations 102 (July 6, 2005 and revised on Sept. 6, 2011).

believes more severe punishment is appropriate, s/he "refers" the case to court-martial (also called "preferring" court-martial charges).[5]

There are three types of courts-martial: (1) Summary, (2) Special, or (3) General. Summary court-martial is available only to resolve charges against enlisted Service members. It consists of one commissioned officer who is charged with "thoroughly and impartially inquir[ing] into both sides of the matter and . . . ensur[ing] that the interest of both the Government and the accused are safeguarded and that justice is done."[6] Special and General courts-martial consist of a military judge, military prosecutor (or "trial counsel"), defense counsel, and court-martial members who perform functions similar to a civilian jury, but with important distinctions.[7] There are at least three officers in a Special court-martial and at least five officers in a General court-martial. An accused before a Special or General court-martial is entitled to free legal representation by military defense counsel, or civilian counsel at his/her own expense.[8]

Before referring a case to a General court-martial, a commander must appoint an officer to conduct a fact-finding investigation, known as an Article 32 hearing, to determine whether reasonable grounds exist to believe an accused committed an offense and, if so, to recommend the appropriate court-martial level.[9] The commander retains full discretion in deciding whether to refer the case to trial, regardless of the investigating officer's recommendation.[10]

---

[5] "Referral" is the order of a convening authority for an accused Service member to be tried by court-martial. The commander must have "reasonable grounds" to refer or "prefer" court-martial charges. U.S. Marine Corps SAPR Response to Request for Documents No. 8.; *MCM* R. 601, at II-52.

[6] *MCM* R. 1301, at II-179-180. The maximum punishment a Summary court-martial may impose is limited and varies with an accused's grade. For grade E-4 and below, the maximum sentence is 30 days of confinement (incarceration), reduction in rank to E-1, and restriction for 60 days. A Summary court-martial cannot sentence an accused of the rank of E-5 or higher to confinement, nor can it reduce the accused's rank by more than one grade. *See Id.*

[7] *MCM* R. 501, at II-42 & R. 805(b), at II-79-80. An accused may request trial by judge alone. If there are court-martial members, an accused may request that it be composed of at least one-third enlisted personnel. *MCM* R. 501(a)(1), at II-42 & R. 503(a)(2), at II-46-47. A Special court-martial sentence is limited to no more than forfeiture of two-thirds basic pay per month for one year, and for enlisted personnel, no more than one year of confinement and/or a bad-conduct discharge. *MCM* R. 1003, at II-126-128. General court-martial allows for the maximum punishment set for each offense, including death (for certain offenses), confinement, a dishonorable or bad-conduct discharge for enlisted personnel, or a dismissal for officers. *MCM* R. 1003, at II-126-128. General court-martial sentences also may include any of the less severe punishments available in a Summary or Special court-martial. *See DoD FY11 Annual Report on Sexual Assault* at 45.

[8] *MCM* R. 506, at II-50.

[9] 10 U.S.C. § 832, UCMJ, Art. 32. An Article 32 hearing affords an accused more rights than a preliminary hearing or a Grand Jury proceeding in the civilian context. An accused has the right to be present, have counsel appointed and present, cross-examine witnesses, call witnesses of his or her own, and make a statement. *Id.*

[10] *MCM* R. 401, at II-31-32.

After pre-trial discovery,[11] the commander selects the court-martial members.[12] The parties may contest the selections through peremptory challenges.[13] Once the court-martial member selection is complete, the trial proceeds. As in civilian cases, the trial counsel (prosecutor) presents evidence on the charges and the accused may confront the evidence, cross-examine any witnesses, and present his/her own evidence. The Military Rules of Evidence closely resemble the Federal Rules of Evidence used by U.S. District Courts in civilian cases, and the military has a version of the "rape shield law" to protect a victim's previous sexual behavior or predisposition.[14]

However, unlike civilian criminal cases, military court-martial members need not reach a unanimous decision. Only a two-thirds majority is needed to convict.[15] If the accused is found guilty, the court-martial members determine the sentence.[16] The accused's commander approves or disapproves the court-martial members' findings of guilt and either approves or reduces the sentence.[17] "The [commander] may for any reason or no reason disapprove the legal sentence in whole or in part, mitigate the sentence, and change a punishment to one of a different nature as long as the severity of the punishment is not increased."[18] Service members convicted of a sexual offense also may be required to register as sex offenders, depending on the charge upon which the conviction was obtained and whether the sentence included confinement.[19]

---

[11] *See MCM* R. 701, 702, 703, at II-56-65.

[12] *MCM* R. 502, at II-42-43.

[13] *MCM* R. 912, at II-103-6.

[14] *MCM* R. 412, at III-21.

[15] *MCM* R. 921(c)(B), at II-119.

[16] *MCM* R. 502, at II-42; *MCM* R. 1001, at II-122; *MCM* R. 1002, at II-125.

[17] *MCM* R. 1107(b)(1), at II-152 ("The action to be taken on the findings and sentence is within the sole discretion of the convening authority . . . [and] is a matter of command prerogative.").

[18] *MCM* R. 1107(d)(1), at II-153; *see MCM* R. 1101(c), at II-138. Commanders have access to judge advocates who advise them regarding the final disposition, including the sentence, for a criminal offense and who is required to forward a recommendation to the commander. *MCM* R. 1106, at II-149-151.

[19] *See* DoD INSTRUCTION 1325.07, ADMINISTRATION OF MILITARY CORRECTIONAL FACILITIES AND CLEMENCY AND PAROLE AUTHORITY 78-82 (Mar. 11, 2013), *available at* http://www.dtic.mil/whs/directives/corres/pdf/132507p.pdf. *See also* OPNAVINST 1752.3, POLICY FOR SEX OFFENDER TRACKING, ASSIGNMENT AND ACCESS RESTRICTIONS WITHIN THE NAVY (May 27, 2009), *available at* http://doni.documentservices.dla.mil/Directives/01000_Military_Personnel_Support/01-700_Morale,Community_and_Religious_Services/1752.3.pdf; NAVAL MILITARY PERSONNEL MANUAL (MPM) 1910-233. MANDATORY SEPARATION PROCESSING (Oct. 18. 2010); MPM 1910-142, SEPARATION BY REASON OF MISCONDUCT – COMMISSION OF A SERIOUS OFFENSE (Nov. 10, 2009). However, according to Professor Dwight Sullivan, if a Service member receives confinement for "any offense that has the word 'indecent' in it," there is

(cont'd)

Characterization of Discharge of Service Members Accused of Sexual Assault

As discussed above, commanders may impose an administrative discharge as a form of adverse administrative action. A Service member facing court-martial for a sexual assault may seek to be administratively discharged in lieu of a court-martial.[20] It is also military service policy that commanders initiate administrative discharges for Service members whose courts-martial or civilian court convictions for sexual assault are final, but are not punitively discharged in connection with such conviction.[21]

When a Service member is administratively discharged, the characterization of discharge is listed as one of three options: (1) Honorable discharge, (2) General discharge under Honorable conditions, or (3) General discharge under Other Than Honorable Conditions.[22] An Honorable

---

(cont'd from previous page)

"mandatory notification to both state and local [sex offender] registration officials." Sullivan testimony, *Briefing Transcript*, at 145-46.

[20] For example, Marine Corps policy provides that a Marine may be separated upon his or her request in lieu of trial court-martial, if it is determined that the Marine is unqualified for further military service. MCO P1900.16F, MARINE CORPS SEPARATION AND RETIREMENT MANUAL, ¶¶4104.4 & 6419. The request for discharge in lieu of court-martial must include an acknowledgement of guilt and a summary of the evidence. *Id.* at ¶¶ 4104.4.b. & 6419.3.e. *See also* AFI 36-3207, SEPARATING COMMISSIONED OFFICERS, para 2.2(July 2004); AFI 36-3208, ADMINISTRATIVE SEPARATION OF AIRMEN, Chapter 4 (July 9, 2004); AR 600-8-24, Officer Transfers and Discharges 49 (Apr.12, 2006); AR 635-200, Active Duty Enlisted Separations 81 (July 6, 2005 and revised on Sept. 6, 2011).

[21] Col. Alan Metzler, in-person interview, Alexandria, VA, Nov. 29, 2012. *See also* SECNAVINST 1920.6C, ADMINISTRATIVE SEPARATION OF OFFICERS (Sept. 20, 2011), Enclosure (8) page 12; OPNAVINST 1752.3, *supra* note 19 at para. 3.D ("Navy members who are convicted of a sex offense while on active duty, or in a reserve status, and who are not punitively discharged, shall be processed for administrative separation"); MARINE ADMINISTRATIVE MESSAGE (MARADMINS) 317/09, POLICY FOR SEX OFFENDER DISCHARGES (May 20, 2009), *available at* http://www.marines.mil/News/Messages/MessagesDisplay/tabid/13286/Article/112596/policy-for-sex-offender-discharges.aspx (providing that the Marine Corps will process an administrative separation for any Marine who, while on active duty or in a reserve status, is convicted of a sex crime as defined by the Sex Offender Registration and Notification Act, whether in a civilian criminal court or a court-martial); AR 600-20, para. 8-5o(34) and 635-200, chapter 14-12c(2)(b)(3) (requiring unit commanders to process for administrative separation all soldiers convicted of sexual assault in any type of court proceeding); MPM 1910-233, MANDATORY SEPARATION PROCESSING (Oct. 18, 2010) para. 1.a.; MPM 1910-142, SEPARATION BY REASON OF MISCONDUCT – COMMISSION OF A SERIOUS OFFENSE (Nov. 10, 2009) para. 3.d. Despite the pre-existing policy, Congress recently mandated that all Service members convicted of sexual assault be discharged. *See* National Defense Authorization Act for Fiscal Year 2013, 10 USCA § 1561 (NOTE), Pub. L. No. 112-239, § 572(a)(2).

[22] Only a court-martial can impose a bad-conduct discharge or a dishonorable discharge. *MCM* R. 1003, at II-127-28

discharge and a General discharge under Honorable conditions entitle a veteran to nearly all benefits; benefits may be limited or precluded for other characterizations of discharge.[23]

Substantiated allegations of sexual assault against a Service member, or even a court-martial conviction for a sex offense, do not necessarily result in a discharge under Other Than Honorable Conditions. The Services' regulations provide conflicting guidance as to when it is appropriate for an administrative discharge based on sexual misconduct to be characterized as under Honorable conditions.[24]

The military does not maintain data that tracks the characterizations of discharges for Service members accused of sexual assault.[25] Therefore, it is impossible to know how often Service members accused of sexual assault were given an Honorable discharge or a General discharge under Honorable conditions either as nonjudicial punishment, in lieu of a court-martial, or after a court-martial conviction for sexual assault.

---

[23] For example, to be eligible for the Post-9/11 GI Bill, a discharge must be Honorable, and not simply a General discharge under Honorable Conditions. U.S. Air Force Office of The Judge Advocate General comments to U.S. Commission on Civil Rights at 5, June 7, 2013, in response to affected agency review.

[24] The separation of an Army officer, for example, will generally be under honorable conditions when the officer "(1) Submits an unqualified resignation . . . under circumstances involving misconduct [or] (2) [i]s separated based on misconduct, including misconduct for which punishment was imposed, which renders the officer unsuitable for further service . . . ." AR 600-8-24, Officer Transfers and Discharges para. 1-22b (Apr.12, 2006). However, "[a]n Army officer will normally receive an "Under Other Than Honorable Conditions" [characterization of a General discharge] when they [sic] – (1) Resign for the good of the service . . . . (3) Are involuntarily separated due to misconduct, moral or professional dereliction . . . . [or] (4) Are discharged following conviction by civilian authorities." *Id.* at para. 1-22c. *See also* AR 635-200, Active Duty Enlisted Separations, para. 3-7a(2)(b)-(c), para. 10-8a, para. 3-7a(2)(d) (July 6, 2005 and revised on Sept. 6, 2011) (providing guidance regarding characterization of administrative discharge of Soldiers); MCO P1900.16F, MARINE CORPS SEPARATION AND RETIREMENT MANUAL, para, 1004, 1004.3 (a Marine may receive an Honorable characterization of discharge or a general discharge under Honorable conditions even when separated in lieu of trial by court-martial "if the Marine's service is otherwise so meritorious that any other characterization would clearly be inappropriate."); MCO P1900.16F, para. 1004.2.a(2) and 1004.2.b(2); SECNAVINST 1920.6C, ADMINISTRATIVE SEPARATION OF OFFICERS (Sept. 20, 2011), Enclosure (3) page 7, Enclosure (5) pages 1-2; MPM 1910-302, GENERAL CONSIDERATIONS ON CHARACTERIZATION OF SERVICE (June 2, 2008); MPM 1910-304, DESCRIPTION OF CHARACTERIZATION OF SERVICE (June 30, 2008); AFI 36-3206, ADMINISTRATIVE DISCHARGE PROCEDURES FOR COMMISSIONED OFFICERS (June 9, 2004); AFI 36-3207, SEPARATING COMMISSIONED OFFICERS (July 9, 2004); AFI 36-3208, ADMINISTRATIVE SEPARATION OF AIRMEN (July 9, 2004); AFI 51-201, ADMINISTRATIVE MILITARY JUSTICE (Oct. 25, 2012).

[25] The Navy explained that it cannot determine how many of its service members were administratively discharged due to a sexual assault because it uses the same Navy Separation Code (SPD Code) for all sexual misconduct, including non-contact offenses, such as viewing pornography. Chief of Naval Operations' Response to the U.S. Commission on Civil Rights' Interrogatory No. 120a.

Commander Discretion

The accused's commander has full discretion in deciding the dispositions of criminal offenses and the punishments imposed.[26] No policy guidance exists specifying that "allegations must be disposed of in a particular manner, [which] predetermined types or amounts of punishments are appropriate, or [if] adverse action is required in all cases or in a particular case."[27] The commander must obtain advice from a judge advocate, but the commander is not obligated to act upon that advice.[28] DoD policy lacks a clear standard for corrective or disciplinary action against commanders making discretionary determinations of whether there is sufficient evidence to support command action. In FY 2011, nearly half of the reported penetration-type sexual offenses, and nearly one-third of reported sexual contact offenses and attempted sexual offenses, were determined to have insufficient evidence to support command action.[29]

A superior officer may not limit the commander's discretion in exercising authority.[30] On the other hand, a superior officer may withhold disposition authority.[31]

A commander with disposition or convening authority "is singularly powerful with respect to his influence over the military justice system."[32] He/she has the power to conduct direct investigations before the case is referred to court-martial, authorize probable cause searches, refer cases to court-martial, grant witnesses immunity, negotiate and approve pretrial

---

[26] *MCM* R. 306(a), at II-25. *See* Memorandum of the Secretary of Defense, Withholding Initial Disposition Authority Under the Uniform Code of Military Justice in Certain Sexual Assault Cases (Apr. 20, 2012), *available at* http://www.dod.gov/dodgc/images/withhold_authority.pdf, *effective by* June 28, 2012.

[27] Dep't of the Army's Response to Request for Document No. 10.

[28] UCMJ App. 2, Sec. 834, Art. 24 ("Before directing the trial of any charge by general court-martial, the convening authority shall refer it to his staff judge advocate for consideration and advice.").

[29] Analysis of the U.S. Commission on Civil Rights. *See* Figure 5.1, *supra* Chapter 5, at 48. A comparison to civilian contexts is difficult because, in the military, substantiated allegations of criminal conduct may be punished without being prosecuted, as discussed in this chapter.

[30] *MCM* R. 306(a), at II-25.

[31] Memorandum of the Secretary of Defense, *supra* note 26 (withholding disposition authority from all commanders below the grade of O-6). The Marine Corps expanded this withholding of disposition authority to include sexual contact offenses. MARADMINS 372/12, WITHHOLD OF INITIAL DISPOSITION AUTHORITY IN CERTAIN SEXUAL ASSAULT CASES (July 13, 2012), *available at* http://www.marines.mil/News/Messages/MessagesDisplay/tabid/13286/Article/110494/withhold-of-initial-disposition-authority-in-certain-sexual-assault-cases.aspx.

[32] Lindsy Nicole Alleman, *Who Is In Charge, and Who Should Be? The Disciplinary Role of the Commander in Military Justice Systems*, 16 DUKE J. OF COMP. & INT'L L. 169, 170 (2006).

agreements, select court-martial members, approve sentences, grant clemency, and grant funding to the prosecution and defense counsel for retaining expert witnesses.[33]

The Manual for Courts-Martial (MCM) directs commanders to dispose of criminal allegations at the *lowest* appropriate level.[34] The only written guidance for deciding the appropriate level states that commanders should consider several factors, including the accused's "character and military service."[35] The MCM establishes the *maximum* penalty for each offense in the UCMJ, but it provides no *minimum* penalty.[36] Therefore, commanders have various factors to consider, along with the advice of a judge advocate, to guide decisions.[37]

A commander may not refer a case to a General court-martial for trial without having been advised by a judge advocate that adequate evidence supports the allegation.[38] However, a commander is free to forego any disciplinary action even if a judge advocate recommends

---

[33] *MCM* R. 303, 315(d), 407(a), 502(a)(1), 703(d), 704(c), 705, 1107(d)(1), 1107(d)(2), at II-19, II-41, II-42, II-63, II-66, II-68 , II-153, III-14, III-15. The commander does not, however, have the power to change an acquittal to a conviction or to increase a sentence. *MCM* R. 1107(d)(2), at II-153.

[34] *MCM* R. 306(b), at II-25 (emphasis added).

[35] *MCM* R. 306(b), at II-25-26 (Other factors include the nature of and circumstances surrounding the offense and the extent of the harm caused by the offense, including the offense's effect on morale, health, safety, welfare, and discipline; when applicable, the views of the victim as to disposition; existence of jurisdiction over the accused and the offense; availability and admissibility of evidence; the willingness of the victim or others to testify; cooperation of the accused in the apprehension or conviction of others; possible improper motives or biases of the person(s) making the allegation(s); availability and likelihood of prosecution of the same or similar and related charges against the accused by another jurisdiction; and, appropriateness of the authorized punishment to the particular accused or offense; and other likely issues.). Military leadership informed the Senate Armed Services Committee that they support removing "military service" as a consideration in the disposition of a sexual offense. *Hearing of the Senate Armed Services Committee*, June 4, 2013, at time marker 1:51-1:54, http://www.senate.gov/isvp/?type=live&comm=armed&filename=armed060413.

[36] *See MCM*, APPENDIX 12, at A12-1-7 (emphasis added). All sexual assault offenses have a maximum punishment of a dishonorable discharge or bad-conduct discharge and confinement terms ranging from one year for wrongful sexual contact to life for rape and forcible sodomy. *Id.*

[37] The Navy's Staff Judge Advocates are instructed to review a list of factors to evaluate sexual assault cases, which are enumerated in a newsmailer (OFFICE OF THE JAG CRIMINAL LAW DIVISION NEWSMAILER 2010-02, GUIDANCE AND TRAINING FOR SJA/TC ON CONSULTING WITH CONVENING AUTHORITIES IN SEXUAL ASSAULT CASES (Feb. 16, 2010)) and in a Sexual Assault Disposition Brief on a secure website accessible to Navy personnel. Chief of Naval Operations' Request for Documents Nos. 8-11.

[38] UCMJ App. 2, Sec. 834, Art. 24(a). The standard of proof applied in a staff judge advocate's advice is probable cause. *MCM* R. 406(b)(2), at II-40.

otherwise.[39] There is no mechanism currently in place to ensure that justice is administered consistently.[40]

<u>Concerns with the Current System</u>

Some social scientists have noted that considering the "character and military service of the accused" when deciding the disposition of a sexual assault allegation may be based on false beliefs about who perpetrates sexual assault.[41] They argue that sexual predators are adept at being likeable to authority figures and are "such masters of the 'hidden persona' . . . that their colleagues and commanders are often happy to offer positive character testimony to investigators and courts-martial."[42] Further, it may be difficult for a commander to be objective due to his or her relationship with the accused or the victim. In a public comment to the Commission, one retired commander explained, "The military is an experience that can create bonds within the ranks—up and down—in extraordinary ways and in extraordinary situations. Each of their lives is in the hands of [the] other, and they can become deeply indebted, consciously or unconsciously, for a lifetime."[43]

Retired Army psychiatrist, Brigadier General Lorree Sutton, believes that more than a decade of war has led military leaders to value achievement in combat above all other characteristics, and that this has created a situation where commanders tend to overlook or tolerate sexually-abusive conduct among subordinates.[44] Also, there may be a disincentive for a commander to uncover these problems if promotion potential or performance evaluations depend upon the

---

[39] DoD's Office of Legal Policy's Response to the U.S. Commission on Civil Rights' Interrogatory No. 118 (citing Nonjudicial Punishment Procedure (Art. 15, UCMJ) Guidance in Part V, *MCM*, at V-1-9); DoD's Office of Legal Policy's Response to the U.S. Commission on Civil Rights' Interrogatory No. 112.

[40] *Report of the Defense Task Force* at 85 (citing as an example, "Service Members from different Services jointly engaging in the same criminal activity may receive disparate treatment from convening authorities from different Services.") *See also* Chief of Naval Operations' Request for Documents Nos. 8-11.

[41] *See* Kristen Houser, *Analysis and Implications of the Omission of Offenders in the DoD Care for Victims of Sexual Assault Task Force Report*, 13 VIOLENCE AGAINST WOMEN 961, 961-70 (2007).

[42] James Kitfield, *The Enemy Within*, NATIONAL JOURNAL, Sept. 13, 2012, http://www.nationaljournal.com/magazine/the-military-s-rape-problem-20120913?mrefid=site_search&page=1 (quoting Russell Strand); Tim Madigan, *Q&A with Russell Strand, Retired Criminal Investigator*, STAR-TELEGRAM, Aug. 20, 2012, http://www.star-telegram.com/2012/08/17/4188015/qa-with-russell-strand-retired.html.

[43] Comment submitted by Lt. Col. Terry Moore, USAF (ret.) to the U.S. Commission on Civil Rights (Feb. 5, 2013).

[44] Gen. Lorree Sutton, telephone interview, Nov. 27, 2012. *See also Report of the Defense Task Force* at 34 ("[S]ome military personnel indicated that predators may believe they will not be held accountable for their misconduct during deployment because commanders' focus on the mission overshadows other concerns.").

conduct and performance of subordinates.[45] A commander might want to paint the most benign picture of his unit, without the negativity of sexual harassment or sexual assault in his or her ranks.

Many victims and victim advocacy groups insist that the disposition of sexual assault reports should be removed from the chain of command and instead be handled by an independent civilian authority.[46] Military law expert, Professor Elizabeth Hillman, and retired General Sutton support such fundamental change.[47] Professor Hillman argued military sexual assault should be prosecuted in civilian courts in order to "help to break the link between war, military service, and sexual violence."[48] Some commanders agree that they are insufficiently trained to make complex legal decisions and that eliminating this responsibility would free them to focus on day-to-day operations.[49]

Professor Eugene Fidell, a military law expert at Yale Law School, agrees that disposition authority must be taken outside the chain of command for all criminal offenses, not just sexual offenses, as is the case in Canada, the United Kingdom, and Israel. He advocates for a single, permanent military convening authority.[50] Professor Hillman agrees with Professor Fidell that a central prosecutorial authority would help to ensure consistency in all military criminal

---

[45] Jackie Speier, *Rapes of Women in Military 'A National Disgrace'*, SFGATE (Apr. 16, 2011), http://www.sfgate.com/opinion/article/Rapes-of-women-in-military-a-national-disgrace-2374845.php. Professor Hillman also testified that the current system fails to protect the rights of minorities within the Armed Forces:

> From the civil rights perspective then, the current system of prosecution within the military fails to protect the rights of many vulnerable minorities, including survivors of rape and sexual assault who suffer disability as a result of those experiences, women whose professional opportunities are limited by the prevalence of sexual assault, men, especially African-American men, who have too often been unfairly singled out for prosecution for these crimes, and gay men and lesbians, historically perceived as sexually deviant and therefore less deserving of protection, whether they have been the targets of or accused of the criminal misconduct themselves.

Elizabeth Hillman testimony, *Briefing Transcript,* at 88.

[46] Jim Forsyth, *House Committee Hearing to Address Sexual Assault in Military*, REUTERS, Jan. 23, 2013, http://www.reuters.com/article/2013/01/23/us-usa-military-sex-hearing-idUSBRE90M09620130123.

[47] Garry Trudeau and Lorree Sutton, *Breaking the Cycle of Sexual Assault in the Military*, WASH. POST, June 29, 2012, http://articles.washingtonpost.com/2012-06-29/opinions/35461103_1_military-sexual-assault-military-culture-trust; Hillman testimony, *Briefing Transcript,* at 92-94.

[48] Statement of Elizabeth L. Hillman, Professor, University of California, Hastings, School of Law, submitted to the U.S. Commission on Civil Rights 5 [hereinafter *Hillman Statement*], *available at* http://www.eusccr.com/msa1.htm.

[49] Comment submitted by Lt. Col. Terry Moore, USAF (ret.) to the U.S. Commission on Civil Rights (Feb. 5, 2013).

[50] Comment of Professor Eugene R. Fidell submitted to the U.S. Commission on Civil Rights (Dec. 11, 2012).

prosecutions.[51] Both Fidell and Hillman argue that the military justice system is "opaque" because of its "decentralized character" in which a different commander controls the course of prosecution in each case.[52] They argue that greater consistency and transparency would equal greater legitimacy.[53]

In April 2013, Secretary of Defense Chuck Hagel asked Congress to amend the UCMJ to limit commanders' discretion in overturning court-martial convictions.[54] The leadership of each of the Services has publicly agreed with this suggestion.[55]

Arguments for Maintaining, and Ways to Strengthen, the Current System

The military's position is that the disposition of sexual assault reports must be handled within the chain of command in order for the commander to maintain "good order and discipline."[56] Vice Admiral Nanette M. DeRenzi, Judge Advocate General of the Navy, testified:

> [C]ommanding officers are responsible for the safety, the welfare and the good order and discipline within their command. They have difficult leadership decisions to make and … [have] experienced judge advocates to advise them in making them, and they make those decisions case by case, day in and day out, on the specific facts and circumstances of each case, and they try to do what's right in each case, not what's easy, not what's expedient, and not what is a perception of what's expected of them.[57]

General Gary S. Patton, Director of DoD's Sexual Assault Prevention and Response Office, testified, "Commanders are going to have to fix this problem, and we need to keep commanders involved in the problem, not less involved."[58] He argued that "[r]emoving a commander from the administration of justice among his or her troops would undercut a commander's authority,

---

[51] *Hillman Statement* at 4.

[52] *Id.*

[53] *Id.*

[54] Craig Whitlock, *Hagel Seeks Changes to Military Code After Outcry Over Handling of Sex-Assault Cases*, WASH. POST (Apr. 8, 2013), *available at* http://www.washingtonpost.com/world/national-security/hagel-seeks-changes-to-military-code-after-outcry-over-handling-of-sex-assault-cases/2013/04/08/5552b8d6-a08a-11e2-ac00-8ef7caef5e00_story.html.

[55] *Hearing of the Senate Armed Services Committee*, June 4, 2013, at time marker 1:42, http://www.senate.gov/isvp/?type=live&comm=armed&filename=armed060413.

[56] *Patton Statement* at 4, 12; *see also* Statement of Dwight H. Sullivan submitted to the U.S. Commission on Civil Rights 4 [hereinafter *Sullivan Statement*], *available at* http://www.euseccr.com/msa1.htm; Patton testimony, *Briefing Transcript,* at 206-9.

[57] DeRenzi testimony, *Briefing Transcript,* at 224-25.

[58] Patton testimony, *Briefing Transcript,* at 207-8.

especially in combat."[59] Lieutenant General Dana Chipman, Judge Advocate General of the Army, added, "The commander's ability to punish quickly, visibly, and locally is essential to maintaining discipline in units. The Uniform Code of Military Justice ensures that commanders can maintain good order and discipline in the force."[60]

Military criminal defense attorney, Major Wilson, also advised against giving a civilian authority the responsibility of determining the disposition of military sexual assault cases. She testified, "I think that the people within this institution have to own it . . . for the process to have credibility. The people in this institution have to be the people who make that change . . . [I]t has to be command driven."[61]

Professor and defense counsel, Dwight H. Sullivan, also cautioned that changes to the UCMJ may have unforeseen and unintended consequences, as altering the military justice system from the outside may raise constitutional questions.[62] He noted that, when Congress amended the UCMJ's sexual assault statute in 2006, it unconstitutionally shifted the burden of one element of the offense to the defendant, which resulted in some convictions being overturned. The 2006 amendments were so problematic that Congress had to overhaul them again in 2011.[63] He also argued that Congress should wait to make any further changes until it has time to evaluate the effectiveness of revisions to the military's sex crime statutes pursuant to the National Defense Authorization Act of 2013.[64]

---

[59] *Patton Statement* at 4. Professor Hillman disagreed: "I consider the imperative to protect commanders' authority to prosecute a Pyrrhic victory at best, because it leaves commanders liable to the scrutiny of the public, to criticism no matter what they do, and it leaves their troops vulnerable to a problem that so far our military has gained little traction over, despite two decades of what I think are serious and comprehensive efforts to address it." Hillman testimony, *Briefing Transcript*, at 91.

[60] Statement of Lt. Gen. Dana K. Chipman, Judge Advocate General of the Army, Submitted to the U.S. Commission on Civil Rights 2, *available at* http://eusccr.com/msa1.

[61] Wilson testimony, *Briefing Transcript*, at 36-37. Congressman Michael R. Turner and Congresswoman Niki Tsongas, who have been outspoken on the need to fully address military sexual assault, agree that altering military culture requires buy-in from the Pentagon, and they support waiting to see how recent changes in law and policy work before taking the issue away from the chain of command. *See* Emily Cadei and Megan Scully, *Grappling With an Epidemic of Assault*, CONG. Q., Oct. 27, 2012, http://public.cq.com/docs/weeklyreport/weeklyreport-000004169541.html.

[62] *Sullivan Statement* at 1-3. Professor Sullivan also noted that Australia's High Court overturned that country's military justice system after it was amended, which caused significant disruption. Sullivan testimony, *Briefing Transcript*, at 124-26, 129; *see also* Weiss v. U.S., 510 U.S. 163 (1994) (finding that military judges who already had been commissioned officers before being assigned to serve as judges did not have to receive a second appointment before assuming their judicial duties).

[63] *Sullivan Statement* at 1-3. *See also* U.S. v. Prather, 69 M.J. 338, 339-340 (C.A.A.F. 2011).

[64] *Sullivan Statement* at 3-4; Sullivan testimony, *Briefing Transcript*, at 84-86.

In order to increase consistency across the Services and provide more guidance to commanders, DoD could provide sentencing guidelines with mandatory minimum sentences.[65] While the MCM sets forth *maximum* punishments for each criminal infraction,[66] there are no *minimum* penalties.[67] The Navy agrees: "Anecdotal insights suggest a potential value for minimum sentencing guidelines for sex crimes under the Uniform Code of Military Justice."[68]

Military law expert, Professor Victor Hansen, also advocates strengthening the current system through greater command accountability. Currently, "dereliction of duty" under UCMJ Article 92 is the primary statutory mechanism to hold a commander accountable for his or her command failings.[69] Hansen argues that this mechanism is inadequate because it merely requires a commander "to avoid willful failures and achieve a level of competency that is somewhere above simple negligence or culpable inefficiency."[70] In order to create adequate "legal incentives to aggressively prevent and suppress [sexual] misconduct," Hansen testified that the UCMJ should include a doctrine that exists in international law known as "command responsibility."[71] Under this doctrine, a commander would be required "to do all that is reasonable within his power and authority to investigate, prevent and suppress sexual assault crimes within the ranks." [72] Hansen argues that holding commanders to this higher standard would help identify the command failings that have contributed to the under-detection of sexual assault.[73]

---

[65] Major General Vaughn Ary, Staff Judge Advocate to the Commandant of the Marine Corps, informed the Commission that the appearance of light sentences may, in part, be due to the fact that court-martial members who vote to acquit, but are outnumbered, still play a role in deciding the sentence. Ary testimony, *Briefing Transcript,* at 222.

[66] *See MCM*, APPENDIX 12, at A12-1-7.

[67] In comparison, for example, civilian federal sentencing guidelines require a minimum sentence of five years imprisonment for criminal sexual abuse. 18 U.S.C. §§ 2241, 3553; 3559(a)(1); U.S. Sentencing Guidelines §5D1.2(a)(1).

[68] Dep't of the Navy, SAPRO, Response to the U.S. Commission on Civil Rights' Interrogatory No. 127. *See also* Hansen testimony, *Briefing Transcript,* at 147-48; Parrish testimony, *Briefing Transcript,* at 68.

[69] *Hansen Statement* at 3.

[70] *Id.*

[71] *Id.* at 2.

[72] *Id.*

[73] *Id. See also* Diane H. Mazur, Capt. U.S. Air Force (Ret.), *Military Values in Law*, 14 DUKE J. GENDER L. & POL'Y 977, 1004 ("If Congress, the military, or critics of military policy are dissatisfied with the performance of military leaders in punishing and preventing sexual assault, they need to hold them accountable for failures of leadership in the same manner in which they would hold them accountable in situations not involving violence against women. The answer is not to . . . relieve military commanders of the obligation to protect the people they lead.") Professor Hillman agreed that "[m]ore robust theories of accountability for higher-ranking officers who neglect or condone military sexual violence would also advance the prosecution of military sexual violence."

(cont'd)

Another way to strengthen the current system is to have a policy encouraging commanders to disclose the dispositions of sexual assault incidents. Commanders generally do not communicate the outcomes of sexual assault reports to members of their command despite a recommendation by the Defense Task Force that they do so in order to control rumors, clarify misperceptions, and reinforce the commander's zero tolerance stance.[74] Similarly, Dr. Lisak testified that he sees "enormous prevention opportunities" in informing Service members of the disciplinary outcomes of sexual assault investigations in their units.[75] Professor Hansen made a similar recommendation that senior military leadership should communicate clearly when there has been a command failure with respect to preventing or responding to sexual assault.[76]

Unlawful Command Influence

As discussed above, the accused's commander has full discretion to decide the disposition and ultimate punishment in all criminal cases. Unlawful command influence occurs when a superior office improperly attempts to direct or influence a subordinate commander's decision or improperly interfere with a criminal investigation or prosecution.[77] Unlawful command influence also may take other forms such as intimidating witnesses, humiliating the accused, or

---

(cont'd from previous page)

Hillman Statement at 4. *See also* Statement of Cindy McNally, Chief Master Sergeant, U.S. Air Force (Ret.) to House Armed Services Committee Hearing on the Review of Sexual Misconduct by Basic Training Instructors at Lackland Air Force Base (Jan. 23, 2009), http://docs.house.gov/meetings/AS/AS00/20130123/100231/HHRG-113-AS00-Wstate-McNallyC-20130123.pdf ("[H]olding our leaders responsible and legally liable for the welfare of their troops is an absolute must.").

[74] *Report of the Defense Task Force* at 82.

[75] Lisak testimony, *Briefing Transcript*, at 142-43.

[76] Professor Hansen testified, "[O]ftentimes the messaging is very inconsistent and there is a cultural unwillingness to broadcast those consequences in a clear way so that the soldiers, the service members understand, and so that other commanders understand specifically what . . . were the command failings, and there's a huge cultural resistance within the military to do that, and I think that needs to change." Hanson testimony, *Briefing Transcript*, at 143-44.

[77] Unlawfully influencing the action of a court is prohibited by Article 37, UCMJ. At a subordinate commander's request, however, a superior commander lawfully may consult with a subordinate about judicial decisions. DoD's Office of Legal Policy's Response to the U.S. Commission on Civil Rights' Interrogatory No. 112. The SAPR training for all Navy leaders includes training on the need to avoid unlawful command influence. The "suggested script" for facilitators of such training includes the following: "Sexual assault cases can be incredibly complicated, and as we've discussed, command leaders must limit their involvement in the cases and simply 'support – report – and initiate an official NCIS investigation.'" Chief of Naval Operations' Response to the U.S. Commission on Civil Rights' Interrogatory No. 105 (citing Navy SAPR-L Facilitation Guide (Fiscal Year 2012)). At the pre-trial stages, the commander lawfully may exercise command control when gathering evidence against members of his or her command, who are suspected of violating the UCMJ, but not once court-martial charges are referred or "preferred." *Id.*

publicly drawing conclusions as to guilt or innocence.[78] A superior commander may, however, lawfully elect to remove or withhold the authority from a subordinate commander to act in a particular case or types of cases.

Some military criminal defense attorneys believe there is unlawful command influence prejudicing those accused of sexual assault.[79] They believe that this, in part, is due to political pressure to increase the number of sexual assault cases referred to court-martial and to increase conviction rates.[80] In some cases, military judges have concurred. After General James Amos, Commandant of the Marine Corps, publically demanded tougher punishment for those accused of sexual misconduct, some military judges found that his statements presented the appearance of unlawful command influence.[81]

Concerns of Diminished Rights of the Accused and Over-Prosecution

Attorneys (judge advocates) who represent the accused in military sexual assault cases believe that political pressure and unlawful command influence are diminishing their clients' ability to mount an adequate defense and causing over-prosecution.

First, alleged perpetrators and their attorneys are concerned that there is a growing disparity in the resources the military provides to criminal defendants and those provided to the prosecution. Professor Sullivan explained,

> The sexual assault prevention legislation has earmarked funds for the prosecution of these offenses, and so we are pumping more money into the prosecution side   . . . . And you don't have a mirror image on the defense side, and the whole idea of the military justice system . . . is that there is supposed to

---

[78] *See* Statement of Phillip D. Cave to the U.S. Commission on Civil Rights 13-14 [hereinafter *Cave Statement*], *available at* http://www.eusccr.com/msa1.htm.

[79] *Cave Statement* at 13-14; *Sullivan Statement* at 6-7; Statement of Bridget Wilson submitted to the U.S. Commission on Civil Rights 1-2 [hereinafter *Wilson Statement*], *available at* http://www.eusccr.com/msa1.htm; Wilson & Cave testimonies, *Briefing Transcript*, at 31-32, 44-46, respectively.

[80] Wilson testimony, *Briefing Transcript*, at 30-32.

[81] Michael Doyle, *Tough Talk by Marine Commandant James Amos Complicates Sexual-Assault Cases*, McClatchy Newspapers, Sept. 13, 2012, http://www.mcclatchydc.com/2012/09/13/168410/tough-talk-by-marine-commandant.html. In response to criticism that he was exerting unlawful command influence, Gen. Amos wrote a White Letter in which he stated, "My intent is not to influence the outcome or response in any particular case, but rather to positively influence the behavior of Marines across our Corps. As senior leaders, we have the inherent responsibility to ensure the sanctity of our justice system, this includes the presumption of innocence unless proven otherwise. . . . . . I expect all Marines involved in the military justice process – from convening authorities, to members, to witnesses – to make their own independent assessment of the facts and circumstances of each case." White Letter No. 3-12 from the Commandant of the Marine Corps on Leadership (July 12, 2012).

be an equality of resources on both sides. And again I think because of the politicization of this issue, you see earmarks going exclusively to the prosecution side.

. . .

[T]he fact [is] that the defense counsel don't even have investigators. I mean, literally something that would be taken for granted in most public defender's offices . . . military defense counsel don't have.[82]

Furthermore, alleged perpetrators are sometimes denied the benefit of an expert because there is insufficient funding or the commander does not believe the defense has provided sufficient justification.[83] Military defense attorney, Philip Cave, explained, "Such an imbalance in resources further negates the actual and perceived fairness of the military justice system."[84] He did acknowledge, however, that "[t]he Services have hired highly qualified experts for the defense in the same manner they are hired for the prosecution."[85]

Second, in defense attorney Major Wilson's opinion, there is concern that the Services' "strategic goal"[86] to increase sexual assault reporting rates may motivate some commanders to take action based on ambiguous information. She explained,

The military way is that if the command wants more reports, they will get those reports, one way or another even if those reports are not accurate. No institution is more single minded in its pursuit of a goal than the armed forces. . . . When those in charge express the "desire" to see something done, it will be done, often without regard for the collateral damage. That is the current approach that we are seeing with regard to sexual assault in the military. Those who would rather not report are being pressured to do so. A junior enlisted woman is lectured by a senior noncommissioned officer that the events of the drunken party were a rape regardless of the misgivings of the woman.[87]

---

[82] Sullivan testimony, *Briefing Transcript*, at 149-50.

[83] *Cave Statement* at 13.

[84] *Id.*

[85] *Id.*

[86] *Wilson Statement* at 1 (citing the Army's FY 2010 report to DoD's Sexual Assault Prevention and Response Office).

[87] *Wilson Statement* at 1.

The increase, since FY 2009, in the percentage of sexual assault reports determined by military criminal investigators to be "unfounded" indicates that concern may be warranted.[88]

Third, some defense attorneys believe the zeal to punish sexual assaulters makes commanders and judge advocates blind to those who intentionally make false accusations.[89] Professor Sullivan argued that "[p]oliticization of the issue of sexual assault in the military threatens [the] goal [of] . . . fairly and accurately distinguish[ing] those Service members who are innocent from those who are guilty."[90] Mr. Cave argued, "Over the last five to seven years it has been increasingly apparent to an accused going into a sexual assault case that he is presumed guilty, that he must prove his innocence, and that background politics play an important role in how the case is to be resolved."[91]

While acknowledging that false accusations are relatively rare,[92] Mr. Cave provided the Commission with an example of a situation where he believed military prosecutors disregarded evidence that allegations were false.[93] He noted a variety of reasons one might make a false accusation, including the desire to obtain an expedited transfer;[94] the hope of delaying punishment for misconduct;[95] or, simply for revenge.[96] Before the ban on gays and lesbians was

---

[88] The percentage of cases determined by a MCIO to be unfounded has risen from 5.2 percent in FY 2009 to 10.7 percent in FY 2010, to 11.9 percent in FY 2011, and to 13.6 percent in FY 2012. *DoD FY09 Annual Report on Sexual Assault in the Military* at 64; DoD, DEPARTMENT OF DEFENSE FISCAL YEAR 2010 ANNUAL REPORT ON SEXUAL ASSAULT IN THE MILITARY 64 (2011) [hereinafter *DoD FY10 Annual Report on Sexual Assault*], *available at* http://www.sapr.mil/media/pdf/reports/fy10_annual_report.pdf; *DoD FY11 Annual Report on Sexual Assault* at 32; *DoD FY12 Annual Report on Sexual Assault, Vol. 1* at 68.

[89] *Cave Statement* at 3-8; *Sullivan Statement* at 6.

[90] *Sullivan Statement* at 6.

[91] *Cave Statement* at 1-2. *See also id.* at 10.

[92] *Cave Statement* at 3. *See also Wilson Statement* at 2. According to Dr. David Lisak, social science research estimates that 2-10 percent of rape allegations are false. *Lisak Statement* at 3. Mr. Cave did not dispute this statistic. Cave testimony, *Briefing Transcript*, at 51. According to a DoD Task Force,

> [Service members] may overestimate the number of false reports for several reasons: the victim may recount the incident differently during the course of the investigation; the case may not have gone to trial due to insufficient evidence; the case may have resulted in an acquittal, or the results of the investigation, trial, or final consequences may not have been published or shared. The distinction between a false report and an unsubstantiated report is usually not obvious.

Report of the Defense Task Force at 33. *See also* Bruce Gross, Ph.D., JD, MBA *False Rape Allegations: An Assault On Justice*, THE FORENSIC EXAMINER, Sept. 15, 2012, *available at* http://www.theforensicexaminer.com/archive/spring09/15/ (describing the difficulties in estimating the rate of false rape allegations).

[93] *Cave Statement* at 5-6.

[94] *Id., see also Wilson Statement* at 2.

[95] The military has a policy of delaying the investigation and disposition of collateral misconduct committed by the Service member who alleges sexual assault until after final disposition of the sexual assault allegation. DoD

(cont'd)

repealed in 2011, some Service members caught engaging in consensual same-sex sexual conduct may have had an incentive to make a false accusation in an attempt to avoid being discharged on the basis of homosexuality.[97]

A final concern of military defense attorneys (judge advocates) and their clients is that sexual assault cases are being referred to court-martial even when the evidence is weak. They expressed the view that, rather than looking critically at the evidence, prosecutors presume the accused to be guilty.[98] According to Mr. Cave, "the perception today, if not the reality is that a sexual assault case is more likely to go to trial despite . . . recommendations from an [investigating officer not to pursue prosecution]."[99] Professor Sullivan agreed with Mr. Cave.[100]

In response, Lieutenant General Richard C. Harding, the Judge Advocate General for the Air Force, noted that "commanders are asked to take an oath before they prefer a charge . . . that based on their personal knowledge or personal investigation of the case, . . . they believe, honestly believe that the charges are true to the best of their knowledge and belief."[101]

While some military prosecutors agree they prosecute sexual assault cases that civilian district court attorneys (DAs) would not, this does not necessarily mean there is over-prosecution.[102] The UCMJ criminalizes all forms of nonconsensual, sexual touching in order to preserve "good

---

(cont'd from previous page)

INSTRUCTION 6495.02, SEXUAL ASSAULT PREVENTION AND RESPONSE PROGRAM PROCEDURE 41-42 (Mar. 28, 2012). Collateral misconduct may include offenses such as underage drinking, fraternization, engaging in consensual sex in the barracks or on a military vessel (a criminal offense under the UCMJ), or adultery in which the victim had engaged at the time of the sexual assault. Bridget Wilson, in-person conversation, Jan. 11, 2013, Washington D.C.; *Cave Statement* at 4. In focus group studies, many male service members expressed the belief that women accused men of sexual assault to avoid discipline for collateral misconduct, but reviews of unrestricted sexual assault reports did not support this belief. *See* Sarah Jane Brubaker, *Sexual Assault Prevalence, Reporting and Policies: Comparing College and University Campuses and Military Service Academies*, 22 SECURITY J. 56, 67 (2009). Consequently, according to Wilson, the military is now less likely to delay discipline for collateral misconduct so as to avoid giving the appearance that the victim has an incentive to give false testimony. Bridget Wilson, in-person conversation, Jan. 11, 2013, Washington D.C.

[96] Cave testimony, *Briefing Transcript*, at 18-20.

[97] *Wilson Statement* at 2.

[98] *Cave Statement* at 1.

[99] *Id.*

[100] Sullivan testimony, *Briefing Transcript,* at 87.

[101] Harding testimony, *Briefing Transcript*, at 220.

[102] *Report of the Defense Task Force* at 81 (quoting a staff judge advocate as stating that Judge Advocates prosecute a lot of cases that their civilian counterparts would not, saying they "ethically could not prosecute because they have serious reservations that enough facts exist to support all elements of the allegation.").

order and discipline"—conduct that civilian authorities may not consider severe enough to devote resources to investigating and prosecuting.

Further, as Major General Vaughn Ary, Staff Judge Advocate to the Commandant of the Marine Corps, noted, DAs must seek re-election based, in part, on conviction records,[103] and as such, this may influence the decision whether to prosecute more challenging cases. Also, civilian prosecutors need a unanimous jury to get a conviction, whereas military prosecutors need only two-thirds to convict.[104]

Lt. Gen. Chipman, Judge Advocate General of the Army, added that the public holds the military to a higher standard than civilian law enforcement, and that Americans have higher expectations that the military will protect their sons and daughters from sexual assault within the ranks.[105]

Nevertheless, a lack of confidence in the military justice system undermines the entire effort to address the problem of sexual assault, as defense attorney Major Wilson explained:

> The good intention of addressing sexual assault in the military is being buried by a campaign that now lacks credibility in the ranks. There is an increasing perception that the deck is stacked against someone accused of a sexual assault.
>
> . . .
>
> The prosecution of sexual assault now is privately being dismissed by many in the armed forces as a political witch hunt, something that will damage the cause of protecting victims for years to come. It will damage the status of women in the institution for years to come. It will give rapists a cover for years to come.[106]

Thus, some Service members accused of sexual assault and the attorneys who represent them are concerned that the heightened attention to the issue is tilting the scales of justice away from the accused.

---

[103] Ary testimony, *Briefing Transcript*, at 222.

[104] *Id.*

[105] Chipman testimony, *Briefing Transcript*, at 223-24. *See also Hansen Statement* at 1 ("Our military has a unique mission and we ask a great deal of our service members. We have a special and critical obligation to protect all of them from these crimes in exchange for the selfless sacrifice that we ask of them.").

[106] *Wilson Statement* at 1. Nancy Parrish, President of Protect Our Defenders, agreed that "Command bias that convicts the innocent is as bad as command bias that wreaks retribution on the victim and ignores the crime." Parrish testimony, *Briefing Transcript*, at 41.

Trends in the Department of Defense's Data on Prosecution and Discipline

Overall, DoD's Annual Reports on Sexual Assault indicate that commanders have been referring more cases to court-martial over the past four years. Of the military subjects whose cases were given to their commander by the MCIO for possible action, the commander referred 21 percent of these cases to court-martial in FY 2009, 27 percent in FY 2010, 32 percent in FY 2011, and 35 percent in FY 2012.[107] For those cases in which commanders decided there was sufficient evidence to take action, court-martial charges accounted for 42 percent of disciplinary actions in FY 2009, 52 percent of disciplinary actions in FY 2010, 62 percent of disciplinary actions in FY 2011, and 68 percent of disciplinary actions in FY 2012.[108]

Of the subjects referred to court-martial whose cases were completed during the listed fiscal year, 72 percent proceeded to trial in FY 2009, 67 percent in FY 2010, 65 percent in FY 2011, and 66 percent in FY 2012. The others either were dismissed due to lack of evidence (18 percent in FY 2009, 23 percent in FY 2010, 24.6 percent in FY 2011, and 19 percent in FY 2012) or the subject was permitted to resign or be discharged in lieu of court-martial (10 percent in FY 2009 and FY 2010, 10.5 percent in FY 2011, and 15 percent in 2012).[109]

The Commission's analysis revealed that, of all the investigations that gathered sufficient evidence to support commander action in FY 2011, just over one-fifth (203 of 989) led to court-martial convictions (191 subjects convicted on a sexual assault charge at court-martial; 12 subjects convicted of some other misconduct charge at court-martial). These convictions represented just over 10% (203 of 2,004) of the total sexual assault subjects with case dispositions reached in FY 2011; however, 486 of these 2,004 subjects were either unidentified

---

[107] *DoD FY09 Annual Report on Sexual Assault* at 64 (of 1,935 subjects reviewed for commander action where the commander made a decision within the fiscal year, 410 had courts-martial charges preferred); *DoD FY10 Annual Report on Sexual Assault* at 71 (of 1,980 subjects reviewed for commander action where the commander made a decision within the fiscal year, 529 had courts-martial charges preferred); *DoD FY11 Annual Report on Sexual Assault* at 32 (of 1,516 subjects reviewed for commander action, 489 had court-martial charges preferred); *DoD FY12 Annual Report on Sexual Assault, Vol. 1* at 68 (of 1,714 subjects reviewed for commander action, 594 had court-martial charges preferred).

[108] *DoD FY09 Annual Report on Sexual Assault* at 64 (of 983 subjects whose commander took action, 410 had courts-martial charges preferred); *DoD FY10 Annual Report on Sexual Assault* at 71 (of 1,025 subjects whose commander took action, 529 had courts-martial charges preferred); *DoD FY11 Annual Report on Sexual Assault* at 32 (of 989 subjects whose commander took action, 489 had court-martial charges preferred); *DoD FY12 Annual Report on Sexual Assault, Vol. 1* at 68 (of 880 subjects whose commander took action, 594 had court-martial charges preferred).

[109] *DoD FY11 Annual Report on Sexual Assault* at 45, 82, 78; *DoD FY12 Annual Report on Sexual Assault, Vol. 1* at 73. Notably, some of the subjects whose court-martial charges were dismissed received nonjudicial punishment based on evidence discovered during the sexual assault investigation. *DoD FY10 Annual Report on Sexual Assault* at 76; *DoD FY11 Annual Report on Sexual Assault* at 45; *DoD FY12 Annual Report on Sexual Assault, Vol. 1* at 73.

or outside the legal authority of the DoD as shown in <u>Figure 6.1</u> below. Evidence supported nonjudicial punishment for nearly 16% of subjects for a sexual offense (156 of 989); 4.9% of subjects (49 of 989) were acquitted of court-martial charges; and 9.2% of subjects (91 of 989) had court-martial charges dismissed. The rest were still pending at the close of the fiscal year.

<u>Figure 6.1</u>
Subject records in investigations of sexual offenses that led to court cases or Article 15, by case disposition and outcome, FY 2011

case disposition	Court Case or Article 15 Outcome							Total records	Records with Court Case or Art. 15 Outcomes
	None	Discharge or Resignation in Lieu of Court Martial	Acquittal	Article 15 punishment imposed	Conviction	Dismissal	Pending adjudication		
Subject outside DOD's legal authority	479		2	3		1	1	486	7
Command Action Precluded	476			1		6		483	7
Action Declined by Commander	47							47	0
Evidence for commander action for sexual assault charge	137	43	58	166	191	74	121	790	653
Court-Martial Charge Preferred	2	40	48	18	190	74	116	488	486
Nonjudicial punishments (Article 15 UCMJ) or adverse administrative action	91		10	148			5	254	163
Administrative discharge	44	3			1			48	4
Evidence for commander action for other criminal offenses	113			80	5			198	85
Probable cause for only non-sexual assault offense	113			80	5			198	85
Total	1252	43	60	250	196	81	122	2004	752
Percents of records...									
All subjects	62.5%	2.1%	3.0%	12.5%	9.8%	4.0%	6.1%	100.0%	37.5%
Those with evidence for commander action, any offense	25.3%	4.4%	5.9%	24.9%	19.8%	7.5%	12.2%	100.0%	74.7%
Those with evidence for commander action, sexual offense	17.3%	5.4%	7.3%	21.0%	24.2%	9.4%	15.3%	100.0%	82.7%

Source: Compiled by USCCR from DOD FY 2011 sexual assault data.

<u>Figure 6.2</u> below illustrates all unrestricted sexual assault reports that reached final disposition in FY 2011, separating penetration offenses from sexual contact and attempted sexual offenses.

<u>Figure 6.2</u>
All unrestricted sexual assault reports reaching final disposition, FY 2011

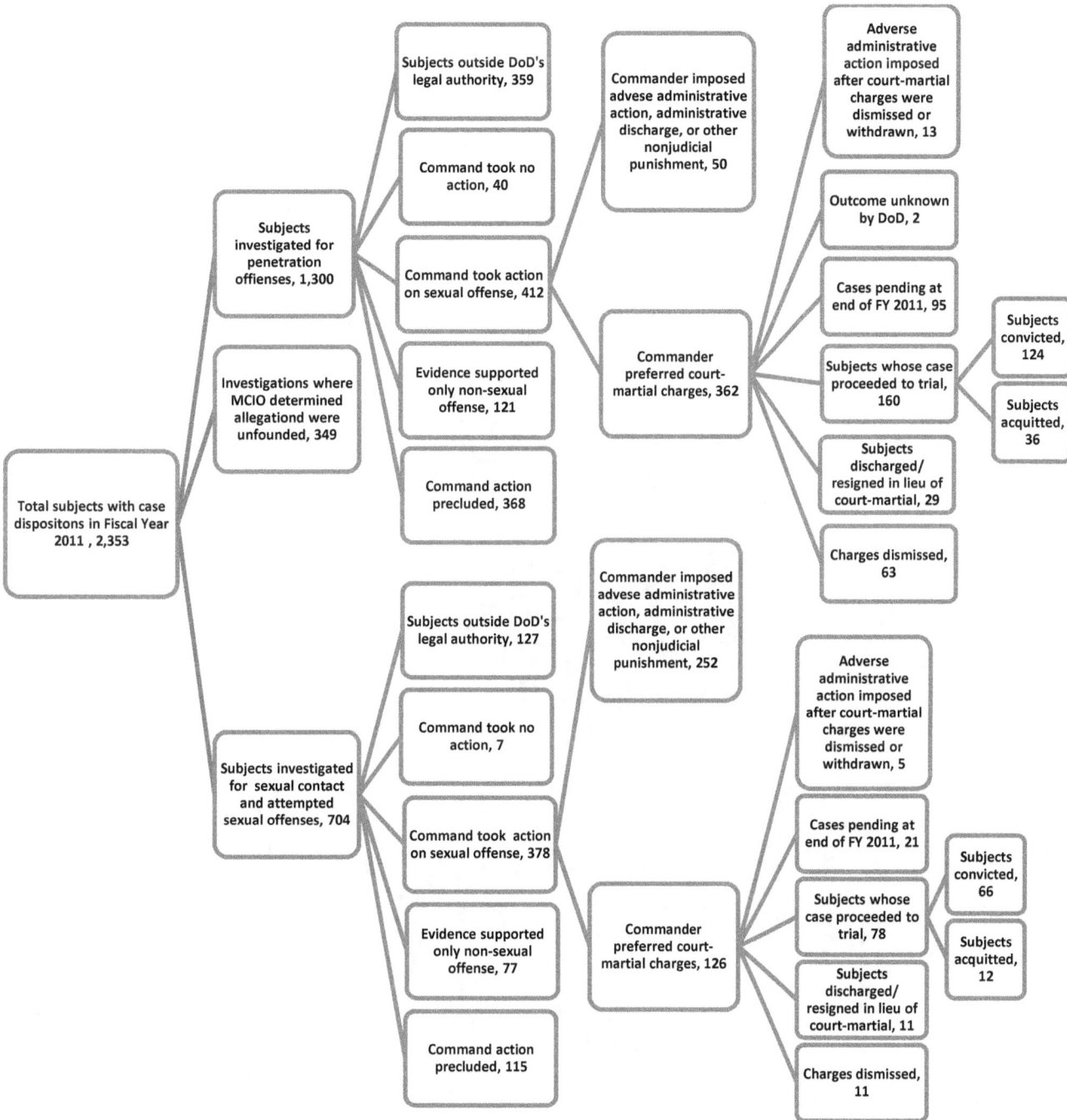

Source: DoD 2011 Annual Report on Sexual Assault in the Military and analysis by U.S. Commission on Civil Rights using DoD FY 2011 sexual assault data.

<u>Figure 6.3</u> differentiates the number of reported allegations of penetration offenses (rape, forcible sodomy, and aggravated sexual assault), which would justify the most severe punishments, from reports of sexual contact offenses or attempted offenses (which might

justify less severe punishments).[110] Of the reported allegations of penetration offenses with sufficient evidence to support commander action for a sexual offense, 88 percent were referred to court-martial. Of the reported allegations of sexual contact offenses and attempted sexual offenses with evidence to support commander action for a sexual offense, 33 percent were referred to court-martial.

Figure 6.3
Case dispositions for records with evidence for commander action for sexual assault offense, FY 2011

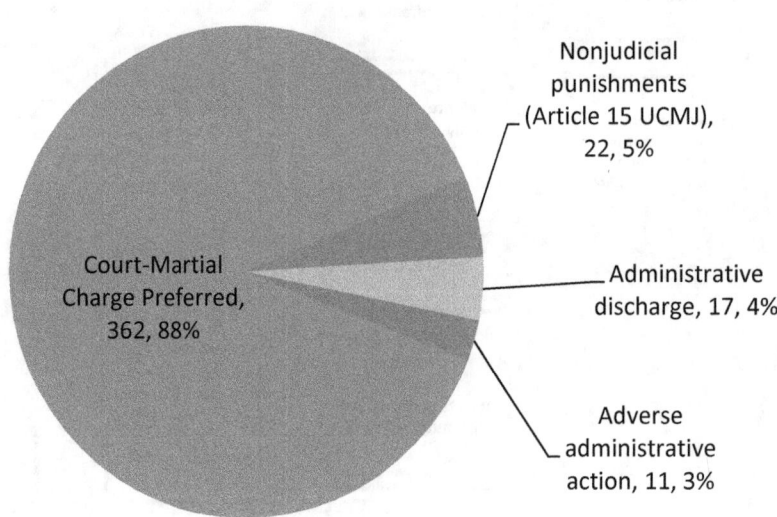

Penetration Offenses

---

[110] Note that DoD's data only provides the most serious sexual offense alleged in the criminal investigation, which is not necessarily the most serious offense for which the subject is charged ultimately and/or convicted.

Sexual Contact and Attempted Sexual Offenses

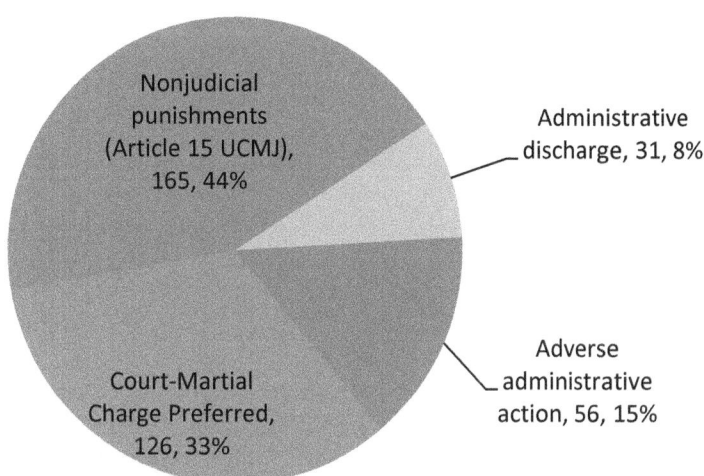

Source: Compiled by USCCR from DOD FY 2011 sexual assault data.

The DoD's data indicates that penetration sexual offenses are more likely to be prosecuted than sexual contact and attempted sexual offenses. But, whether the prosecution rates are appropriate cannot be ascertained from the DoD's data. Professor Sullivan expressed the view that the military "is more willing to prosecute sexual assault cases than are state criminal justice systems; the military not infrequently tries off-base sexual assault allegations that state prosecutors declined to prosecute."[111] A comparison to data of civilian prosecution rates suggests that military prosecution rates for penetration offenses are similar, but the Commission's research did not uncover data from the civilian context that would allow an exact comparison.[112] Comparisons to civilian prosecution rates also are complicated by the fact that Service members can be disciplined for criminal offenses through the use of nonjudicial punishments or adverse administrative actions without being prosecuted in court.

---

[111] *Sullivan Statement* at 6.

[112] *See, e.g.,* ERICA L. SMITH ET AL., U.S. DEP'T OF JUST., OFF. OF JUST. PROGRAMS, BUREAU OF JUST. STATISTICS, STATE COURT PROCESSING OF DOMESTIC VIOLENCE CASES (2008), *available at* http://www.ovw.usdoj.gov/docs/bjs-specialreport.pdf (comparing prosecution rates of sexual assault cases where the defendant was a member of the victim's family or household or the victim's intimate partner to those where the defendant did not have such a relationship with the victim; finding 89 percent and 73 percent prosecution rates, respectively).

APPENDIX A: RELEVANT STATUTES

Statute	Statutory Language	Public Law that last amended statute
Definitions of Sexual Offenses		
10 U.S.C. §920(a)	**Rape**—Any person subject to this chapter who commits a sexual act upon another person by— (1) using unlawful force against that other person; (2) using force causing or likely to cause death or grievous bodily harm to any person; (3) threatening or placing that other person in fear that any person will be subjected to death, grievous bodily harm, or kidnapping; (4) first rendering that other person unconscious; or (5) administering to that other person by force or threat of force, or without the knowledge or consent of that person, a drug, intoxicant, or other similar substance and thereby substantially impairing the ability of that other person to appraise or control conduct; is guilty of rape and shall be punished as a court-martial may direct	Pub. L. No. 112-81, §541 (2012)
10 U.S.C. §920(b)	**Sexual Assault**—Any person subject to this chapter who-- (1) commits a sexual act upon another person by-- (A) threatening or placing that other person in fear; (B) causing bodily harm to that other person; (C) making a fraudulent representation that the sexual act serves a professional purpose; or (D) inducing a belief by any artifice, pretense, or concealment that the person is another person; (2) commits a sexual act upon another person when the person knows or reasonably should know that the other person is asleep, unconscious, or otherwise unaware that the sexual act is occurring; or (3) commits a sexual act upon another person when the other person is incapable of consenting to the sexual act due to-- (A) impairment by any drug, intoxicant, or other similar substance, and that condition is known or reasonably should be known by the person; or (B) a mental disease or defect, or physical disability, and that condition is known or reasonably should be known by the person; is guilty of sexual assault and shall be punished as a court-martial may direct.	Pub. L. No. 112-81, §541 (2012)
10 U.S.C. §920(c)	(c) **Aggravated Sexual Contact**— Any person subject to this chapter who commits or causes sexual contact upon or by another person, if to do so would violate subsection (a) (rape) had the sexual contact been a sexual act, is guilty of aggravated sexual contact and shall be punished as a court-martial may direct.	Pub. L. No. 112-81, §541 (2012)

Statute	Statutory Language	Public Law that last amended statute
10 U.S.C. §920(e)	(e) **Proof of Threat—** In a prosecution under this section, in proving that a person made a threat, it need not be proven that the person actually intended to carry out the threat or had the ability to carry out the threat.	Pub. L. No. 112-81, §541 (2012)
10 U.S.C. §920(g)	(1) **Sexual act—** The term "sexual act" means— (A) contact between the penis and the vulva or anus or mouth, and for purposes of this subparagraph contact involving the penis occurs upon penetration, however slight; or (B) the penetration, however slight, of the vulva or anus or mouth, of another by any part of the body or by any object, with an intent to abuse, humiliate, harass, or degrade any person or to arouse or gratify the sexual desire of any person. (2) **Sexual contact—** The term "sexual contact" means— (A) touching, or causing another person to touch, either directly or through the clothing, the genitalia, anus, groin, breast, inner thigh, or buttocks of any person, with an intent to abuse, humiliate, or degrade any person; or (B) any touching, or causing another person to touch, either directly or through the clothing, any body part of any person, if done with an intent to arouse or gratify the sexual desire of any person. (6) **Unlawful force—** The term "unlawful force" means an act of force done without legal justification or excuse.	Pub. L. No. 112-81, §541 (2012)
10 U.S.C. §925(a)	**Sodomy—**(a) Any person subject to this chapter who engages in unnatural carnal copulation with another person of the same or opposite sex or with an animal is guilty of sodomy. Penetration, however slight, is sufficient to complete the offense.	Pub. L. No. 84-1028, (1956)
10 U.S.C. §920(g)(8)	**Consent—**(A) The term "consent" means a freely given agreement to the conduct at issue by a competent person. An expression of lack of consent through words or conduct means there is no consent. Lack of verbal or physical resistance or submission resulting from the use of force, threat of force, or placing another person in fear does not constitute consent. A current or previous dating or social or sexual relationship by itself or the manner of dress of the person involved with the accused in the conduct at issue shall not constitute consent. (B) A sleeping, unconscious, or incompetent person cannot consent. A person cannot consent to force causing or likely to cause death or grievous bodily harm or to being rendered unconscious. A person cannot consent while under threat or in fear or [when the perpetrator makes "a fraudulent representation that the sexual act serves a professional purpose;" or "induc[es] a belief by any artifice, pretense, or concealment that the person is another person"].	Pub. L. No. 109-163, (2006)
Sexual Assault Prevention and Response		
10 U.S.C. §113	(a) **Comprehensive Policy on Prevention and Response to Sexual** Assaults. — (1) Not later than January 1, 2005, the Secretary of Defense	Pub. L. No. 108-375,

Statute	Statutory Language	Public Law that last amended statute

	shall develop a comprehensive policy for the Department of Defense on the prevention of and response to sexual assaults involving members of the Armed Forces.
	
	(2) The policy shall be based on the recommendations of the Department of Defense Task Force on Care for Victims of Sexual Assaults and on such other matters as the Secretary considers appropriate.
	(3) Before developing the comprehensive policy required by paragraph (1) The Secretary of Defense shall develop a definition of sexual assault. The definition so developed shall be used in the comprehensive policy under paragraph (1) and otherwise within the Department of Defense and Coast Guard in matters involving members of the Armed Forces. The definition shall be uniform for all the Armed Forces and shall be developed in consultation with the Secretaries of the military departments and the Secretary of Homeland Security with respect to the Coast Guard.
	(b) Elements of Comprehensive Policy.--The comprehensive policy developed under subsection (a) shall, at a minimum, address the following matters:
	    (1) Prevention measures.
	    (2) Education and training on prevention and response.
	    (3) Investigation of complaints by command and law enforcement personnel.
	    (4) Medical treatment of victims.
	    (5) Confidential reporting of incidents.
	    (6) Victim advocacy and intervention.
	    (7) Oversight by commanders of administrative and disciplinary actions in response to substantiated incidents of sexual assault.
	    (8) Disposition of victims of sexual assault, including review by appropriate authority of administrative separation actions involving victims of sexual assault.
	    (9) Disposition of members of the Armed Forces accused of sexual assault.
	    (10) Liaison and collaboration with civilian agencies on the provision of services to victims of sexual assault.
	    (11) Uniform collection of data on the incidence of sexual assaults and on disciplinary actions taken in substantiated cases of sexual assault.
	(c) Report on Improvement of Capability To Respond to Sexual Assaults.--Not later than March 1, 2005, the Secretary of Defense shall submit to Congress a proposal for such legislation as the Secretary considers necessary to enhance the capability of the Department of Defense to address matters relating to sexual assaults involving members of the Armed Forces.
	(d) Application of Comprehensive Policy To Military Departments.--The Secretary of Defense shall ensure that, to the maximum extent practicable, the policy developed under subsection (a) is implemented
		§577 (2005)

Statute	Statutory Language	Public Law that last amended statute
	uniformly by the military departments. (e) Policies and Procedures of Military Departments.--(1) Not later than March 1, 2005, the Secretaries of the military.	

10 U.S.C. §1561	**Complaints of sexual harassment: investigation by commanding officers —**
	(a) In General.--The Secretary of Defense shall standardize, assess, and monitor the quality assurance programs of the military departments to evaluate the following in the performance of their duties (including duties under chapter 61 of title 10, United States Code):
	   (1) Medical Evaluation Boards.
	   (2) Physical Evaluation Boards.
	   (3) Physical Evaluation Board Liaison Officers.
	  (b) Objectives.--The objectives of the quality assurance program shall be as follows:
	   (1) To ensure accuracy and consistency in the determinations and decisions of Medical Evaluation Boards and Physical Evaluation Boards.
	   (2) To otherwise monitor and sustain proper performance of the duties of Medical Evaluation Boards and Physical Evaluation Boards, and of Physical Evaluation Board Liaison Officers.
	   (3) Such other objectives as the Secretary shall specify for purposes of the quality assurance program.
	   (c) Reports.--
	   (1) Report on implementation.--Not later than 180 days after the date of the enactment of this Act, the Secretary shall submit to the appropriate committees of Congress a report setting forth the plan of the Secretary for the implementation of the requirements of this section.
	   (2) Annual reports.--Not later than one year after the date of the submittal of the report required by paragraph (1), and annually thereafter for the next four years, the Secretary shall submit to the appropriate committees of Congress a report setting forth an assessment of the implementation of the requirements of this section during the one-year period ending on the date of the report under this paragraph. Each report shall include, in particular, an assessment of the extent to which the quality assurance program under the requirements of this section meets the objectives specified in subsection (b).
	   (3) Appropriate committees of congress defined.--In this subsection, the term ``appropriate committees of Congress" means--
	    (A) the Committee on Armed Services and the Committee on Veterans' Affairs of the Senate; and
	    (B) the Committee on Armed Services and the Committee on Veterans' Affairs of the House of Representatives.
		Pub. L. No. 112-239, §574 (2013)

10 U.S.C.	**Legal Assistance for Sexual Assault Victims**—Not later than 180 days after the	Pub. L. No.

Statute	Statutory Language	Public Law that last amended statute
§1565b NOTE	date of the enactment of this Act, the Secretaries of the military departments shall prescribe regulations on the provision of legal assistance to victims of sexual assault. Such regulations shall require that legal assistance be provided by military or civilian legal assistance counsel pursuant to section 1044 of title 10, United States Code.	112-81, §581 (2012)
10 U.S.C. §1565b	(a) **Availability of Legal Assistance and Victim Advocate Services** — (1) A member of the armed forces, or a dependent of a member, who is the victim of a sexual assault may be provided the following: (A) Legal assistance provided by military or civilian legal assistance counsel pursuant to section 1044 of this title. (B) Assistance provided by a Sexual Assault Response Coordinator. (C) Assistance provided by a Sexual Assault Victim Advocate. (2) A member of the armed forces or dependent who is the victim of sexual assault shall be informed of the availability of assistance under paragraph (1) as soon as the member or dependent seeks assistance from a Sexual Assault Response Coordinator, a Sexual Assault Victim Advocate, a military criminal investigator, a victim/witness liaison, or a trial counsel. The member or dependent shall also be informed that the legal assistance and the services of a Sexual Assault Response Coordinator or a Sexual Assault Victim Advocate under paragraph (1) are optional and may be declined, in whole or in part, at any time. (3) Legal assistance and the services of Sexual Assault Response Coordinators and Sexual Assault Victim Advocates under paragraph (1) shall be available to a member or dependent regardless of whether the member or dependent elects unrestricted or restricted (confidential) reporting of the sexual assault. (b) RESTRICTED REPORTING.--(1) Under regulations prescribed by the Secretary of Defense, a member of the armed forces, or a dependent of a member, who is the victim of a sexual assault may elect to confidentially disclose the details of the assault to an individual specified in paragraph (2) and receive medical treatment, legal assistance under section 1044 of this title, or counseling, without initiating an official investigation of the allegations. (2) The individuals specified in this paragraph are the following: (A) A Sexual Assault Response Coordinator. (B) A Sexual Assault Victim Advocate. (C) Healthcare personnel specifically identified in the regulations required by paragraph (1).	Pub. L. No. 112-81, §581 (2012)
10 U.S.C. §673	**Expedited Transfer** Consideration of application for permanent change of station or unit transfer based on humanitarian conditions for victim of sexual assault or related offense.	Pub. L. No. 112-81, §582 (2012)
10 U.S.C. §1561	(a) **Comprehensive Prevention and Response Policy—** (1) Policy required.--The Secretary of Defense shall develop a	Pub. L. No. 112-239,

Statute	Statutory Language	Public Law that last amended statute
	comprehensive policy to prevent and respond to sexual harassment in the Armed Forces. The policy shall provide for the following: Training for members of the Armed Forces on the prevention of sexual harassment. (B) Mechanisms for reporting incidents of sexual harassment in the Armed Forces, including procedures for reporting anonymously. (C) Mechanisms for responding to and resolving incidents of alleged sexual harassment incidences involving members of the Armed Forces, including through the prosecution of offenders. (2) Report.--Not later than one year after the date of the enactment of this Act, the Secretary of Defense shall submit to the Committees on Armed Services of the Senate and the House of Representatives a report setting forth the policy required by paragraph (1). (3) Consultation.--The Secretary of Defense shall prepare the policy and report required by this subsection in consultation with the Secretaries of the military departments and the Equal Opportunity Office of the Department of Defense. (b) Data Collection and Reporting Regarding Substantiated Incidents of Sexual Harassment.-- (1) Plan required.--The Secretary of Defense shall develop a plan to collect information and data regarding substantiated incidents of sexual harassment involving members of the Armed Forces. The plan shall specifically deal with the need to identify cases in which a member is accused of multiple incidents of sexual harassment. (2) Submission of plan.--Not later than June 1, 2013, the Secretary of Defense shall submit to the Committees on Armed Services of the Senate and the House of Representatives the plan developed under paragraph (1). (3) Reporting requirement.--As part of the reports required to be submitted in 2014 under section 1631 of the Ike Skelton National Defense Authorization Act for Fiscal Year 2011 (Public Law 111-383; 124 Stat. 4433; 10 U.S.C. 1561 note), the Secretary of Defense shall include information and data collected under the plan during the preceding year regarding substantiated incidents of sexual harassment involving members of the Armed Forces.	§579 (2013)
10 U.S.C. §113	**Comprehensive policy on Prevention and Response to Sexual Assaults —** (1) Not later than January 1, 2005, the Secretary of Defense shall develop a comprehensive policy for the Department of Defense on the prevention of and response to sexual assaults involving members of the Armed Forces. (2) The policy shall be based on the recommendations of the Department of Defense Task Force on Care for Victims of Sexual Assaults and on such other matters as the Secretary considers appropriate. (3) Before developing the comprehensive policy required by paragraph (1), the Secretary of Defense shall develop a definition of sexual assault. The definition so	Pub. L. No. 108–375, §577 (2005)

Statute	Statutory Language	Public Law that last amended statute
	developed shall be used in the comprehensive policy under paragraph (1) and otherwise within the Department of Defense and Coast Guard in matters involving members of the Armed Forces. The definition shall be uniform for all the Armed Forces and shall be developed in consultation with the Secretaries of the military departments and the Secretary of Homeland Security with respect to the Coast Guard. (b) ELEMENTS OF COMPREHENSIVE POLICY.—The comprehensive policy developed under subsection (a) shall, at a minimum, address the following matters: (1) Prevention measures. (2) Education and training on prevention and response. (3) Investigation of complaints by command and law enforcement personnel. (4) Medical treatment of victims. (5) Confidential reporting of incidents. (6) Victim advocacy and intervention. (7) Oversight by commanders of administrative and disciplinary actions in response to substantiated incidents of sexual assault. (8) Disposition of victims of sexual assault, including review by appropriate authority of administrative separation actions involving victims of sexual assault. (9) Disposition of members of the Armed Forces accused of sexual assault. (10) Liaison and collaboration with civilian agencies on the provision of services to victims of sexual assault. (11) Uniform collection of data on the incidence of sexual assaults and on disciplinary actions taken in substantiated cases of sexual assault. (c) REPORT ON IMPROVEMENT OF CAPABILITY TO RESPOND TO SEXUAL ASSAULTS.—Not later than March 1, 2005, the Secretary of Defense shall submit to Congress a proposal for such legislation as the Secretary considers necessary to enhance the capability of the Department of Defense to address matters relating to sexual assaults involving members of the Armed Forces. (d) APPLICATION OF COMPREHENSIVE POLICY TO MILITARY DEPARTMENTS.—The Secretary of Defense shall ensure that, to the maximum extent practicable, the policy developed under subsection (a) is implemented uniformly by the military departments. (e) POLICIES AND PROCEDURES OF MILITARY DEPARTMENTS.—(1) Not later than March 1, 2005, the Secretaries of the military departments shall prescribe regulations, or modify current regulations, on the policies and procedures of the military departments on the prevention of and response to sexual assaults involving members of the Armed Forces in order— (A) to conform such policies and procedures to the policy developed under subsection (a); and (B) to ensure that such policies and procedures include the elements specified in paragraph (2). (2) The elements specified in this paragraph are as follows: (A) A program to promote awareness of the incidence of sexual assaults involving	

Statute	Statutory Language	Public Law that last amended statute
	members of the Armed Forces.	

members of the Armed Forces.

(B) A program to provide victim advocacy and intervention for members of the Armed Force concerned who are victims of sexual assault, which program shall make available, at home stations and in deployed locations, trained advocates who are readily available to intervene on behalf of such victims.

(C) Procedures for members of the Armed Force concerned to follow in the case of an incident of sexual assault involving a member of such Armed Force, including—

(i) specification of the person or persons to whom the alleged offense should be reported;

(ii) specification of any other person whom the victim should contact;

(iii) procedures for the preservation of evidence; and

(iv) procedures for confidential reporting and for contacting victim advocates.

(D) Procedures for disciplinary action in cases of sexual assault by members of the Armed Force concerned.

(E) Other sanctions authorized to be imposed in substantiated cases of sexual assault, whether forcible or nonforcible, by members of the Armed Force concerned.

(F) Training on the policies and procedures for all members of the Armed Force concerned, including specific training for members of the Armed Force concerned who process allegations of sexual assault against members of such Armed Force.

(G) Any other matters that the Secretary of Defense considers appropriate.

(f) ANNUAL REPORT ON SEXUAL ASSAULTS.—(1) Not later than January 15 of each year, the Secretary of each military department shall submit to the Secretary of Defense a report on the sexual assaults involving members of the Armed Forces under the jurisdiction of that Secretary during the preceding year. In the case of the Secretary of the Navy, separate reports shall be prepared for the Navy and for the Marine Corps.

(2) Each report on an Armed Force under paragraph (1) shall contain the following:

(A) The number of sexual assaults against members of the Armed Force, and the number of sexual assaults by members of the Armed Force, that were reported to military officials during the year covered by such report, and the number of the cases so reported that were substantiated.

(B) A synopsis of, and the disciplinary action taken in, each substantiated case.

(C) The policies, procedures, and processes implemented by the Secretary concerned during the year covered by such report in response to incidents of sexual assault involving members of the Armed Force concerned.

(D) A plan for the actions that are to be taken in the year following the year covered by such report on the prevention of and response to sexual assault involving members of the Armed Forces concerned.

(3) Each report under paragraph (1) for any year after 2005 shall include an assessment by the Secretary of the military department submitting the report of the implementation during the preceding fiscal year of the policies and procedures of such department on the prevention of and response to sexual assaults involving

Statute	Statutory Language	Public Law that last amended statute
	members of the Armed Forces in order to determine the effectiveness of such policies and procedures during such fiscal year in providing an appropriate response to such sexual assaults. (4) The Secretary of Defense shall submit to the Committees on Armed Services of the Senate and House of Representatives each report submitted to the Secretary under this subsection, together with the comments of the Secretary on the report. The Secretary shall submit each such report not later than March 15 of the year following the year covered by the report. (5) For the report under this subsection covering 2004, the applicable date under paragraph (1) is April 1, 2005, and the applicable date under paragraph (4) is May 1, 2005.	
10 U.S.C. §4331	**Improved Prevention and Response to Allegations of Sexual Assault involving members of the armed forces—** (a) Prevention and Response Plan. Not later than 180 days after the date of the enactment of this Act, the Secretary of Defense shall submit to the Committees on Armed Services of the Senate and the House of Representatives a revised plan for the implementation of policies aimed at preventing and responding effectively to sexual assaults involving members of the Armed Forces. The revised implementation plan shall include, at a minimum, the following elements: (1) New initiatives aimed at reducing the number of sexual assaults, including timelines for implementation of such initiatives. (2) Requirements for monitoring and reporting on progress in implementation of such initiatives and methods to measure the effectiveness of plans that implement the policies of the Department of Defense regarding sexual assaults involving members of the Armed Forces. (3) Training programs for judge advocates, criminal investigators, commanders, prospective commanding officers, senior enlisted members, and personnel with less than six months of active-duty service. (4) Information about the status of implementation, funding requirements and budgetary implications, and overall utility of data reporting systems on incidents of sexual assault involving members of the Armed Forces. (5) Actions taken to implement recommendations of the Defense Task Force on Sexual Assault in the Military Services established pursuant to section 576 of the Ronald W. Reagan National Defense Authorization Act for Fiscal Year 2005 (Public Law 108-375; 10 U.S.C. 4331 note). (6) Information about the funding needed to fully implement initiatives aimed at preventing and responding to sexual assault involving members of the Armed Forces. (b) Sexual Assault Medical Forensic Examinations.-- (1) Capability to conduct timely sexual assault medical forensic examinations in combat zones.-- Deadline. Not later than 180 days after the date of	Pub. L. No. 111-84, §567 (2010)

Statute	Statutory Language	Public Law that last amended statute

	the enactment of this Act, the Secretary of Defense shall submit to the Committees on Armed Services of the Senate and the House of Representatives a report evaluating the protocols and capabilities of the Armed Forces to conduct timely and effective sexual assault medical forensic examinations in combat zones. The report shall include, at a minimum, the following:
	
	      (A) The current availability of sexual assault medical forensic examination protocols, trained personnel, and requisite equipment in combat zones.
	
	      (B) An assessment of the barriers to providing timely sexual assault medical forensic examinations to victims of sexual assault at all echelons of care in combat zones.
	
	      (C) Recommendations regarding improved capability to conduct timely and effective sexual assault medical forensic examinations in combat zones.
	
	      (2) Tricare coverage for forensic medical examinations following sexual assaults.--Deadline. Not later than 30 days after the date of the enactment of this Act, the Secretary of Defense shall submit to the Committees on Armed Services of the Senate and the House of Representatives a report describing the progress made in implementing section 1079(a)(17) of title 10, United States Code, as added by section 701 of the John Warner National Defense Authorization Act for Fiscal Year 2007 (Public Law 109-364; 120 Stat. 2279).
	
	  (c) 10 USC 113 note. Military Protective Orders.--
	
	    (1) Requirement for data collection.--
	
	      (A) In general.--Pursuant to regulations prescribed by the Secretary of Defense, information shall be collected on--
	
	        (i) whether a military protective order was issued that involved either the victim or alleged perpetrator of a sexual assault; and
	
	        (ii) whether military protective orders involving members of the Armed Forces were violated in the course of substantiated incidents of sexual assaults against members of the Armed Forces.
	
	      (B) Submission of data.--The data required to be collected under this subsection shall be included in the annual report submitted to Congress on sexual assaults involving members of the Armed Forces.
	
	    (2) Information to members.--
	
	  Deadline. Not later than 180 days after the date of the enactment of this Act, the Secretary of Defense shall submit to the Committees on Armed Services of the Senate and the House of Representatives a report explaining the measures being taken to ensure that, when a military protective order has been issued, the member of the Armed Forces who is protected by the order is informed, in a timely manner, of the member's option to request transfer from the command to which the member is assigned.
	
	  (d) Comptroller General Report.--
	
	    (1) Report required.--Not later than one year after the date of the enactment of this Act, the Comptroller General shall	

Statute	Statutory Language	Public Law that last amended statute
	submit to the Committees on Armed Services of the Senate and the House of Representatives a report containing a review of the capability of each of the Armed Forces to timely and effectively investigate and adjudicate allegations of sexual assault against members of the Armed Forces. The Comptroller General shall determine whether existing policies and implementation plans of the Department of Defense, and the resources devoted for this purpose, are adequate or negatively affect the ability of each of the Armed Forces to facilitate the prevention, investigation, and adjudication of such allegations under the Uniform Code of Military Justice. (2) Elements of report.--The report required by paragraph (1) shall refer to and incorporate the recommendations of the Defense Task Force on Sexual Assault in the Military Services regarding investigation and adjudication of sexual assault, and include a review of the following: (A) The procedures required by each of the Armed Forces for responding to allegations of sexual assault (including guidance to commanding officers, standard operating and reporting procedures, and related matters), and the personnel (including judge advocates) and budgetary resources available to each of the Armed Forces to respond to allegations of sexual assault. (B) The scope and effectiveness of personnel training methods regarding investigation and adjudication of sexual assault cases. (C) The capability to investigate and adjudicate sexual assault cases in combat zones. (D) An assessment whether the existing policies of the Department of Defense aimed at preventing and responding to incidents of sexual assault are adequate.	
10 U.S.C. §585	**Training and Education Program for Sexual Assault Prevention and Response Program—** (a) Sexual Assault Prevention and Response Training and Education.-- (1) Development of curriculum.--Not later than one year after the date of the enactment of this Act, the Secretary of each military department shall develop a curriculum to provide sexual assault prevention training and education for members of the Armed Forces under the jurisdiction of the Secretary and civilian employees of the military department to strengthen individual knowledge, skills, and capacity to prevent and respond to sexual assault. In developing the curriculum, the Secretary shall work with experts	Pub. L. No. 112-81, §585 (2012)

Statute	Statutory Language	Public Law that last amended statute
	outside of the Department of Defense who are experts sexual assault prevention and response training. (2) Scope of training and education.--The sexual assault prevention and response training and education shall encompass initial entry and accession programs, annual refresher training, professional military education, peer education, and specialized leadership training. Training shall be tailored for specific leadership levels and local area requirements. (3) Consistent training.--The Secretary of Defense shall ensure that the sexual assault prevention and response training provided to members of the Armed Forces and Department of Defense civilian employees is consistent throughout the military departments. (b) Inclusion in Professional Military Education.--The Secretary of Defense shall provide for the inclusion of a sexual assault prevention and response training module at each level of professional military education. The training shall be tailored to the new responsibilities and leadership requirements of members of the Armed Forces as they are promoted. (c) Inclusion in First Responder Training.-- (1) In general.--The Secretary of Defense shall direct that managers of specialty skills associated with first responders described in paragraph (2) integrate sexual assault response training in initial and recurring training courses. (2) Covered first responders.--First responders referred to in paragraph (1) include firefighters, emergency medical technicians, law enforcement officers, military criminal investigators, healthcare personnel, judge advocates, and chaplains.	
10 U.S.C. §156	**Enhancement to Training and Education for Sexual Assault Prevention and Response—** (d) Commanders' Training.--The Secretary of Defense shall provide for the inclusion of a sexual assault prevention and response training module in the training for new or prospective commanders at all levels of command. The training shall be tailored to the responsibilities and leadership requirements of members of the Armed Forces as they are assigned to command positions. Such training shall include the following: (1) Fostering a command climate that does not tolerate sexual assault. (2) Fostering a command climate in which persons assigned to the command are encouraged to intervene to prevent potential incidents of sexual assault. (3) Fostering a command climate that encourages victims of Sexual assault to	Pub. L. No. 112-239, §574 (2013)

Statute	Statutory Language	Public Law that last amended statute

	report any incident of sexual assault.
	
	    (4) Understanding the needs of, and the resources available to, the victim after an incident of sexual assault.
	
	    (5) Use of military criminal investigative organizations for the investigation of alleged incidents of sexual assault.
	
	    (6) Available disciplinary options, including court-martial, non-judicial punishment, administrative action, and deferral of discipline for collateral misconduct, as appropriate.
	
	    (e) Explanation to Be Included in Initial Entry and Accession Training.--
	
	    (1) Requirement.--The Secretary of Defense shall require that the matters specified in paragraph (2) be carefully explained to each member of the Army, Navy, Air Force, and Marine Corps at the time of (or within fourteen duty days after)--
	
	    (A) the member's initial entrance on active duty; or
	
	    (B) the member's initial entrance into a duty status with a reserve component.
	
	    (2) Matters to be explained.--This subsection applies with respect to the following:
	
	    (A) Department of Defense policy with respect to sexual assault.
	
	    (B) The resources available with respect to sexual assault reporting and prevention and the procedures to be followed by a member seeking to access those resources.	

10 USCA §1561 NOTE	(a) **Sexual Assault Prevention and Response Training and Education**
	
	    (1) DEVELOPMENT OF CURRICULUM.--Not later than one year after the date of the enactment of this Act, the Secretary of each military department shall develop a curriculum to provide sexual assault prevention and response training and education for members of the Armed Forces under the jurisdiction of the Secretary and civilian employees of the military department to strengthen individual knowledge, skills, and capacity to prevent and respond to sexual assault. In developing the curriculum, the Secretary shall work with experts outside of the Department of Defense who are experts sexual assault prevention and response training.
	
	    (2) SCOPE OF TRAINING AND EDUCATION.--The sexual assault prevention and response training and education shall encompass initial entry and accession programs, annual refresher training, professional military education, peer education, and specialized leadership training. Training shall be tailored for specific leadership levels and local area requirements.
	
	    (3) CONSISTENT TRAINING.--The Secretary of Defense shall ensure that the sexual assault prevention and response training provided to members of the Armed Forces and Department of Defense civilian employees is consistent throughout the military departments.
	
	    (b) INCLUSION IN PROFESSIONAL MILITARY EDUCATION.--The
		Pub. L. No. 112-81, §585 (2012)

Statute	Statutory Language	Public Law that last amended statute

	Secretary of Defense shall provide for the inclusion of a sexual assault prevention and response training module at each level of professional military education. The training shall be tailored to the new responsibilities and leadership requirements of members of the Armed Forces as they are promoted.
	    (c) INCLUSION IN FIRST RESPONDER TRAINING.--
	    (1) IN GENERAL.--The Secretary of Defense shall direct that managers of specialty skills associated with first responders described in paragraph (2) integrate sexual assault response training in initial and recurring training courses.
	    (2) COVERED FIRST RESPONDERS.--First responders referred to in paragraph (1) include firefighters, emergency medical technicians, law enforcement officers, military criminal investigators, healthcare personnel, judge advocates, and chaplains.	

10 U.S.C. §113 NOTE	**Comprehensive Policy on Prevention and Response to Sexual Assaults —**
	(1) Not later than January 1, 2005, the Secretary of Defense shall develop a comprehensive policy for the Department of Defense on the prevention of and response to sexual assaults involving members of the Armed Forces.
	(2) The policy shall be based on the recommendations of the Department of Defense Task Force on Care for Victims of Sexual Assaults and on such other matters as the Secretary considers appropriate.
	(3) Before developing the comprehensive policy required by paragraph (1), the Secretary of Defense shall develop a definition of sexual assault. The definition so developed shall be used in the comprehensive policy under paragraph (1) and otherwise within the Department of Defense and Coast Guard in matters involving members of the Armed Forces. The definition shall be uniform for all the Armed Forces and shall be developed in consultation with the Secretaries of the military departments and the Secretary of Homeland Security with respect to the Coast Guard.
	    (b) ELEMENTS OF COMPREHENSIVE POLICY.—The comprehensive policy developed under subsection (a) shall, at a minimum, address the following matters:
	    (1) Prevention measures.
	    (2) Education and training on prevention and response.
	    (3) Investigation of complaints by command and law enforcement personnel.
	    (4) Medical treatment of victims.
	    (5) Confidential reporting of incidents.
	    (6) Victim advocacy and intervention.
	    (7) Oversight by commanders of administrative and disciplinary actions in response to substantiated incidents of sexual assault.
	    (8) Disposition of victims of sexual assault, including review by appropriate authority of administrative separation actions involving victims of sexual assault.
	    (9) Disposition of members of the Armed Forces accused of sexual
		Pub. L. No. 108-375 §577 (2004)

Statute	Statutory Language	Public Law that last amended statute
	assault.	

(10) Liaison and collaboration with civilian agencies on the provision of services to victims of sexual assault.

(11) Uniform collection of data on the incidence of sexual assaults and on disciplinary actions taken in substantiated cases of sexual assault.

(c) REPORT ON IMPROVEMENT OF CAPABILITY TO RESPOND TO SEXUAL ASSAULTS.—Not later than March 1, 2005, the Secretary of Defense shall submit to Congress a proposal for such legislation as the Secretary considers necessary to enhance the capability of the Department of Defense to address matters relating to sexual
assaults involving members of the Armed Forces.

(d) APUBLICATION OF COMPREHENSIVE POLICY TO MILITARY DEPARTMENTS.—The Secretary of Defense shall ensure that, to the maximum extent practicable, the policy developed under subsection (a) is implemented uniformly by the military departments.

(e) POLICIES AND PROCEDURES OF MILITARY DEPARTMENTS.—

(1) Not later than March 1, 2005, the Secretaries of the military, on the policies and procedures of the military departments on the prevention of and response to sexual assaults involving members of the Armed Forces in order—

(A) to conform such policies and procedures to the policy developed under subsection (a); and

(B) to ensure that such policies and procedures include the elements specified in paragraph (2).

(2) The elements specified in this paragraph are as follows:

(A) A program to promote awareness of the incidence of sexual assaults involving members of the Armed Forces.

(B) A program to provide victim advocacy and intervention for members of the Armed Force concerned who are victims of sexual assault, which program shall make available, at home stations and in deployed locations, trained advocates who are readily available to intervene on behalf of such victims.

(C) Procedures for members of the Armed Force concerned to follow in the case of an incident of sexual assault involving a member of such Armed Force, including—

(i) specification of the person or persons to whom the alleged offense should be reported;

(ii) specification of any other person whom the victim should contact;

(iii) procedures for the preservation of evidence; and

(iv) procedures for confidential reporting and for contacting victim advocates.

(D) Procedures for disciplinary action in cases of sexual assault by members of the Armed Force concerned.

(E) Other sanctions authorized to be imposed in substantiated

Statute	Statutory Language	Public Law that last amended statute
	cases of sexual assault, whether forcible or nonforcible, by members of the Armed Force concerned. (F) Training on the policies and procedures for all members of the Armed Force concerned, including specific training for members of the Armed Force concerned who process allegations of sexual assault against members of such Armed Force. (G) Any other matters that the Secretary of Defense considers Appropriate. (f) ANNUAL REPORT ON SEXUAL ASSAULTS.—(1) Not later than January 15 of each year, the Secretary of each military department shall submit to the Secretary of Defense a report on the sexual assaults involving members of the Armed Forces under the jurisdiction of that Secretary during the preceding year. In the case of the Secretary of the Navy, separate reports shall be prepared for the Navy and for the Marine Corps. (2) Each report on an Armed Force under paragraph (1) shall contain the following: (A) The number of sexual assaults against members of the Armed Force, and the number of sexual assaults by members of the Armed Force, that were reported to military officials during the year covered by such report, and the number of the cases so reported that were substantiated. (B) A synopsis of, and the disciplinary action taken in, each substantiated case. (C) The policies, procedures, and processes implemented by the Secretary concerned during the year covered by such report in response to incidents of sexual assault involving members of the Armed Force concerned one year following the year covered by such report on the prevention of and response to sexual assault involving members of the Armed Forces concerned. (3) Each report under paragraph (1) for any year after 2005 shall include an assessment by the Secretary of the military department submitting the report of the implementation during the preceding fiscal year of the policies and procedures of such department on the prevention of and response to sexual assaults involving members of the Armed Forces in order to determine the effectiveness of such policies and procedures during such fiscal year in providing an appropriate response to such sexual assaults. (4) The Secretary of Defense shall submit to the Committees on Armed Services of the Senate and House of Representatives each report submitted to the Secretary under this subsection, together with the comments of the Secretary on the report. The Secretary shall submit each such report not later than March 15 of the year following the year covered by the report. (5) For the report under this subsection covering 2004, the applicable date under paragraph (1) is April 1, 2005, and the applicable date under paragraph (4) is May 1, 2005.	

Statute	Statutory Language	Public Law that last amended statute
10 U.S.C. §1561	**Complaints of sexual harassment: investigation by commanding officers—** (a) Action on complaints alleging sexual harassment.--A commanding officer or officer in charge of a unit, vessel, facility, or area of the Army, Navy, Air Force, or Marine Corps who receives from a member of the command or a civilian employee under the supervision of the officer a complaint alleging sexual harassment by a member of the armed forces or a civilian employee of the Department of Defense shall carry out an investigation of the matter in accordance with this section. (b) Commencement of investigation.--To the extent practicable, a commanding officer or officer in charge receiving such a complaint shall, within 72 hours after receipt of the complaint-- (1) forward the complaint or a detailed description of the allegation to the next superior officer in the chain of command who is authorized to convene a general court-martial; (2) commence, or cause the commencement of, an investigation of the complaint; and (3) advise the complainant of the commencement of the investigation. (c) Duration of investigation.--To the extent practicable, a commanding officer or officer in charge receiving such a complaint shall ensure that the investigation of the complaint is completed not later than 14 days after the date on which the investigation is commenced. (d) Report on investigation.--To the extent practicable, a commanding officer or officer in charge receiving such a complaint shall-- (1) submit a final report on the results of the investigation, including any action taken as a result of the investigation, to the next superior officer referred to in subsection (b)(1) within 20 days after the date on which the investigation is commenced; or (2) submit a report on the progress made in completing the investigation to the next superior officer referred to in subsection (b)(1) within 20 days after the date on which the investigation is commenced and every 14 days thereafter until the investigation is completed and, upon completion of the investigation, then submit a final report on the results of the investigation, including any action taken as a result of the investigation, to that next superior officer. (e) Sexual harassment defined.--In this section, the term "sexual harassment" means any of the following: (1) Conduct (constituting a form of sex discrimination) that-- (A) involves unwelcome sexual advances, requests for sexual favors, and deliberate or repeated offensive comments or gestures of a sexual nature when-- (i) submission to such conduct is made either explicitly or implicitly a term or condition of a person's job, pay, or career; (ii) submission to or rejection of such conduct by a person is used as a basis for career or employment decisions affecting that person; or	Pub. L. No. 105-85 (1997)

Statute	Statutory Language	Public Law that last amended statute
	(iii) such conduct has the purpose or effect of unreasonably interfering with an individual's work performance or creates an intimidating, hostile, or offensive working environment; and (B) is so severe or pervasive that a reasonable person would perceive, and the victim does perceive, the work environment as hostile or offensive. (2) Any use or condonation, by any person in a supervisory or command position, of any form of sexual behavior to control, influence, or affect the career, pay, or job of a member of the armed forces or a civilian employee of the Department of Defense. (3) Any deliberate or repeated unwelcome verbal comment or gesture of a sexual nature in the workplace by any member of the armed forces or civilian employee of the Department of Defense.	
10 U.S.C. §1044	**Legal assistance-** (a) Subject to the availability of legal staff resources, the Secretary concerned may provide legal assistance in connection with their personal civil legal affairs to the following persons: (1) Members of the armed forces who are on active duty. (2) Members and former members entitled to retired or retainer pay or equivalent pay. (3) Officers of the commissioned corps of the Public Health Service who are on active duty or entitled to retired or equivalent pay. (4) Members of reserve components not covered by paragraph (1) or (2) following release from active duty under a call or order to active duty for more than 30 days issued under a mobilization authority (as determined by the Secretary), for a period of time (prescribed by the Secretary) that begins on the date of the release and is not less than twice the length of the period served on active duty under that call or order to active duty. (5) Dependents of members and former members described in paragraphs (1), (2), (3), and (4). (6) Survivors of a deceased member or former member described in paragraphs (1), (2), (3), and (4) who were dependents of the member or former member at the time of the death of the member or former member, except that the eligibility of such survivors shall be determined pursuant to regulations prescribed by the Secretary concerned. (7) Civilian employees of the Federal Government serving in locations where legal assistance from non-military legal assistance providers is not reasonably available, except that the eligibility of civilian employees shall be determined pursuant to regulations prescribed by the Secretary concerned. (b) Under such regulations as may be prescribed by the Secretary concerned, the Judge Advocate General (as defined in section 801(1) of this title) under the jurisdiction of the Secretary, and within the Marine Corps the Staff Judge Advocate to the Commandant of the Marine Corps, is responsible for the establishment and	Pub. L. No. 112-239, §531(d)(2) (2013)

Statute	Statutory Language	Public Law that last amended statute

	supervision of legal assistance programs under this section.
	(c) This section does not authorize legal counsel to be provided to represent a member or former member of the uniformed services described in subsection (a), or the dependent of such a member or former member, in a legal proceeding if the member or former member can afford legal fees for such representation without undue hardship.
	(d)
	    (1) Notwithstanding any law regarding the licensure of attorneys, a judge advocate or civilian attorney who is authorized to provide military legal assistance is authorized to provide that assistance in any jurisdiction, subject to such regulations as may be prescribed by the Secretary concerned.
	    (2) Military legal assistance may be provided only by a judge advocate or a civilian attorney who is a member of the bar of a Federal court or of the highest court of a State.
	    (3) In this subsection, the term "military legal assistance" includes—
	        (A) legal assistance provided under this section; and
	        (B) legal assistance contemplated by sections 1044a, 1044b, 1044c, and 1044d of this title.
	(e) The Secretary concerned shall define "dependent" for the purposes of this section.	

10 U.S.C. §4331	**Improved Prevention and Response to Allegations of Sexual Assault Involving Members of the Armed Forces-**
	(1) Requirement for data collection.--
	    (A) In general.--Pursuant to regulations prescribed by the Secretary of Defense, information shall be collected on--
	        (i) whether a military protective order was issued that involved either the victim or alleged perpetrator of a sexual assault; and
	        (ii) whether military protective orders involving members of the Armed Forces were violated in the course of substantiated incidents of sexual assaults against members of the Armed Forces.
	    (B) Submission of data.--The data required to be collected under this subsection shall be included in the annual report submitted to Congress on sexual assaults involving members of the Armed Forces.
	    (2) Information to members.--
	    Deadline. Not later than 180 days after the date of the enactment of this Act, the Secretary of Defense shall submit to the Committees on Armed Services of the Senate and the House of Representatives a report explaining the measures being taken to ensure that, when a military protective order has been issued, the member of the Armed Forces who is protected by the order is informed, in a timely manner, of the member's option to request transfer from the command to which the member is assigned.
		Pub. L. No. 111-84 §567(c) (2010)

10 U.S.C.	(a) **Restricting Communications With Members of Congress and Inspector**	Pub. L. No.

Statute	Statutory Language	Public Law that last amended statute
§1034	**General Prohibited—** (1) No person may restrict a member of the armed forces in communicating with a Member of Congress or an Inspector General. (2) Paragraph (1) does not apply to a communication that is unlawful. (b) Prohibition of Retaliatory Personnel Actions.— (1) No person may take (or threaten to take) an unfavorable personnel action, or withhold (or threaten to withhold) a favorable personnel action, as a reprisal against a member of the armed forces for making or preparing— (A) a communication to a Member of Congress or an Inspector General that (under subsection (a)) may not be restricted; or (B) a communication that is described in subsection (c)(2) and that is made (or prepared to be made) to— (i) a Member of Congress; (ii) an Inspector General (as defined in subsection (i)) or any other Inspector General appointed under the Inspector General Act of 1978; (iii) a member of a Department of Defense audit, inspection, investigation, or law enforcement organization; (iv) any person or organization in the chain of command; or (v) any other person or organization designated pursuant to regulations or other established administrative procedures for such communications. (2) Any action prohibited by paragraph (1) (including the threat to take any unfavorable action and the withholding or threat to withhold any favorable action) shall be considered for the purposes of this section to be a personnel action prohibited by this subsection. (c) Inspector General Investigation of Allegations of Prohibited Personnel Actions.— (1) If a member of the armed forces submits to an Inspector General an allegation that a personnel action prohibited by subsection (b) has been taken (or threatened) against the member with respect to a communication described in paragraph (2), the Inspector General shall take the action required under paragraph (3). (2) A communication described in this paragraph is a communication in which a member of the armed forces complains of, or discloses information that the member reasonably believes constitutes evidence of, any of the following: (A) A violation of law or regulation, including a law or regulation prohibiting sexual harassment or unlawful discrimination. (B) Gross mismanagement, a gross waste of funds, an abuse of authority, or a substantial and specific danger to public health or safety. (C) A threat by another member of the armed forces or employee of the Federal Government that indicates a determination or intent to kill or cause serious bodily injury to members of the armed forces or civilians or damage to military, Federal, or civilian property. (3)	112-239 §1054 (2013)

Statute	Statutory Language	Public Law that last amended statute
	(A) An Inspector General receiving an allegation as described in paragraph (1) shall expeditiously determine, in accordance with regulations prescribed under subsection (h), whether there is sufficient evidence to warrant an investigation of the allegation.	

(B) If the Inspector General receiving such an allegation is an Inspector General within a military department, that Inspector General shall promptly notify the Inspector General of the Department of Defense of the allegation. Such notification shall be made in accordance with regulations prescribed under subsection (h).

(C) If an allegation under paragraph (1) is submitted to an Inspector General within a military department and if the determination of that Inspector General under subparagraph (A) is that there is not sufficient evidence to warrant an investigation of the allegation, that Inspector General shall forward the matter to the Inspector General of the Department of Defense for review.

(D) Upon determining that an investigation of an allegation under paragraph (1) is warranted, the Inspector General making the determination shall expeditiously investigate the allegation. In the case of a determination made by the Inspector General of the Department of Defense, that Inspector General may delegate responsibility for the investigation to an appropriate Inspector General within a military department.

(E) In the case of an investigation under subparagraph (D) within the Department of Defense, the results of the investigation shall be determined by, or approved by, the Inspector General of the Department of Defense (regardless of whether the investigation itself is conducted by the Inspector General of the Department of Defense or by an Inspector General within a military department).

(4) Neither an initial determination under paragraph (3)(A) nor an investigation under paragraph (3)(D) is required in the case of an allegation made more than 60 days after the date on which the member becomes aware of the personnel action that is the subject of the allegation.

(5) The Inspector General of the Department of Defense, or the Inspector General of the Department of Homeland Security (in the case of a member of the Coast Guard when the Coast Guard is not operating as a service in the Navy), shall ensure that the Inspector General conducting the investigation of an allegation under this subsection is outside the immediate chain of command of both the member submitting the allegation and the individual or individuals alleged to have taken the retaliatory action.

(d) Inspector General Investigation of Underlying Allegations.— Upon receiving an allegation under subsection (c), the Inspector General receiving the allegation shall conduct a separate investigation of the information that the member making the allegation believes constitutes evidence of wrongdoing (as described in subparagraph (A) or (B) of subsection (c)(2)) if there previously has not been such an investigation or if the Inspector General determines that the original investigation was biased or otherwise inadequate. In the case of an allegation received by the Inspector General of the Department of Defense, the Inspector

Statute	Statutory Language	Public Law that last amended statute
	General may delegate that responsibility to the Inspector General of the armed force concerned. (e) Reports on Investigations.— (1) After completion of an investigation under subsection (c) or (d) or, in the case of an investigation under subsection (c) by an Inspector General within a military department, after approval of the report of that investigation under subsection (c)(3)(E), the Inspector General conducting the investigation shall submit a report on the results of the investigation to the Secretary of Defense (or to the Secretary of Homeland Security in the case of a member of the Coast Guard when the Coast Guard is not operating as a service in the Navy) and shall transmit a copy of the report on the results of the investigation to the member of the armed forces who made the allegation investigated. The report shall be transmitted to the Secretary, and the copy of the report shall be transmitted to the member, not later than 30 days after the completion of the investigation or, in the case of an investigation under subsection (c) by an Inspector General within a military department, after approval of the report of that investigation under subsection (c)(3)(E). (2) In the copy of the report transmitted to the member, the Inspector General shall ensure the maximum disclosure of information possible, with the exception of information that is not required to be disclosed under section 552 of title 5. However, the copy need not include summaries of interviews conducted, nor any document acquired, during the course of the investigation. Such items shall be transmitted to the member, if the member requests the items, with the copy of the report or after the transmittal to the member of the copy of the report, regardless of whether the request for those items is made before or after the copy of the report is transmitted to the member. (3) If, in the course of an investigation of an allegation under this section, the Inspector General determines that it is not possible to submit the report required by paragraph (1) within 180 days after the date of receipt of the allegation being investigated, the Inspector General shall provide to the Secretary of Defense (or to the Secretary of Homeland Security in the case of a member of the Coast Guard when the Coast Guard is not operating as a service in the Navy) and to the member making the allegation a notice— (A) of that determination (including the reasons why the report may not be submitted within that time); and (B) of the time when the report will be submitted. (4) The report on the results of the investigation shall contain a thorough review of the facts and circumstances relevant to the allegation and the complaint or disclosure and shall include documents acquired during the course of the investigation, including summaries of interviews conducted. The report may include a recommendation as to the disposition of the complaint. (f) Correction of Records When Prohibited Action Taken.— (1) A board for the correction of military records acting under section 1552 of this title, in resolving an application for the correction of records made by a member or	

Statute	Statutory Language	Public Law that last amended statute
	former member of the armed forces who has alleged a personnel action prohibited by subsection (b), on the request of the member or former member or otherwise, may review the matter. (2) In resolving an application described in paragraph (1), a correction board— (A) shall review the report of the Inspector General submitted under subsection (e)(1); (B) may request the Inspector General to gather further evidence; and (C) may receive oral argument, examine and cross-examine witnesses, take depositions, and, if appropriate, conduct an evidentiary hearing. (3) If the board elects to hold an administrative hearing, the member or former member who filed the application described in paragraph (1)— (A) may be provided with representation by a judge advocate if— (i) the Inspector General, in the report under subsection (e)(1), finds that there is probable cause to believe that a personnel action prohibited by subsection (b) has been taken (or threatened) against the member with respect to a communication described in subsection (c)(2); (ii) the Judge Advocate General concerned determines that the case is unusually complex or otherwise requires judge advocate assistance to ensure proper presentation of the legal issues in the case; and (iii) the member is not represented by outside counsel chosen by the member; and (B) may examine witnesses through deposition, serve interrogatories, and request the production of evidence, including evidence contained in the investigatory record of the Inspector General but not included in the report submitted under subsection (e)(1). (4) The Secretary concerned shall issue a final decision with respect to an application described in paragraph (1) within 180 days after the application is filed. If the Secretary fails to issue such a final decision within that time, the member or former member shall be deemed to have exhausted the member's or former member's administrative remedies under section 1552 of this title. (5) The Secretary concerned shall order such action, consistent with the limitations contained in sections 1552 and 1553 of this title, as is necessary to correct the record of a personnel action prohibited by subsection (b). (6) If the Board determines that a personnel action prohibited by subsection (b) has occurred, the Board may recommend to the Secretary concerned that the Secretary take appropriate disciplinary action against the individual who committed such personnel action. (g) Review by Secretary of Defense.— Upon the completion of all administrative review under subsection (f), the member or former member of the armed forces (except for a member or former member of the Coast Guard when the Coast Guard is not operating as a service in the Navy) who made the allegation referred to in subsection (c)(1), if not satisfied with the disposition of the matter, may submit the matter to the Secretary of Defense. The Secretary shall make a decision to reverse or uphold the decision of the Secretary of the military department concerned in the	

Statute	Statutory Language	Public Law that last amended statute
	matter within 90 days after receipt of such a submittal. (h) Regulations.— The Secretary of Defense, and the Secretary of Homeland Security with respect to the Coast Guard when it is not operating as a service in the Navy, shall prescribe regulations to carry out this section. (i) Definitions.— In this section: (1) The term "Member of Congress" includes any Delegate or Resident Commissioner to Congress. (2) The term "Inspector General" means any of the following: (A) The Inspector General of the Department of Defense. (B) The Inspector General of the Department of Homeland Security, in the case of a member of the Coast Guard when the Coast Guard is not operating as a service in the Navy. (C) Any officer of the armed forces or employee of the Department of Defense who is assigned or detailed to serve as an Inspector General at any level in the Department of Defense. (3) The term "unlawful discrimination" means discrimination on the basis of race, color, religion, sex, or national origin.	

10 U.S.C. §1561	**Involuntary Separation**
	(a) Review Required.--The Secretary of Defense shall develop a policy to require a general officer or flag officer of the Armed Forces to review the circumstances of, and grounds for, the proposed involuntary separation of any member of the Armed Forces who--
	    (1) made an Unrestricted Report of a sexual assault;
	    (2) within one year after making the Unrestricted Report of a sexual assault, is recommended for involuntary separation from the Armed Forces; and
	    (3) requests the review on the grounds that the member believes the recommendation for involuntary separation from the Armed Forces was initiated in retaliation for making the report.
	    (b) Concurrence Required.--If a review is requested by a member of the Armed Forces as authorized by subsection (a), the concurrence of the general officer or flag officer conducting the review of the proposed involuntary separation of the member is required in order to separate the member.
	    (c) Submission of Policy.--Not later than 180 days after the date of the enactment of this Act, the Secretary of Defense shall submit to the Committees on Armed Services of the Senate and the House of Representatives a report containing the policy developed under subsection (a).
	    (d) Application of Policy.--The policy developed under subsection (a) shall take effect on the date of the submission of the policy to Congress under subsection (c) and apply to members of the Armed Forces described in subsection (a) who are proposed to be involuntarily separated from the Armed Forces on or after that date.
		Pub. L. No. 112-239, §567(c), (2013)

10 U.S.C. §1561	**Establishment of Special Victim Capabilities within the Military Departments to Respond to allegations of Certain Special Victim Offenses—**	Pub. L. No. 112-239,

Statute	Statutory Language	Public Law that last amended statute
	(a) ESTABLISHMENT REQUIRED.—Under regulations prescribed by the Secretary of Defense, the Secretary of each military department shall establish special victim capabilities for the purposes of— (1) investigating and prosecuting allegations of child abuse, serious domestic violence, or sexual offenses; and (2) providing support for the victims of such offenses. (b) PERSONNEL.—The special victim capabilities developed under subsection (a) shall include specially trained and selected— (1) investigators from the Army Criminal Investigative Command, Naval Criminal Investigative Service, or Air Force Office of Special Investigations; (2) judge advocates; (3) victim witness assistance personnel; and (4) administrative paralegal support personnel. (c) TRAINING, SELECTION, AND CERTIFICATION STANDARDS.—The Secretary of Defense shall prescribe standards for the training, selection, and certification of personnel who will provide special victim capabilities for a military department. (d) DISCRETION REGARDING EXTENT OF CAPABILITIES.— (1) IN GENERAL.—Subject to paragraph (2), the Secretary of a military department shall determine the extent to which special victim capabilities will be established within the military department and prescribe regulations for the management and use of the special victim capabilities. (2) REQUIRED ELEMENTS.—At a minimum, the special victim capabilities established within a military department must provide effective, timely, and responsive world-wide support for the purposes described in subsection (a). (e) TIME FOR ESTABLISHMENT.— (1) IMPLEMENTATION PLAN.—Not later than 270 days after the date of the enactment of this Act, the Secretary of Defense shall submit to the Committees on Armed Services of the Senate and the House of Representatives a report containing— (A) the plans and time lines of the Secretaries of the military departments for the establishment of the special victims capabilities; and (B) an assessment by the Secretary of Defense of the plans and time lines. (2) INITIAL CAPABILITIES.—Not later than one year after the date of the enactment of this Act, the Secretary of each military department shall have available an initial special victim capability consisting of the personnel specified in subsection (b). (f) EVALUATION OF EFFECTIVENESS.—Not later than 180 days after the date of the enactment of this Act, the Secretary of Defense shall— (1) prescribe the common criteria to be used by the Secretaries of the military departments to measure the effectiveness and impact of the special victim capabilities from the investigative, prosecutorial, and victim's perspectives; and (2) require the Secretaries of the military departments to collect and report the data	§573 (2013)

Statute	Statutory Language	Public Law that last amended statute
	used to measure such effectiveness and impact. (g) SPECIAL VICTIM CAPABILITIES DEFINED.—In this section, the term "special victim capabilities" means a distinct, recognizable group of appropriately skilled professionals who work collaboratively to achieve the purposes described in subsection (a). This section does not require that the special victim capabilities be created as separate military unit or have a separate chain of command.	
38 U.S.C. §1720D	**Counseling and Treatment of Sexual Trauma—** (a) (1) The Secretary shall operate a program under which the Secretary provides counseling and appropriate care and services to veterans who the Secretary determines require such counseling and care and services to overcome psychological trauma, which in the judgment of a mental health professional employed by the Department, resulted from a physical assault of a sexual nature, battery of a sexual nature, or sexual harassment which occurred while the veteran was serving on active duty or active duty for training. (2) In furnishing counseling to a veteran under this subsection, the Secretary may provide such counseling pursuant to a contract with a qualified mental health professional if (A) in the judgment of a mental health professional employed by the Department, the receipt of counseling by that veteran in facilities of the Department would be clinically inadvisable, or (B) Department facilities are not capable of furnishing such counseling to that veteran economically because of geographical inaccessibility. (b) (1) The Secretary shall give priority to the establishment and operation of the program to provide counseling and care and services under subsection (a). In the case of a veteran eligible for counseling and care and services under subsection (a), the Secretary shall ensure that the veteran is furnished counseling and care and services under this section in a way that is coordinated with the furnishing of such care and services under this chapter. (2) In establishing a program to provide counseling under subsection (a), the Secretary shall— (A) provide for appropriate training of mental health professionals and such other healthcare personnel as the Secretary determines necessary to carry out the program effectively; (B) seek to ensure that such counseling is furnished in a setting that is therapeutically appropriate, taking into account the circumstances that resulted in the need for such counseling; and (C) provide referral services to assist veterans who are not eligible for services under this chapter to obtain those from sources outside the Department. (c) The Secretary shall provide information on the counseling and treatment available to veterans under this section. Efforts by the Secretary to provide such	Pub. L. No. 102-585 (2012)

Statute	Statutory Language	Public Law that last amended statute
	information— (1) shall include availability of a toll-free telephone number (commonly referred to as an 800 number); (2) shall ensure that information about the counseling and treatment available to veterans under this section— (A) is revised and updated as appropriate; (B) is made available and visibly posted at appropriate facilities of the Department; and (C) is made available through appropriate public information services; and (3) shall include coordination with the Secretary of Defense seeking to ensure that individuals who are being separated from active military, naval, or air service are provided appropriate information about programs, requirements, and procedures for applying for counseling and treatment under this section. (d) (1) The Secretary shall carry out a program to provide graduate medical education, training, certification, and continuing medical education for mental health professionals who provide counseling, care, and services under subsection (a). (2) In carrying out the program required by paragraph (1), the Secretary shall ensure that— (A) all mental health professionals described in such paragraph have been trained in a consistent manner; and (B) training described in such paragraph includes principles of evidence-based treatment and care for sexual trauma and post-traumatic stress disorder. (e) Each year, the Secretary shall submit to Congress an annual report on the counseling, care, and services provided to veterans pursuant to this section. Each report shall include data for the year covered by the report with respect to each of the following: (1) The number of mental health professionals, graduate medical education trainees, and primary care providers who have been certified under the program required by subsection (d) and the amount and nature of continuing medical education provided under such program to such professionals, trainees, and providers who are so certified. (2) The number of women veterans who received counseling and care and services under subsection (a) from professionals and providers who received training under subsection (d). (3) The number of graduate medical education, training, certification, and continuing medical education courses provided by reason of subsection (d). (4) The number of trained full-time equivalent employees required in each facility of the Department to meet the needs of veterans requiring treatment and care for sexual trauma and post-traumatic stress disorder. (5) Such recommendations for improvements in the treatment of women veterans with sexual trauma and post-traumatic stress disorder as the Secretary considers appropriate.	

Statute	Statutory Language	Public Law that last amended statute
	(6) Such other information as the Secretary considers appropriate. (f) In this section, the term "sexual harassment" means repeated, unsolicited verbal or physical contact of a sexual nature which is threatening in character.	
10 U.S.C. §1561	**Retention of Certain Forms in Connection with Restricted Reports on Sexual Assault at Request of the Member of the Armed Forces making the Report—** (a) Period of Retention.--At the request of a member of the Armed Forces who files a Restricted Report on an incident of sexual assault involving the member, the Secretary of Defense shall ensure that all copies of Department of Defense Form 2910 and Department of Defense Form 2911 filed in connection with the Restricted Report be retained for the longer of-- (1) 50 years commencing on the date of signature of the member on Department of Defense Form 2910; or (2) the time provided for the retention of such forms in connection with Unrestricted Reports on incidents of sexual assault involving members of the Armed Forces under Department of Defense Directive-Type Memorandum (DTM) 11-062, entitled ``Document Retention in Cases of Restricted and Unrestricted Reports of Sexual Assault'', or any successor directive or policy. (b) Protection of Confidentiality.--Any Department of Defense form retained under subsection (a) shall be retained in a manner that protects the confidentiality of the member of the Armed Forces concerned in accordance with procedures for the protection of confidentiality of information in Restricted Reports under Department of Defense memorandum JTF-SAPR-009, relating to the Department of Defense policy on confidentiality for victims of sexual assault, or any successor policy or directive.	Pub. L. No. 112-239, §577 (2013)
10 U.S.C. §1561	**Retention of Certain Forms in Connection with Restricted Reports on Sexual Assault at Request of the Member of the Armed Forces Making the Report—** (a) PERIOD OF RETENTION.—At the request of a member of the Armed Forces who files a Restricted Report on an incident of sexual assault involving the member, the Secretary of Defense shall ensure that all copies of Department of Defense Form 2910 and Department of Defense Form 2911 filed in connection with the Restricted Report be retained for the longer of— (1) 50 years commencing on the date of signature of the member on Department of Defense Form 2910; or (2) the time provided for the retention of such forms in connection with Unrestricted Reports on incidents of sexual assault involving members of the Armed Forces under Department of Defense Directive–Type Memorandum (DTM) 11–062, entitled "Document Retention in Cases of Restricted and Unrestricted Reports of Sexual Assault", or any successor directive or policy. (b) PROTECTION OF CONFIDENTIALITY.—Any Department of Defense form	Pub. L. No. 112-239, §577 (2013)

Statute	Statutory Language	Public Law that last amended statute
	retained under subsection (a) shall be retained in a manner that protects the confidentiality of the member of the Armed Forces concerned in accordance with procedures for the *1763 protection of confidentiality of information in Restricted Reports under Department of Defense memorandum JTF–SAPR–009, relating to the Department of Defense policy on confidentiality for victims of sexual assault, or any successor policy or directive.	
10 U.S.C. §1561 NOTE	**Independent Reviews and Assessments of Uniform Code of Military Justice and Judicial Proceedings of Sexual Assault Cases—** (a) Independent Reviews and Assessments Required.-- (1) Response systems to adult sexual assault crimes.--The Secretary of Defense shall establish a panel to conduct an independent review and assessment of the systems used to investigate, prosecute, and adjudicate crimes involving adult sexual assault and related offenses under section 920 of title 10, United States Code (article 120 of the Uniform Code of Military Justice), for the purpose of developing recommendations regarding how to improve the effectiveness of such systems. (2) Judicial proceedings since fiscal year 2012 amendments.-- The Secretary of Defense shall establish a panel to conduct an independent review and assessment of judicial proceedings conducted under the Uniform Code of Military Justice involving adult sexual assault and related offenses since the amendments made to the Uniform Code of Military Justice by section 541 of the National Defense Authorization Act for Fiscal Year 2012 (Public Law 112-81; 125 Stat. 1404) for the purpose of developing recommendations for improvements to such proceedings. (b) Establishment of Independent Review Panels.-- (1) Composition.-- (A) Response systems panel.--The panel required by subsection (a)(1) shall be composed of nine members, five of whom are appointed by the Secretary of Defense and one member each appointed by the chairman and ranking member of the Committees on Armed Services of the Senate and the House of Representatives. Judicial proceedings panel.--The panel required by subsection (a)(2) shall be appointed by the Secretary of Defense and consist of five members, two of whom must have also served on the panel established under subsection (a)(1). (2) Qualifications.--The members of each panel shall be selected from among private United States citizens who collectively possess expertise in military law, civilian law, the investigation, prosecution, and adjudication of sexual assaults in State and Federal criminal courts, victim advocacy, treatment for victims, military justice, the organization and missions of the Armed Forces, and offenses relating to rape, sexual assault, and other adult sexual assault crimes. (3) Chair.--The chair of each panel shall be appointed by the Secretary of	Pub. L. No. 112-239, §576 (2013)

Statute	Statutory Language	Public Law that last amended statute
	Defense from among the members of the panel. (4) Period of appointment; vacancies.--Members shall be appointed for the life of the panel. Any vacancy in a panel shall be filled in the same manner as the original appointment. (5) Deadline for appointments.-- (A) Response systems panel.--All original appointments to the panel required by subsection (a)(1) shall be made not later than 120 days after the date of the enactment of this Act. Judicial proceedings panel.--All original appointments to the panel required by subsection (a)(2) shall be made before the termination date of the panel established under subsection (a)(1), but no later than 30 days before the termination date. (6) Meetings.--A panel shall meet at the call of the chair. (7) First meeting.--The chair shall call the first meeting of a panel not later than 60 days after the date of the appointment of all the members of the panel. (c) Reports and Duration.-- (1) Response systems panel.--The panel established under subsection (a)(1) shall terminate upon the earlier of the following: (A) Thirty days after the panel has submitted a report of its findings and recommendations, through the Secretary of Defense, to the Committees on Armed Services of the Senate and the House of Representatives. (B) Eighteen months after the first meeting of the panel, by which date the panel is expected to have made its report. (2) Judicial proceedings panel.-- (A) First report.--The panel established under subsection (a)(2) shall submit a first report, including any proposals for legislative or administrative changes the panel considers appropriate, to the Secretary of Defense and the Committees on Armed Services of the Senate and the House of Representatives not later than 180 days after the first meeting of the panel. (B) Subsequent reports.--The panel established under subsection (a)(2) shall submit subsequent reports during fiscal years 2014 through 2017. (C) Termination.--The panel established under subsection (a)(2) shall terminate on September 30, 2017. (d) Duties of Panels.-- (1) Response systems panel.--In conducting a systemic review and assessment, the panel required by subsection (a)(1) shall provide recommendations on how to improve the effectiveness of the investigation, prosecution, and adjudication of crimes involving adult sexual assault and related offenses under section 920 of title 10, United States Code (article 120 of the Uniform Code of Military Justice). The review shall include the following: (A) Using criteria the panel considers appropriate, an assessment of the strengths and weaknesses of the systems, including the administration of the Uniform Code of the Military Justice, and the investigation, prosecution, and	

Statute	Statutory Language	Public Law that last amended statute
	adjudication, of adult sexual assault crimes during the period 2007 through 2011.	

(B) A comparison of military and civilian systems for the investigation, prosecution, and adjudication of adult sexual assault crimes. This comparison shall include an assessment of differences in providing support and protection to victims and the identification of civilian best practices that may be incorporated into any phase of the military system.

(C) An assessment of advisory sentencing guidelines used in civilian courts in adult sexual assault cases and whether it would be advisable to promulgate sentencing guidelines for use in courts-martial.

(D) An assessment of the training level of military defense and trial counsel, including their experience in defending or prosecuting adult sexual assault crimes and related offenses, as compared to prosecution and defense counsel for similar cases in the Federal and State court systems.

(E) An assessment and comparison of military court-martial conviction rates with those in the Federal and State courts and the reasons for any differences.

(F) An assessment of the roles and effectiveness of commanders at all levels in preventing sexual assaults and responding to reports of sexual assault.

(G) An assessment of the strengths and weakness of proposed legislative initiatives to modify the current role of commanders in the administration of military justice and the investigation, prosecution, and adjudication of adult sexual assault crimes.

(H) An assessment of the adequacy of the systems and procedures to support and protect victims in all phases of the investigation, prosecution, and adjudication of adult sexual assault crimes, including whether victims are provided the rights afforded by section 3771 of title 18, United States Code, Department of Defense Directive 1030.1, and Department of Defense Instruction 1030.2.

(I) Such other matters and materials the panel considers appropriate.

(2) Judicial proceedings panel.--The panel required by subsection (a)(2) shall perform the following duties:

(A) Assess and make recommendations for improvements in the implementation of the reforms to the offenses relating to rape, sexual assault, and other sexual misconduct under the Uniform Code of Military Justice that were enacted by section 541 of the National Defense Authorization Act for Fiscal Year 2012 (Public Law 112-81; 125 Stat. 1404).

(B) Review and evaluate current trends in response to sexual assault crimes whether by courts-martial proceedings, non-judicial punishment and administrative actions, including the number of punishments by type, and the consistency and appropriateness of the decisions, punishments, and administrative actions based on the facts of individual cases.

(C) Identify any trends in punishments rendered by military courts, including general, special, and summary courts-martial, in response to sexual assault, including the number of punishments by type, and the consistency of the punishments, based on the facts of each case compared with the punishments

Statute	Statutory Language	Public Law that last amended statute
	rendered by Federal and State criminal courts. (D) Review and evaluate court-martial convictions for sexual assault in the year covered by the most-recent report required by subsection (c)(2) and the number and description of instances when punishments were reduced or set aside upon appeal and the instances in which the defendant appealed following a plea agreement, if such information is available. (E) Review and assess those instances in which prior sexual conduct of the alleged victim was considered in a proceeding under section 832 of title 10, United States Code (article 32 of the Uniform Code of Military Justice), and any instances in which prior sexual conduct was determined to be inadmissible. (F) Review and assess those instances in which evidence of prior sexual conduct of the alleged victim was introduced by the defense in a court-martial and what impact that evidence had on the case. (G) Building on the data compiled as a result of paragraph (1)(D), assess the trends in the training and experience levels of military defense and trial counsel in adult sexual assault cases and the impact of those trends in the prosecution and adjudication of such cases. (H) Monitor trends in the development, utilization and effectiveness of the special victims capabilities required by section 573 of this Act. (I) Monitor the implementation of the April 20, 2012, Secretary of Defense policy memorandum regarding withholding initial disposition authority under the Uniform Code of Military Justice in certain sexual assault cases. (J) Consider such other matters and materials as the panel considers appropriate for purposes of the reports. (3) Utilization of other studies.--In conducting reviews and assessments and preparing reports, a panel may review, and incorporate as appropriate, the data and findings of applicable ongoing and completed studies. (e) Authority of Panels.-- (1) Hearings.--A panel may hold such hearings, sit and act at such times and places, take such testimony, and receive such evidence as the panel considers appropriate to carry out its duties under this section. (2) Information from federal agencies.--Upon request by the chair of a panel, a department or agency of the Federal Government shall provide information that the panel considers necessary to carry out its duties under this section. (f) Personnel Matters.-- (1) Pay of members.--Members of a panel shall serve without pay by reason of their work on the panel. (2) Travel expenses.--The members of a panel shall be allowed travel expenses, including per diem in lieu of subsistence, at rates authorized for employees of agencies under subchapter I of chapter 57 of title 5, United States Code, while away from their homes or regular places of business in the performance or services for the panel.	

Statute	Statutory Language	Public Law that last amended statute
	(3) Staffing and resources.--The Secretary of Defense shall provide staffing and resources to support the panels, except that the Secretary may not assign primary responsibility for such staffing and resources to the Sexual Assault Prevention and Response Office.	
10 U.S.C. §1561	(a) **Action on complaints alleging sexual harassment**. —A commanding officer or officer in charge of a unit, vessel, facility, or area of the Army, Navy, Air Force, or Marine Corps who receives from a member of the command or a civilian employee under the supervision of the officer a complaint alleging sexual harassment by a member of the armed forces or a civilian employee of the Department of Defense shall carry out an investigation of the matter in accordance with this section. (b) Commencement of investigation.--To the extent practicable, a commanding officer or officer in charge receiving such a complaint shall, within 72 hours after receipt of the complaint-- (1) forward the complaint or a detailed description of the allegation to the next superior officer in the chain of command who is authorized to convene a general court-martial; (2) commence, or cause the commencement of, an investigation of the complaint; and (3) advise the complainant of the commencement of the investigation. (c) Duration of investigation.--To the extent practicable, a commanding officer or officer in charge receiving such a complaint shall ensure that the investigation of the complaint is completed not later than 14 days after the date on which the investigation is commenced. (d) Report on investigation.--To the extent practicable, a commanding officer or officer in charge receiving such a complaint shall-- (1) submit a final report on the results of the investigation, including any action taken as a result of the investigation, to the next superior officer referred to in subsection (b)(1) within 20 days after the date on which the investigation is commenced; or (2) submit a report on the progress made in completing the investigation to the next superior officer referred to in subsection (b)(1) within 20 days after the date on which the investigation is commenced and every 14 days thereafter until the investigation is completed and, upon completion of the investigation, then submit a final report on the results of the investigation, including any action taken as a result of the investigation, to that next superior officer. (e) Sexual harassment defined.--In this section, the term "sexual harassment" means any of the following: (1) Conduct (constituting a form of sex discrimination) that-- (A) involves unwelcome sexual advances, requests for sexual favors, and deliberate or repeated offensive comments or gestures of a sexual nature when-- (i) submission to such conduct is made either explicitly or implicitly a term or condition of a person's job, pay, or career;	Pub. L. No. 112-239, §576 (2013)

Statute	Statutory Language	Public Law that last amended statute
	(ii) submission to or rejection of such conduct by a person is used as a basis for career or employment decisions affecting that person; or (iii) such conduct has the purpose or effect of unreasonably interfering with an individual's work performance or creates an intimidating, hostile, or offensive working environment; and (B) is so severe or pervasive that a reasonable person would perceive, and the victim does perceive, the work environment as hostile or offensive. (2) Any use or condonation, by any person in a supervisory or command position, of any form of sexual behavior to control, influence, or affect the career, pay, or job of a member of the armed forces or a civilian employee of the Department of Defense. (3) Any deliberate or repeated unwelcome verbal comment or gesture of a sexual nature in the workplace by any member of the armed forces or civilian employee of the Department of Defense.	

APPENDIX B: DOD DATA PROVIDED TO COMMISSION

Figure B.1
CASES: Number of alleged perpetrators per case by branch of service, FY 2011

Service	1	2	3	4	5	6	9	Total number of cases (or records)	Number of multiple perpetrator cases (or records)
Air Force	402	18	4	1				425	23
Army	746	45	14	4		2	1	812	66
Marine Corps	222	12	5	2	1			242	20
Navy	316	18	3					337	21
Number of Cases	1686	93	26	7	1	2	1	1816	130
Number of Records	1686	186	78	28	5	12	9	2004	318

Source: Compiled by USCCR from DOD FY 2011 sexual assault data.

Figure B.2
RECORDS: Subject's gender by number of alleged perpetrators per case, FY 2011

Number of Perpetrators per Case	Female	Male	Unknown	Total Number of Records
1	27	1551	108	1686
2	5	161	20	186
3	3	69	6	78
4		20	8	28
5		5		5
6		6	6	12
9		9		9
Total records involving multiple subjects	8	270	40	318
Total	35	1821	148	2004

Source: Compiled by USCCR from DOD FY 2011 sexual assault data.

Figure B.3
The Department of Defense's groupings of case dispositions

DOD's Groupings of Case Disposition	Case Disposition
Report against the subject was unfounded	
	Case Unfounded by MCIO
Subject outside DOD's legal authority	
	Subject unknown
	Civilian or foreign authority--person NOT subject to the UCMJ
	Civilian or foreign authority--person subject to the UCMJ
	Civilian or foreign prosecution of person NOT subject to UCMJ
	Civilian or foreign prosecution of person subject to UCMJ
	Subject deceased or deserted
Cases that DID NOT go forward for disciplinary action	
Command Action Precluded	
	Victim declined to participate in military justice action
	Insufficient evidence of any offense
	Statute of limitations expired
	Victim deceased
Action Declined by Commander	
	Case unfounded by Command*
Cases that DID go forward for disciplinary action	
Evidence for commander action	
Commander Action for Sexual Assault Charge	
	Court-Martial Charge Preferred
	Non-judicial punishments (Article 15 UCMJ)
	Administrative discharge
	Adverse administrative action
Commander Action for Other Criminal Offenses	
	Probable cause for only non-sexual assault offense(s)

* As noted in Chapter 3, since 2012 any unrestricted report triggers a referral to the MCIO and an investigation, so the "Case Unfounded by Commander" option no longer exists.

Source: U.S. Department of Defense, Annual Report on Sexual Assault in the Military, FY 2011, April 2012, Exhibit 1, p. 32.

Figure B.4
Case disposition by victim's gender, FY 2011

Case disposition	Number of subject records						Percent of subject records					
	Female	Male	Multiple victims - female	Multiple victims - male	Multiple victims - male & female	TOTAL	Female	Male	Multiple victims - female	Multiple victims - male	Multiple victims - male & female	TOTAL
Action declined by Commander	43	4	0	0	0	47	2.5%	2.5%	0.0%	0.0%	0.0%	2.3%
Command action precluded	445	25	12	1	0	483	26.0%	15.5%	12.8%	3.1%	0.0%	24.1%
Insufficient evidence of sexual offense	268	20	7	0	0	295	15.6%	12.4%	7.4%	0.0%	0.0%	14.7%
Other command action precluded	2	1	1	0	0	4	0.1%	60.0%	1.1%	0.0%	0.0%	0.2%
Victim declined to participate in military justice action	175	4	4	1	0	184	10.2%	2.5%	4.3%	3.1%	0.0%	9.2%
Evidence for commander action	813	82	62	27	4	988	47.5%	50.9%	66.0%	84.4%	100.0%	49.3%
Administrative discharge	35	5	6	2	0	48	2.0%	3.1%	6.4%	6.3%	0.0%	2.4%
Commander action for other criminal offenses	179	13	4	2	0	198	10.4%	8.1%	4.3%	6.3%	0.0%	9.9%
Court-martial charge preferred	407	32	40	6	3	488	23.8%	19.9%	42.6%	18.8%	75.0%	24.4%
Nonjudicial punishments or adverse administrative action	192	32	12	17	1	254	11.2%	19.9%	12.8%	53.1%	25.0%	12.7%
Subject outside DOD's legal authority	412	50	20	4	0	486	24.1%	31.1%	21.3%	12.5%	0.0%	24.3%
Civilian or foreign subject or prosecuting authority	220	15	13	3	0	251	12.8%	9.3%	13.8%	9.4%	0.0%	12.5%
Subject unknown, deceased, or deserted	192	35	7	1	0	235	11.2%	21.7%	7.4%	3.1%	0.0%	11.7%
TOTAL RECORDS	1713	161	94	32	4	2004	100%	100%	100%	100%	100%	100%

Source: Compiled by USCCR from DOD FY 2011 sexual assault data.

Figure B.5
Subject records with evidence for Commander action on any offense, by subject's pay grade and by nonjudicial punishment or court-martial outcome, FY 2011

Subject pay grade	Subject records with evidence for commander action, any offense								Subject records not designated as having evidence for commander action				
	None	Acquittal	Article 15 punishment imposed	Conviction	Discharge or resignation in lieu of court-martial	Dismissal	Pending adjudication	TOTAL records with evidence	Subject records for which Commander declined taking action	Command action precluded	Subject outside DOD's legal authority	Those with one or more punishments despite not having evidence for Commander action	TOTAL – ALL RECORDS
All subjects													
Cadet/midshipman	3	0	4	1	0	0	0	8	0	5	3	0	16
Junior enlisted member	127	36	141	126	21	45	78	574	20	277	88	8	967
Noncommissioned officer	91	19	88	55	18	19	37	327	12	116	41	4	500
Warrant officer	2	0	1	1	0	2	0	6	0	0	2	0	8
Officer	22	1	10	12	4	4	6	59		14	6	2	81
Unknown	2	2	2	1	0	3	0	10	15	50	219	0	294
US civilian, foreign national, or foreign military	3	0	0	0	0	1	0	4	0	14	120	0	138
TOTAL, all subjects	250	58	246	196	43	74	121	988	47	476	479	14	2004
Subjects investigated for penetration offenses													
Cadet/midshipman	2	0	2	1	0	0	0	5	0	4	2	0	11
Junior enlisted member	48	27	48	89	19	44	68	33	18	218	75	5	659
Noncommissioned officer	35	8	29	30	10	13	23	148	9	81	34	3	275
Warrant officer	1	0	1	0	0	2	0	4	0	0	2	0	6
Officer	7	0	3	8	1	1	4	24	0	8	5	1	38
Unknown	1	2	2	1	0	2	0	8	13	43	179	0	243
US civilian, foreign national, or foreign military	0	0	0	0	0	1	0	1	0	9	58	0	68
TOTAL, penetration offenses	94	37	85	129	30	63	95	533	40	363	355	9	1300
Subjects investigated for sexual contact and attempts													
Cadet/midshipman	1	0	2	0	0	0	0	3	0	1	1	0	5
Junior enlisted member	79	9	93	37	2	1	10	231	2	59	13	3	307
Noncommissioned officer	56	11	59	25	8	6	14	179	3	35	7	1	225
Warrant officer	1	0	0	1	0	0	0	2	0	0	0	0	2
Officer	15	1	7	4	3	3	2	35	0	6	1	1	44
Unknown	1	0	0	0	0	1	0	2	2	7	40	0	51
US civilian, foreign national, or foreign military	3	0	0	0	0	0	0	3	0	5	62	0	70
TOTAL, sexual contact and attempts	156	21	161	67	13	11	26	455	7	113	124	5	704

Source: Compiled by USCCR from DOD FY 2011 sexual assault data.

Figure B.6
Subject records with evidence for Commander action on a sexual offense, by subject's pay grade and by non-judicial punishment or court-martial outcome, FY 2011

Subject pay grade	Subject records with evidence for commander action, sexual offense								Commander action for other criminal (i.e., non-sexual offenses)	TOTAL – ALL RECORDS
	None	Acquittal	Article 15 punishment imposed	Conviction	Discharge or resignation in lieu of court-martial	Dismissal	Pending adjudication	TOTAL records with evidence for sexual offense		
All subjects										
Cadet/midshipman	3	0	2	1	0	0	0	6	2	16
Junior enlisted member	80	36	97	125	21	45	78	482	92	967
Noncommissioned officer	41	19	56	52	18	19	37	242	85	500
Warrant officer	1	0	1	1	0	2	0	5	1	8
Officer	10	1	8	12	4	4	6	45	14	81
Unknown	2	2	2	0	0	3	0	9	1	294
US civilian, foreign national, or foreign military	0	0	0	0	0	1	0	1	3	138
TOTAL, all subjects	137	58	166	191	43	74	121	790	198	2004
Subjects investigated for penetration offenses										
Cadet/midshipman	2	0	0	1	0	0	0	3	2	11
Junior enlisted member	22	27	14	88	19	44	68	282	61	659
Noncommissioned officer	8	8	9	28	10	13	23	99	49	275
Warrant officer	0	0	1	0	0	2	0	3	1	6
Officer	2		1	8	1	1	4	17	7	38
Unknown	1	2	2	0	0	2	0	7	1	243
US civilian, foreign national, or foreign military	0	0	0	0	0	1	0	1	0	68
TOTAL, penetration offenses	35	37	27	125	30	63	95	412	121	1300
Subjects investigated for sexual contact and attempts										
Cadet/midshipman	1	0	2	0	0	0	0	3	0	5
Junior enlisted member	58	9	83	37	2	1	10	200	31	308
Noncommissioned officer	33	11	47	24	8	6	14	143	36	225
Warrant officer	1	0	0	1	0	0	0	2	0	2
Officer	8	1	7	4	3	3	2	28	7	43
Unknown	1	0	0	0	0	1	0	2	0	51
US civilian, foreign national, or foreign military	0	0	0	0	0	0	0	0	3	70
TOTAL, sexual contact and attempts	102	21	139	66	13	11	26	378	77	704

Source: Compiled by USCCR from DOD FY 2011 sexual assault data.

Figure B.7
Punishments by penetration offense versus sexual contact or attempted sexual offense and by evidence to support command action, FY 2011

Punishment type	Subjects overall						Subjects in records with evidence for commander action for any offense				Subjects in records with evidence for commander action for sexual offense			
	Subjects receiving such punishment	Percent of total records	Those for penetration offenses	Those for sexual contact and attempts	Percent of records with penetration offenses	Percent of records with sexual contact and attempts	Those for penetration offenses	Those for sexual contact and attempts	Percent of records with penetration offenses	Percent of records with sexual contact and attempts	Those for penetration offenses	Those for sexual contact and attempts	Percent of records with penetration offenses	Percent of records with sexual contact and attempts
Adverse administrative action	168	8.4%	55	113	4.2%	16.1%	47	95	8.8%	20.9%	10	54	2.4%	14.3%
Cadet/midshipman disciplinary system	1	0.0%	0	1	0.0%	0.1%	0	1	0.0%	0.2%	0	1	0.0%	0.3%
Letter of admonishment	5	0.2%	0	5	0.0%	0.7%	0	5	0.0%	1.1%	0	0	0.0%	0.0%
Letter of counseling	23	1.1%	3	20	0.2%	2.8%	3	20	0.6%	4.4%	1	9	0.2%	2.4%
Letter of reprimand	88	4.4%	34	54	2.6%	7.7%	30	53	5.6%	11.6%	3	32	0.7%	8.5%
Other administrative action	51	2.5%	18	33	1.4%	4.7%	14	16	2.6%	3.5%	6	12	1.5%	3.2%
Administrative Discharge	111	5.5%	70	41	5.4%	5.8%	55	41	10.3%	9.0%	45	40	10.9%	10.6%
General	24	1.2%	11	13	0.8%	1.8%	10	13	1.9%	2.9%	4	13	1.0%	3.4%
Honorable	2	0.1%	1	1	0.1%	0.1%	1	1	0.2%	0.2%	1	0	0.2%	0.0%
LOR (Letter of reprimand)	2	0.1%	0	2	0.0%	0.3%	0	2	0.0%	0.4%	0	2	0.0%	0.5%
Under other than honorable conditions	82	4.1%	58	24	4.5%	3.4%	44	24	8.3%	5.3%	40	24	9.7%	6.3%
Resignation in lieu of court-martial	1	0.0%	0	1	0.0%	0.1%	0	1	0.0%	0.2%	0	1	0.0%	0.3%
Fines and forfeitures	321	16.0%	157	164	12.1%	23.3%	154	163	28.9%	35.8%	118	146	28.6%	38.6%
Confinement or restriction	352	17.6%	187	165	14.4%	23.4%	185	163	34.7%	35.8%	140	151	34.0%	39.9%
Reduction in rank	355	17.7%	174	181	13.4%	25.7%	172	180	32.3%	39.6%	124	160	30.1%	42.3%
Court-martial discharge	150	7.5%	99	51	7.6%	7.2%	99	51	18.6%	11.2%	98	50	23.8%	13.2%
NUMBER OF PUNISHED SUBJECTS	689	34.4%	326	363	25.1%	51.6%	300	343	56.3%	75.4%	202	278	49.0%	73.5%
TOTAL SUBJECT RECORDS	2004		1300	704			533	455			412	378		

Note: Subjects receiving multiple punishments are counted once for each type of punishment they received. Overall 60.7 percent of the subjects who were punished received multiple types of punishments.

Source: Compiled by USCCR from DOD FY 2011 sexual assault data.

APPENDIX C: DOD INSTRUCTIONS FOR DATA COLLECTION

<u>Figure C.1</u>
Instructions for Entering Information in Data Fields for DOD's SAPRO Reports, FY 2011

Field	Instructions:
No.	Column A – Synopsis Number: This is a number assigned to the synopsis by your Service for purposes of referring to these synopses in the spreadsheet only. Numbers should be 1, 2, 3, 4, etc. Note that this year the Department is reporting specific case outcomes of reports that were not determined to be unfounded at any point in the investigative process. As a result, please report dispositions for all multiple subject investigations by adding an "A", "B", "C", etc. after the number. In example synopsis number 2, there were two subjects. As a result, the Service reporting the case will have a synopsis numbered 2A and a synopsis numbered 2B to capture dispositions for both subjects. While each subject's separate demographic and disposition information is likely to be different, case synopsis information in Column K [sic, Column Q, which is the brief synopsis field in the 2011 instructions] may be copied and pasted for each subject if the information is essentially similar for all subjects.
Offense Investigated	Column B - Offense Investigated: Please enter the offense investigated by your Service. This should be the same offense that is reported for the subject and victim(s) on Worksheet 1b, Unrestricted Reports (F-G). This spreadsheet column contains a drop down menu listing the offenses below. If there were multiple charges, please select the most serious offense investigated. Please select from one of the following: • Rape (Article 120, UCMJ) • Aggravated sexual assault (Article 120, UCMJ) • Aggravated sexual contact (Article 120, UCMJ) • Abusive sexual contact (Article 120, UCMJ) • Wrongful sexual contact (Article 120, UCMJ) • Forcible sodomy (Article 125, UCMJ) • Indecent assault (Article 134, UCMJ for incidents occurring prior to FY08) • An attempt to commit any of these offenses (Article 80, UCMJ) • State/Local Sexual offense Not Specified Exclude all cases involving a child (i.e., A person who at the time of the assault had not yet attained the age of 16).
Location	Column C – Location of Offense: Please select "CONUS", "OCONUS", or the appropriate Combat Area of Interest country to report the location where the offense occurred. For cases that were reported as having occurred in a Combat Area of Interest, select the appropriate country from the list.
Subject Grade	Column D – Subject Grade: Please select the subject's grade from drop down menu.
Subject Gender	Column E – Subject Gender: Please select the subject's gender from the drop down menu
Victim Grade	Column F – Victim Grade: Please select the victim's grade from the drop down menu. For cases with more than one victim, select "Multiple Victims."
Victim Gender	Column G – Victim Gender: Please select the victim's gender from the drop down menu. For reports with more than one victim, select the appropriate category of multiple victims. For multiple victim reports that involved all female victims, select, "Multiple Victims – Female." For multiple victim reports that involved all male victims, select "Multiple Victims – Male." For multiple victim reports that involved victims of both genders, select "Multiple Victims."
Quarter	Column H - Quarter Disposition Completed: Please select from the drop down menu

Field	Instructions:
Disposition Completed	the quarter in which final disposition for the case was reported. Generally, final disposition will be reported when a case has been adjudicated and punishment assigned. For cases where command action was precluded or declined, report the quarter that decision was reported. For cases with unknown subjects, report the quarter the investigation was investigatively closed.
Case Disposition	Column I - Disposition: This spreadsheet column contains a drop-down menu listing of the final dispositions for subjects. Include only investigations of Unrestricted Reports with following final dispositions. Select one of the following: • Case Unfounded by MCIO [Added in 2011] • Subject unknown • Civilian or Foreign Authority-person subject to the UCMJ • Civilian or Foreign Authority-person not subject to the UCMJ • Subject deceased or deserted • Victim deceased • Victim declined to participate in the military justice action • Insufficient evidence of any offense • Statute of limitations expired • Commander Declined Action, RCM 306c1 • Probable cause for only non-sexual assault offense • Case Unfounded by Command [Added in 2011] • Court-Martial Charges Preferred • Nonjudicial Punishment (Article 15) • Administrative Discharge • Adverse Administrative Action
Court Case or Article 15 Outcome	Column J – Court Case or Article 15 Outcome: Only for subjects who had court-martial charges preferred or Article 15 punishment imposed. Select one of the following outcomes: • Dismissal – For subjects where court-martial charges were dismissed or withdrawn at any point in the military justice process (after charges were preferred, after the Article 32 hearing, prior to trial, etc.), and were NOT awarded Article 15 punishment. • Acquittal – For cases where the subject was found not guilty of sexual assault charges. • Conviction – For cases where the subject was found guilty of sexual assault charges. • Discharge or Resignation in Lieu of Court-Martial - For cases where the subject was allowed to separate or resign instead of being court-martialed. • Pending Adjudication - For cases where charges have been preferred, but the case has not yet been tried. • Article 15 Punishment Imposed – For subjects where Article 15 punishment was imposed as the primary disciplinary action OR where court charges were dismissed and an Article 15 punishment was administered instead. • Leave blank for subjects with dispositions other than those with court or Article 15 outcomes. • DO NOT REPORT CASES/SUBJECTS ON THIS WORKSHEET THAT ARE AWAITING COMMAND ACTION OR FINAL DISPOSITION.
Confinement or Restriction	Column K – Confinement or Restriction: ONLY FOR CASES WHERE COURT CASE OUTCOME IS "Conviction" or DISPOSITION IS "Nonjudicial Punishment." Enter: • "YES" for cases where a confinement sentence was imposed (For sexual assault reporting purposes, these sentences may involve any form of confinement, restriction

Field	Instructions:
	or limitations on freedom imposed by the court or command)
	o Ensure confinement sentence details are included in the case synopsis narrative
	• Leave blank for cases where confinement was not imposed.
Fines and Forfeitures	Column L – Fines & Forfeitures: ONLY FOR CASES WHERE COURT CASE OUTCOME IS "Conviction" or DISPOSITION IS "Nonjudicial Punishment." Enter: • "YES" for cases where fines and forfeitures were imposed. o Ensure fines and forfeiture details are included in the case synopsis narrative • Leave blank for cases where fines and forfeitures were not imposed.
Reduction in Rank	Column M – Reduction in Rank: ONLY FOR CASES WHERE COURT CASE OUTCOME IS "Conviction" or DISPOSITION IS "Nonjudicial Punishment." Enter: • "YES" for cases where a reduction in rank was imposed. o Ensure reduction in rank details are included in the case synopsis narrative • Leave blank for cases where a reduction in rank was not imposed.
Court-Martial Discharge	Column N – Court-Martial Discharge Type: ONLY FOR CASES WHERE COURT CASE OUTCOME IS "Conviction." Enter: • "YES" for cases where a punitive discharge was imposed by a Court-Martial (Dishonorable Discharge, Bad Conduct Discharge) or the result of a Court-Martial (e.g. Chapter 10 for the Army). o Ensure reduction in rank details are included in the case synopsis narrative • Leave blank for cases where a punitive discharge was not imposed.
Adverse Administrative Action Type	Column O – Administrative Action Type: ONLY FOR CASES WHERE DISPOSITION IS "Adverse Administrative Action." Enter: • Letter of Reprimand (LOR) • Letter of Admonishment (LOA) • Letter of Counseling (LOC) • Cadet/Midshipman Disciplinary System (for Military Service Academy subjects only) • Select "Other" for all other actions
Administrative Discharge Type	Column P – Administrative Discharge Type: ONLY FOR CASES WHERE DISPOSITION IS "Administrative Discharge." Enter: • Under Other than Honorable Conditions (UOTHC) • General • Honorable • Resignation in Lieu of Court-Martial (RILO)
Case Synopsis	2011 Instructions: Column Q - Brief Synopses: Please use the examples provided below as your guide. Be sure to identify the location and circumstances of the offense, as appropriate for your Service. Please ensure conviction and other punitive action details are described.[1]

[1] The examples were not in the 2011 spreadsheet that DOD provided to the U.S. Commission on Civil Rights. The examples appearing in the 2010 spreadsheet were: "• On-base offense where subject used alcohol to incapacitate and rape victim at a base residence;" "• Off-base offense where victim awoke to find that subject had entered her apartment illegally and was touching and kissing victim's breasts;" "• On-base offense where subject grabbed victim's breast while at indoor swimming pool. Foreign national subject was placed in host nation military jail for a week and will be dealt with by host nation military;" and "• Off-base offense. Victim alleged he was at a local disco and sexually assaulted in the restroom by another military member in her [sic] unit. Subject admitted culpability and was found guilty by court-martial." DOD FY 2011 sexual assault data.

Source: Compiled by USCCR from DOD FY 2011 sexual assault data.

COMMISSIONER STATEMENTS AND REBUTTALS

Statement of
Chairman Martin R. Castro, Commissioner Roberta Achtenberg, Commissioner David Kladney, & Commissioner Michael Yaki

**Four-Commissioner Statement Concerning the
U.S. Commission on Civil Rights'
2013 Statutory Enforcement Report,**

"Sexual Assault in the Military"

August 4, 2013

I.   Introduction

The United States Commission on Civil Rights[1] ("Commission") adopted Sexual Assault in the Military as the 2013 Statutory Enforcement Report topic[2] in the summer of 2012 because the Commission recognized its serious and pervasive nature.[3] After a year-long investigation, the Commission issued "Sexual Assault in the Military: U.S. Commission on Civil Rights 2013 Statutory Enforcement Report"[4] ("Report"). The Report is a comprehensive exploration of the

---

[1] Public Law 103-419 (S.2372). The Civil Rights Act of 1957 created the U.S. Commission on Civil Rights. Since then, Congress has reauthorized or extended the legislation creating the Commission several times; the most recent reauthorization was by virtue of the Civil Rights Commission Amendments Act of 1994. Established as an independent, bipartisan, fact-finding federal agency, our mission is to inform the development of national civil rights policy and enhance enforcement of federal civil rights laws.

[2] Public Law 103-419 (S.2372) Sec. 3 U.S.C. 1975a(d)(1).

[3] Since then, several high-profile incidents and renewed debate on Capitol Hill have again elevated awareness of the problems in the public consciousness. *See* Molly O'Toole, *Pentagon Officials Defend Sexual Assault Response, Pledge to Eliminate Problem*, HuffingtonPost.com, July 3, 2013, http://www.huffingtonpost.com/2013/07/03/pentagon-sexual-assault_n_3530082.html; Kristin Davis, *Ex-SAPRO Chief Heads to Trial to Face Sexual Battery Charge*, MilitaryTimes.com, July 17, 2013, http://www.militarytimes.com/article/20130717/NEWS06/307170026/Ex-SAPRO-chief-heads-trial-face-sexual-battery-charge; and Darren Samuelsohn, *Kirsten Gillibrand Intensifies Effort on Sexual-Assault Bill*, Politico.com, July 31, 2013, http://www.politico.com/story/2013/07/kirstin-gillibrand-intensifies-effort-on-sex-assault-bill-95014.html?hp=l4

[4] U.S. Commission on Civil Rights, 2013 Statutory Enforcement Report, Sexual Assault in the Military (2013) [hereinafter "the Report"] *available at* http://www.eusccr.com/msa1.htm. We thank the Commission staff members who worked diligently on this project. The Commission's thorough investigation included input from DoD, members of the advocacy sector, U.S. Armed Services veterans, and others. The Commission received voluminous documents from DoD through our discovery process. We heard detailed statements from, and engaged in vigorous discussion with, a variety of military and civilian stakeholders at the briefing which we convened in Washington, D.C. on January 11, 2013. The transcript of the Commission's January 2013 briefing *available at*

(cont'd)

nature and extent of sexual assault in the military and the military's response to it. The Report and the full record of our inquiry provide a range of information and raise a variety of questions. Without doubt, the Report provides ample support for the findings and recommendations that we offer.

Young Americans often enlist in our all-volunteer Armed Forces in order to improve their opportunities in life as they serve in defense of our nation. They risk life-altering injury and even death. The Department of Defense ("DoD") recognizes that it owes our Service members the highest duty of care to prevent sexual assault and to respond promptly, fairly, and efficiently when it does occur. As Major General Gary Patton, Director of DoD's Sexual Assault Prevention and Response Office, stated emphatically and unequivocally at our January 11, 2013 briefing, "Our troops take care of each other on the battlefield better than any other military in the world. This same ethos of care must extend to combating sexual assault within our ranks."[5]

The thought that those who enlist are at risk of being sexually assaulted by their comrades in arms –- and of suffering retaliatory actions for reporting the crimes -- is antithetical to the ideals for which our country and our military stand. All efforts must be made to understand and resolve all aspects of this troubling issue.

The Commission's investigation determined that perpetrators commit criminal sexual offenses at alarming rates within the ranks of our Armed Forces, and the number of reports continues to rise.[6] No credible argument to the contrary exists. DoD has repeatedly publicly acknowledged the difficult and complex problem of sexual assault within its ranks since the Tailhook scandal in 1991.[7] Nonetheless, the intractable phenomenon of sexual assault in the military still plagues

---

(cont'd from previous page)

http://www.eusccr.com/msa1.htm. We also received and reviewed many very informative public comments from active duty Service members and veterans.

[5] Major General Gary Patton, Director, Department of Defense's Sexual Assault Prevent and Response Office, testimony, *Briefing Transcript for U.S. Commission on Civil Rights, Washington, D.C.*, Jan. 11, 2013, transcript, p. 158, l. 23. [*"Briefing Transcript"*], *available at* http://www.eusccr.com/msa1.htm.

[6] See, e.g., Courtney Kube and Jim Miklaszewski, *Pentagon's annual report on sex assault shows alarming rise*, NBCNews.com, May 5, 2013, http://usnews.nbcnews.com/_news/2013/05/06/18090415-pentagons-annual-report-on-sexual-assault-shows-alarming-rise?lite; and DEPARTMENT OF DEFENSE, DEPARTMENT OF DEFENSE FISCAL YEAR 2012 ANNUAL REPORT ON SEXUAL ASSAULT IN THE MILITARY (2013), available at http://www.sapr.mil/public/docs/reports/FY12_DoD_SAPRO_Annual_Report_on_Sexual_Assault-VOLUME_ONE.pdf.

[7] See, e.g., *Tailhook '91, The Navy Blues*, Frontline PBS, October 14, 1996, http://www.pbs.org/wgbh/pages/frontline/shows/navy/tailhook/; Michael Winerip, *Revisiting the Military's Tailhook Scandal*, NYTimes.com, May 13, 2013, http://www.nytimes.com/2013/05/13/booming/revisiting-the-militarys-tailhook-scandal-video.html?_r=0.

the Armed Forces[8] and deeply concerns us. We are keenly aware that additional study and further reform will be necessary to halt military sexual assault.

Our inquiry demonstrated that DoD and the Armed Forces still uniformly express a strong desire to address and eliminate the problems. The high-level military representatives who appeared at our briefing spoke resolutely in these terms.[9] We understand that, in accord with their statements from 1991 through 2013, DoD and the Armed Forces have taken steps that will move them toward resolution. We commend DoD and the Armed Forces for many of the efforts that they have made to take responsibility for, and to address, the problems.

Surviving sexual assault in the military does not simply mean living through the incident. We are deeply concerned that for many Service members, it also means enduring re-victimization by the military structure. Our record is replete with examples of informal retaliation undertaken by peers and commanders toward Military Sexual Trauma ("MST") victims who report their abusers.[10]

Even more disturbing are credible allegations of institutional retribution and retaliation against MST victims who report assaults. These include assertions that the military initiates mental health evaluations of MST victims that lead to the misapplication of personality disorder and adjustment disorder diagnoses.[11] There are also indications that the military uses those diagnoses to discharge MST victims with a status that denies them access to Veterans Administration ("VA") health services to treat the long-term physical and emotional wounds which result from the assault itself.[12] Inaccurate diagnoses also create barriers to the MST

---

[8] DoD and the Armed Forces continued to express a desire to improve the dire situation right through the more recent sexual assault scandals at Lackland Air Force Base and Fort Carson. *See, e.g., 31 Female Victims Identified so far in Sex Scandal, Air Force says, FoxNews.com, June 30, 2012,* http://www.foxnews.com/us/2012/06/28/air-force-investigates-sexual-assault-31-women-by-trainers-during-training/; and *Fort Carson Investigates Alleged Sexual Misconduct,* HuffingtonPost.com, July 24, 2013, http://www.huffingtonpost.com/2013/07/24/fort-carson-investigates-_0_n_3646143.html.

[9] See, e.g., Major General Patton, testimony, *Briefing Transcript*, p. 156; Lieutenant General Richard C. Harding, Judge Advocate General, U.S. Department of the Air Force, testimony, *Briefing Transcript,* p. 166, *available at* http://www.eusccr.com/msa1.htm.

[10] *Id.* at 109. See also *Briefing transcript,* p. 13.

[11] Report, pp. 33 – 35, *available at* http://www.eusccr.com/msa1.htm.

[12] *Id.,* p. 35, fn. 31.

Some allege that, since the cited reports, GOVERNMENT ACCOUNTABILITY OFFICE, DEFENSE HEALTH CARE: ADDITIONAL EFFORTS NEEDED TO ENSURE COMPLIANCE WITH PERSONALITY DISORDER SEPARATION REQUIREMENTS, GAO-09-31 (Oct. 31, 2008) and GOVERNMENT ACCOUNTABILITY OFFICE, DEFENSE HEALTH CARE STATUS OF EFFORTS TO ADDRESS LACK OF COMPLIANCE WITH PERSONALITY DISORDER SEPARATION REQUIREMENTS, GAO-10-1013T (Sep 15, 2010) ,were issued, the military may have shifted from incorrectly diagnosing MST victims with personality disorders to incorrectly diagnosing adjustment disorders in order to achieve the same type of discharges without veterans benefits. See, e.g., Natelson Statement p. 4.

(cont'd)

victim-veterans' successful reintegration into civilian society by increasing the difficulty of securing jobs, maximizing income, acquiring housing, and solidifying family arrangements such as court-ordered custody of children.[13]

The VA estimates that approximately 67,000 Americans who have served in the U.S. military were homeless in 2011.[14] We cannot help but wonder how many of these veterans began their downward spiral when sexual assault and inaccurate mental health diagnoses made re-entry into civilian life more difficult.[15] At the very least, a discharge based upon mental health "profiling" of MST victims is a grave affront.

The plight of MST victim-veterans who were discharged under these circumstances is further complicated by the Services' current discharge upgrade request process. That system is difficult for veterans without financial means to access, and very few prevail.[16] Clearly, a more accessible and successful process could help many MST victim-veterans mitigate some of the damage done to them.

Sexual assault in the military harms not only victims, but also DoD and the Armed Forces as a whole. The Report notes that "[m]ilitary sexual assault also impairs military readiness and disrupts unit cohesion."[17] Many Service members who are sexually assaulted are victimized at their military installations. Victims may now request expedited transfers,[18] although both informal and institutional re-victimization still threaten to impair victims' job performance and compromise mission readiness. Service members who have not been sexually assaulted fear

---

(cont'd from previous page)

If indeed the military has shifted any common misdiagnosis of MST victims from personality disorder to adjustment disorder, such a shift may well be difficult to detect. This is because, as defined, a personality disorder exists before enlistment whereas an adjustment disorder can arise in response to events which take place after enlistment. See Report pp. 33 – 36.

[13] See, e.g., Nancy J. Parrish, President, Protect Our Defenders, "Before the U.S. Commission on Civil Rights," January 11 2013, p. 10.

[14] See, e.g., U.S. Department of Housing and Urban Development, Office of Community Planning and Development, "The 2011 Point-in-Time Estimates of Homelessness: Supplement to the Annual Homeless Assessment Report," December 2011, p. 1, available at https://www.onecpd.info/resources/documents/PIT-HIC_SupplementalAHARReport.pdf.

[15] Panelist Natelson stated that "There are enormously elevated rates of homelessness among woman veterans, that far outstrip comparable rates among non-veteran women and male veterans, and a very high percentage of homeless women veterans … have histories of sexual assault in the military." Rachel Natelson, Legal Director, Service Women's Action Network, testimony, *Briefing Transcript*, p. 60, l. 4, *available at* http://www.eusccr.com/msa1.htm.

[16] Report, pp. 41 – 42.

[17] *Id.*, p. 3.

[18] *Id.*, pp. 19 – 20.

being victimized. Others expend time and energy assisting those who have been assaulted. These distractions disrupt unit cohesion and diminish focus on mission readiness.

For these reasons and for numerous others with which our record is replete, the Democratic Caucus questions the overall effectiveness of the U.S. military's efforts to date. Therefore, we add our voices to the call for meaningful, comprehensive, and sustainable reform to address these long-standing problems.

DoD should implement the below proposed recommendations over which it currently has jurisdiction. To the extent that DoD does not act voluntarily or does not have jurisdiction, Congress and the President should enact legislation consistent with our proposed recommendations.

II.   Democratic Caucus Proposed Findings

Our inquiry revealed the following specific concerns about the manner in which the U.S. military addresses issues related to sexual assault within its ranks:

A.   UCMJ Definitions of Sexual Assault Crimes

The generalized manner in which the Uniform Code of Military Justice ("UCMJ") defines "sexual assault" fails to draw fine distinctions between different forms of impermissible sexual contact. DoD and the UCMJ do not break down sexual assault crimes into categories which define the specific elements of each offense as clearly as does civilian criminal law.[19] This makes it impossible to determine exactly what offenses occur, how often they occur, and the range of dispositions for each of the offenses. The net effect is that DoD cannot know whether its efforts to realize its "zero tolerance" goal regarding sexual assault is fair and effective for victims and accused alike.

B.   Data Collection and Research:

DoD does not maintain sufficient information about Service members who report sexual assault to facilitate determination of whether anecdotal accounts of retaliation represent the exception or the norm.

DoD has not comprehensively evaluated each Branch's sexual assault prevention and response ("SAPR") training programs and initiatives, nor has it required that Branches adopt those practices that have been deemed most effective.

---

[19] UCMJ Arts. 120; 10 U.S.C §§ 920, 925 (2013). These statutes and others relevant to sexual assault in the military are listed in Appendix A to this report and *available at* http://www.euscor.com/msa1.htm. *See also* DoD Directive 6495.01, Sexual Assault Prevention and Response Program 17 (Jan. 23, 2012, Incorporating Change 1, Apr. 30, 2013), *available at* http://www.dtic.mi/whs/directives/corres/pdf/649501p.pdf.

C.   Resource Allocation & Military Justice:

The Services do not consistently implement the mandate of the National Defense Authorization Act for Fiscal Year 2012 which requires that sexual assault victims must be provided with legal counsel.[20]

D.   Confidentiality:

Neither Service members' dependents nor civilian DoD personnel have the option of making restricted reports of sexual assault, even though they rely on the military for health care and psychological care.

Under military policy, MST victims lose the ability to make restricted reports if they disclose their assaults to anyone other than a SAPR victim advocate, a sexual assault response coordinator, or a health care provider.[21]

Under current military policy, the allegations made in restricted reports do not trigger investigations.[22]

E.   Commander Discretion:

Investigation and disposition decisions of sexual assault cases across the Service branches have been inconsistent due to wide commander discretion. Such discretion produces varying results for similar charges across commands.[23]

---

[20] Public Law 112-81, Section 581.

[21] Natelson testimony, *Briefing Transcript*, p. 15, *available at* http://www.eusccr.com/msa1.htm.

[22] DoD Directive 6495.01, Sexual Assault Prevention and Response Program (SAPR) 17 (Jan. 23, 2012, Incorporating Change 1, Apr. 30, 2013); Lt. Commander Ann M. Vallandingham JAGC, USN, *Department of Defense's Sexual Assault Policy: Recommendations for a More Comprehensive and Uniform Policy*, 54 NAVAL L. REV. 205, 228-232 (2007) (arguing that the restricted reporting option should be available to civilian DoD employees and military dependents); Sexual assault victims who seek medical care or sexual assault forensic exams in the state of California, however, cannot make a restricted report because state law mandates reporting by healthcare providers. *See* Cal.Penal Code § 11160. Victims in Arizona may also be subject to California's reporting law if the nearest military treatment facility is in California. DEPARTMENT OF DEFENSE, DEPARTMENT OF DEFENSE FISCAL YEAR 2011 ANNUAL REPORT ON SEXUAL ASSAULT IN THE MILITARY 70 (2012).

[23] Lindsy Nicole Alleman, *Who Is In Charge, and Who Should Be? The Disciplinary Role of the Commander in Military Justice Systems*, 16 DUKE J. OF COMP. & INT'L L. 169, 170 (2006); MCM R. 303, 315(d), 407(a), 502(a)(1), 703(d), 704(c), 705, 1107(d)(1), 1107(d)(2), at II-19, II-41, II-42, II-63, II-66, II-68 , II-153, III-14, III-15. The commander does not, however, have the power to change an acquittal to a conviction or to increase a sentence. MCM R. 1107(d)(2), at II-153; *See* DEPARTMENT OF DEFENSE, DEPARTMENT OF DEFENSE FISCAL YEAR 2011 ANNUAL REPORT ON SEXUAL ASSAULT IN THE MILITARY 47 (2012), *available at* http://www.sapr.mil/media/pdf/reports/Department_of_Defense_Fiscal_Year_2011_Annual_Report_on_Sexual_A ssault_in_the_Military.pdf. The severity of nonjudicial punishment that a commander may impose is based on the rank of an accused and the rank of a commander. MCM, at V-4-5; JUDGE ADVOCATE GENERAL INSTRUCTION

(cont'd)

Commanders are not required to communicate the final disposition of sexual assault allegations to Service members in their units.

The Manual for Courts-Martial currently requires that the "character and military service" of Armed Forces members who are accused of sexual assault must be considered in the disposition of those allegations.[24]

F.   Conflict of Interest:

Commanders face an inherent conflict of interest because they must investigate reports of sexual assault within their units. When commanders determine that allegations merit further action, their superiors may believe that the occurrence of sexual assault within the unit indicates that the commander is ineffective in maintaining unit cohesion and mission readiness. Commanders may allow this tension to influence decisions about investigations of potential charges under Article 15, charging of Courts-martial offenses, and whether to amend dispositions.[25]

G.   Consistency:[26]

DoD has issued no uniform standard of proof to all the Branches regarding the imposition of nonjudicial punishment in sexual assault cases.

The Branches are not consistent in their policies and practices for screening recruits for pre-military histories of civil liability involving sexual assault offenses and sexual harassment or for pre-military histories of convictions for domestic violence and sexual offenses.

(cont'd from previous page)

5800.7F, Section 0111. "Conditions that subject soldiers to discharge" include a pattern of minor disciplinary infractions as well as commission of a serious military or civil offense. *See, e.g.,* ARMY REGULATION 635-200, ACTIVE DUTY ENLISTED SEPARATIONS 102 (June 6, 2005).

[24] Manual for Courts-Martial, R. 306(b), at II-25-II-26 (Joint Service Committee on Military Justice 2012), *available at* http://www.loc.gov/rr/frd/Military_Law/pdf/MCM-2012.pdf (emphasis added). Military leadership informed the Senate Armed Services Committee that they support removing "military service" as a consideration in the disposition of a sexual offense. *Hearing of the Senate Armed Services Committee*, June 4, 2013, at time marker 1:51-1:54, http://www.senate.gov/isvp/?type=live&comm=armed&filename=armed060413; *See* Manual for Courts-Martial, Appendix 12, at A12-1-A12-7 (Joint Service Committee on Military Justice 2012), *available at* http://www.loc.gov/rr/frd/Military_Law/pdf/MCM-2012.pdf. All sexual assault offenses have a maximum punishment of a dishonorable discharge or bad conduct discharge and confinement terms ranging from 1 year from wrongful sexual contact to life for rape and forcible sodomy.

[25] See, e.g., Parrish testimony, *Briefing Transcript*, p. 23, *available at* http://www.eusccr.com/msa1.htm.

[26] 10 U.S.C. §113. These statutes and others relevant to sexual assault in the military are listed in Appendix A to this report *available at* http://www.eusccr.com/msa1.htm.

The Services lack uniformity in the implementation of standardized criterion for selection of sexual assault response coordinators and victim advocates, contrary to DoD Instruction 6495.02, paragraph E3.2.6.1.

Compounding the fact that the UCMJ does not define sexual assault offenses with sufficient specificity (as set forth above), the Manual for Courts-Martial does not provide specific minimum and maximum sentencing guidelines for clearly-defined sexual assault offenses.

H.   Discharges and Benefits:

Victims of military sexual assault have been administratively discharged under Other Than Honorable Conditions, or otherwise, with adjustment disorder or personality disorder diagnoses despite having service-related diagnoses of Post-Traumatic Stress Disorder ("PTSD") rooted in the military sexual traumas that they have suffered.

Access to veterans' health benefits for treatment of psychological trauma resulting from sexual assault is often denied to veterans who were sexually assaulted during their military service and who were improperly administratively discharged on the basis of personality disorder or adjustment disorder diagnoses related to the sexual assault.[27]

I.   Accountability:

Under UCMJ Article 92, "dereliction of duty" is the primary statutory mechanism for holding a commander accountable for his or her command failings.[28]

The standard of "dereliction of duty" under UCMJ Article 92 has not been an adequate mechanism to hold commanders accountable for their command failings with respect to preventing and responding to sexual assault.

The doctrine of command responsibility imposes a higher standard of duty upon commanders. This doctrine is widely utilized in international law, international treaties, and other countries'

---

[27] Government Accountability Office, Military Personnel: DoD Has Taken Steps to Meet the Health Needs of Deployed Servicewomen, but Actions Are Needed to Enhance Care for Sexual Assault Victims 17 (2013), *available at* http://www.gao.gov/assets/660/651624.pdf; *see also:* One veteran explained that the psychiatrists "basically throw you sleeping pills [and] anti-depressants, and send you back to continue what you were doing." Irina Sadovich Gillett, et al., Female Veterans and Military Sexual Trauma, 3 J. DIVERSE SOCIAL WORK 50 (Spring 2012). Some male victims only had the option for treatment at a women's health clinic. Report of the Defense Task Force on Sexual Assault (2009) at 73; *see also* DEPARTMENT OF VETERANS AFFAIRS, MILITARY SEXUAL TRAUMA/SEXUAL TRAUMA RESIDENTIAL TREATMENT RESOURCES, http://www.ncdsv.org/images/VAMHS_MST-SexualTraumaResidentialTreatmentResources_10-2010.pdf (noting that there is only one all-male facility for military sexual assault victims).

[28] See, e.g. Professor Elizabeth Hillman, University of California, Hastings, School of Law, testimony, *Briefing Transcript*, pp. 97-100, available at http://www.eusccr.com/msa1.htm.

military structures. The doctrine of command responsibility requires commanders to take all possible actions to prevent and punish violations of military law.[29]

The U.S. Army is the only branch of the Services that has implemented a policy that requires the performance evaluation process to evaluate commanders on achieving the goals of the Equal Opportunity and Equal Employment Opportunity programs.[30]

III.   Democratic Caucus Proposed Recommendations

In light of the high duty of care owed to all Service members, the persistence of high rates of sexual assault, and the decades during which DoD and the Services have tried to solve this problem, we offer the following recommendations:

A.   Investigative and prosecutorial authority and discretion should be removed from the military and vested in an independent authority.

Congress should pass, and the President should sign, legislation creating an authority outside of the military in which is vested the power to investigate, prosecute, try, and impose sentence upon conviction in all sexual assault cases which arise within the military's ranks.

In generating specific proposals, Congress should examine modified systems of military justice which other countries such as Canada, Great Britain, Australia have adopted.[31] Congress should create its own options for debate and possible implementation.

Congress and the President should require this body to keep statistical data concerning each offense defined in the UCMJ as sexual harassment, indecent exposure, voyeurism, sexual assault, rape, and related offenses.

Congress and the President should require this body to report regularly and in detail upon its operations to Congress, the Secretary of Defense, and the President.

B.   In the alternative, sexual assault investigations and prosecutions within each Service branch should be centralized.

In the event that the military retains jurisdiction to investigate and prosecute sexual assault allegations within its ranks, Congress should pass, and the President should sign, legislation establishing within each branch of the military a centralized legal body. Each of these bodies would have authority to investigate all reported sexual assault offenses within its Branch, to file

---

[29] See, e.g. Professor Victor Hansen, testimony, *Id.,* p. 99, *available at* http://www.euscccr.com/msa1.htm.

[30] Army Regulation 600-20, Army Command Policy [March 18, 2008], para. 6-11a.

[31] See, e.g., Natelson testimony, *Briefing Transcript,* pp. 46-47.

charges, and to pursue prosecutions of those allegations in cases where the potential punishment of a perpetrator is not less than imprisonment of six months. In cases where the maximum punishment for upon conviction is imprisonment of less than six months, these bodies shall return the case to command for Article 15 proceedings.

C. **A high-level Department of Defense Sexual Assault Prevention Board should be established to investigate, report, and recommend additional practices that address the problems of sexual assault in the military.**

If the military is to retain jurisdiction to investigate and prosecute sexual assault allegations within its ranks, then either Congress and the President should create through legislation, or the Department of Defense should promptly create, a Sexual Assault Prevention Board which is similar in form and function to DoD's 2012 - 2013 Defense Legal Policy Board Subcommittee on Military Justice in Combat Zones.[32] The Board shall be comprised of, at a minimum, equal numbers of high-level military officials, JAG and civilian lawyers, and mental health experts. The Board shall investigate all aspects of the manner in which the military handles sexual assault within its ranks. Within one year of its creation, the Board shall report its findings and recommendations to the President, Congress, and the Secretary of Defense regarding ways in which the military will:

1) diminish the occurrence of military sexual assault;

2) increase reporting rates of assaults that do occur;

3) increase victims' confidentiality safeguards;

4) increase victims' protections against all forms of retaliation;

5) increase victims' advocacy resources;

6) improve training of investigators and prosecutors; and

7) improve the accuseds' access to experts and specially trained investigators and military defense lawyers with expertise in sexual assault cases.

---

[32] On July 30, 2012, then-Secretary of Defense Leon Panetta created the Defense Legal Policy Board Subcommittee on Military Justice in Combat and appointed a panel of experts to serve on it. Secretary Panetta charged the new Subcommittee with "review[ing] and assess[ing] … military justice in cases of U.S. Service members alleged to have caused the death, injury, or abuse of non-combatants in Iraq or Afghanistan…." Secretary of Defense Memorandum, Military Justice in Combat Zones (July 30, 2012), *available at* http://www.caaflog.com/wpcontent/uploads/Military_Justice_in_Combat_Zones.pdf.). The Subcommittee issued its comprehensive Final Report on May 30, 2013. (DEFENSE LEGAL POLICY BOARD, REPORT OF THE SUBCOMMITTEE ON MILITARY JUSTICE IN COMBAT ZONES, Military Justice in Cases of U.S. Service Members Alleged to Have Caused the Death, Injury, or Abuse of Non-Combatants in Iraq or Afghanistan (May 30, 2013), *available at* http://www.caaflog.com/wp-content/uploads/20130531-Subcommittee-Report-REPORT-OF-THE-SUBCOMMITTEE-ON-MILITARY-JUSTICE-IN-COMBAT-ZONES-31-May-13-2.pdf).

D. A high-level Department of Defense Restorative Justice Discharge Review Board should be created to investigate, review, and resolve claims of veteran-victims of Military Sexual Trauma who were discharged with inaccurate psychological diagnoses which impede access to veterans' benefits and stigmatize them in civilian life.

DoD should create a Restorative Justice Discharge Review Board. The purpose of this Board should be to address the profiling of MST victim-veterans and resolve past injustices which limit their access to VA benefits. This Board shall create and implement a comprehensive system to review promptly discharge upgrade requests and records correction requests from MST victim-veterans whose discharges are of less-than-Honorable status. This Board should be comprised of independent mental health experts and high-ranking DoD and Armed Forces officials. If DoD does not create such a Board, then Congress and the President should enact legislation which does so.

This Board shall have the authority to evaluate claims and discharges of any age. Its process should make advance funding available to claimants, at a minimum, for legal services, expert witness services, and travel and lodging expenses involved in the filing, processing, and hearing of discharge upgrade and records correction claims. Veterans whose claims for discharge upgrade or records correction succeed shall not be required to refund monies expended for their intended purposes. The new discharge upgrade and records correction claim review process should allow the claimant to prevail upon a showing of a preponderance of the evidence. This Board shall be required to report regularly and in detail to Congress, the Secretary of Defense, and the President.

E. Additional Recommendations for Improvement to The Military's Current Systems for Resolution of Issues Related To Sexual Assault Within Its Ranks

1. Commander Discretion:

The Department of Defense (DoD) and Armed Forces should strip commanders of discretion in the investigation and disposition decisions of sexual assault cases in the military. The DoD and Armed Forces should instead work to establish uniform guidelines that will set forth requirements for investigations and evidence gathering and set minimum and maximum sentencing guidelines which do not allow for commander discretion. This should be done by vesting control of investigations, trials and sentencing in a neutral third party.[33]

---

[33] MANUAL FOR COURTS-MARTIAL, R. 306(a), at II-25 (Joint Service Committee on Military Justice 2012), *available at* http://www.loc.gov/rr/frd/Military_Law/pdf/MCM-2012.pdf; ("Each commander has discretion to

(cont'd)

In the alternative, in circumstances where the accused's immediate supervisor has a grade of O-6 or higher and has at least Special court-martial convening authority, the disposition authority of sexual assault allegations should be withheld from the supervisor and vested in the commanding General/Admiral of the duty station where the offenses occurred. Should the General/Admiral amend the disposition of a sentence imposed by a Courts Martial, she/he shall send a letter of specific explanation to the Chairman of the Joint Chiefs of Staff, the Secretary of Defense, and the President.[34]

DoD should amend the Manual for Courts-Martial to indicate that a Service member's character and military service can be considered to either increase toward the maximum or reduce toward the minimum the sentence of the convicted person, but that those factors may not lower a sentence below a minimum required guideline. These factors also should be made unavailable to the commanding General of the duty station as justification for changing disposition of courts martial.

DoD should change the UCMJ to raise commanders' standard of duty from the mere "dereliction of duty" standard embodied in Article 92 to reflect the common international standard of "command responsibility."

Within the requirements of laws applicable to Service members' privacy rights, DoD should establish a policy that Commanders must clearly and timely communicate the final disposition and resolution of sexual assault allegations to Service members in their command.

(cont'd from previous page)

dispose of offenses by members of that command.") (Memorandum from the Secretary of Defense (Apr. 20, 2012), *available at* http://www.dod.gov/dodgc/images/withhold_authority.pdf., *effective by*, June 28, 2012); *See also* MCM R. 306(b), at II-25; *See also* MANUAL FOR COURTS-MARTIAL, R. 306(b), at II-25-II-26 (Joint Service Committee on Military Justice 2012), *available at* http://www.loc.gov/rr/frd/Military_Law/pdf/MCM-2012.pdf (emphasis added; *See also* REPORT OF THE DEFENSE TASK FORCE ON SEXUAL ASSAULT IN THE MILITARY SERVICES 34 (2009), *available at* http://www.ncdsv.org/images/SAPR_DTFSAMS_Report_Dec_2009.pdf ("[S]ome military personnel indicated that predators may believe they will not be held accountable for their misconduct during deployment because commanders' focus on the mission overshadows other concerns."); *See also* Hillman testimony, *Briefing transcript* at 88.

[34] Secretary of Defense Memorandum, "Withholding Initial Disposition Authority Under the Uniform Code of Military Justice in Certain Sexual Assault Cases" (April 20, 2012), *available at* http://www.dod.gov/dodgc/images/withhold_authority.pdf. The Marine Corps expanded this withholding of disposition authority to include sexual contact offenses. MARINE ADMINISTRATIVE MESSAGE (MARADMINS) 372/12, WITHHOLD OF INITIAL DISPOSITION AUTHORITY IN CERTAIN SEXUAL ASSAULT CASES (July 13, 2012), *available at* http://www.marines.mil/News/Messages/MessagesDisplay/tabid/13286/Article/110494/withhold-of-initial-disposition-authority-in-certain-sexual-assault-cases.aspx.

2.   Confidentiality:

Reports of sexual assault in the military, whether made as restricted or unrestricted, should trigger official investigations. Any investigations made of allegations raised as restricted reports should be conducted within parameters necessary to protect victim confidentiality.[35]

Service members' dependents, civilian DoD personnel, and anyone else who relies on the military for health care and psychological care should have the option of making a restricted report of sexual assault.

DoD policy should revise its policy to allow victims of military sexual assault to seek support from a close friend, family member, therapist, member of the clergy, and/or other confidante without losing the ability to make restricted sexual assault reports.

3.   Discharges, Discharge Reviews, and Benefits:

The Veterans Benefits Administration should implement expedited discharge upgrade and correction of record request review processes for MST victim-veterans who were discharged without access to disability benefits, psychological care, and/or medical care for conditions related to the sexual trauma. Veterans who apply for discharge upgrades or records corrections should have immediate access to all appropriate care through the Veterans Administration health services from the time of application until the resolution of their claims, including appeals.

Congress and the President should ensure that veterans who were sexually assaulted during their military service and were subsequently administratively discharged have full access to veterans' health benefits for treatment of psychological trauma resulting from the sexual assault, regardless of the characterization of their discharge.

Congress and the President should ensure the ongoing inclusion of independent mental health experts on Discharge Review Boards.[36]

---

[35] Defense Manpower Data Center (DMDC), 2010 Workplace and Gender Relations Survey of Active Duty Members: Overview Report on Sexual Assault 43 (2011) [hereinafter *2010 DoD Gender Relations Survey*], *available at* http://servicewomen.org/SAPROpercent20Reports/DMDC_2010_WGRA_Overview_Report_of_Sexual_Assault.pdf. In DoD's 2012 anonymous survey, 51 percent of women stated they did not report their sexual assault for fear their information would not remain confidential; the relatively small number of male Service members who participated in the 2012 survey may have contributed to a lack of statistically significant response numbers for this question on the survey questionnaire. *See DoD 2012 Gender Relations Survey* at 106-7; *See also DoD FY12 Annual Report on Sexual Assault* at 18; *See also* DOD DIRECTIVE 6495.01, SEXUAL ASSAULT PREVENTION AND RESPONSE (SAPR) PROGRAM 11, 14 (Jan. 23, 2012, Incorporating Change 1, Apr. 30, 2013), *available at* http://www.dtic.mil/whs/directives/corres/pdf/649501p.pdf.

4.   Consistency:

Congress should require DoD to have a consistent policy across all Service branches requiring expanded screening of recruits' history for sexual assault and domestic violence. DoD should require legal review of, and consider disqualification of, recruits who have been convicted in civilian criminal court of, or held liable in civil tort actions for, sexual offenses.[37]

DoD should establish standardized criteria for the selection of sexual assault response coordinators and victim advocates based on input from existing sexual assault response coordinators from each of the Services and other identified stakeholders.

Congress should appoint a civilian task force to audit military sexual assault cases to determine whether the dispositions were appropriate and whether there is consistency both within and among Service branches in the dispositions and sentencing of such cases.

The Manual for Courts-Martial should provide more specific guidelines for the disposition of sexual offenses to ensure more consistency across installations and across Services.

The Manual for Courts-Martial should provide sentencing guidelines with mandatory minimum sentences for Service members convicted of sexual offenses.

5.   Accountability:

Congress should incorporate heightened command responsibility into the UCMJ to further ensure that commanders to reduce the incidence of, and pursue appropriate investigation and disposition of reports of, sexual assault. Congress should also ensure that the Department of Defense provides for more severe penalties than currently in place for commanders who fail to discharge all duties with regard to processing of sexual assault reports.

DoD should strengthen the Army's policy of encouraging that the performance evaluation process should appraise commanders' achievement of the goals of the Equal Opportunity and Equal Employment Opportunity programs to require such evaluation, and it should make this tool mandatory for all other Service branches.

(cont'd from previous page)

[36] Report at p. 42 *available at* http://www.eusccr.com/msa1.htm (See discussion of Servicemember Mental Health Review Act, S. 628, 113th Congress (2013-2014) and H.R. 975, 113th Congress (2013-2015)).

[37] S. 548, Military Sexual Assault Prevention Act of 2013, 113th Congress (2013-2015) (seeks to prohibit enlistment or commission of those convicted of sexual assault crimes in civilian criminal courts, *available at* http://bit.ly/16UftTS).

DoD should regulate the possession of pornography on military property through consistent compliance with the Military Honor and Decency Act of 1996.[38]

In cases where sexual assault allegations against a Service member are substantiated and that Service member is not discharged, his or her personnel records should include all prior sexual assault incident reports, especially where incidents were fully investigated and the Service member was found liable. Commanders of such Service members' future posts should be required to review this personnel history promptly upon the member's transfer.[39] This is particularly important when an accused Service member is transferred prior to resolution of a pending case. At a minimum, DoD and the Armed Forces should keep records for evaluative purposes and to take into consideration when the service members are up for promotion or for benefits evaluations after disengaging from military service.[40]

6. Resource Allocation & Military Justice:

The military criminal justice system should ensure that defendants accused of sexual assault have all appropriate resources to defend themselves, including access to investigators, experts, and attorneys with expertise in defending the accused sexual assault cases.

DoD and the Armed Forces should move away from isolating sexual assault victims. DoD and the Armed Forces should establish a uniform plan of action to accommodate victims' ongoing needs for support from military personnel, healthcare professionals and family and friends. This

---

[38] Kristin Davis, *Welsh Battles Culture of Disrespect for Women*, AIR FORCE TIMES, Dec. 10, 2012. A January 2013 inspection found 33,216 items offensive or inappropriate items in Air Force installations, including items specific to military history such as patches, coins, log books, and song books. U.S. Air Force, *Air Force Releases Results of Health and Welfare Inspection*, Jan. 18, 1013, http://www.af.mil/news/story.asp?id=123333057; The Navy explained that it cannot determine how many of its service members were administratively discharged due to a sexual assault because it uses the same Navy Separation Code (SPD Code) for all sexual misconduct, including non-contact offenses, such as viewing pornography. Chief of Naval Operations' Response to the U.S. Commission on Civil Rights' Interrogatory No. 120a.

[39] See S. 548, Military Sexual Assault Prevention Act of 2013, 113th Congress (2013-2015).

[40] MCM R. 921(c)(B), at II-119; *See also* MCM R. 1001, at II-122; MCM R. 1002, at II-125. If the accused pleads guilty to some or all charges and the military judge accepts the guilty plea, the accused decides whether to be sentenced by a military judge or by the court-martial members. MCM R. 406, at II-40; *See* MCM R. 1007(b)(1), at II-136 ("The action to be taken on the findings and sentence is within the sole discretion of the convening authority . . . [and] is a matter of command prerogative."); *See, e.g.,* MCM R. 1107(d)(1), at II-153; S*ee also* MCM R. 1101(c), at II-138. Commanders have access to judge advocates who advise them regarding the final disposition, including the sentence, for a criminal offense; See, e.g. Dr. Nate Galbreath, Highly Qualified Expert, Department of Defense's Sexual Assault Prevention and Response Office, testimony, Briefing transcript, pp. 215, lines 9-24 and page 216, lines 1-24.

includes timely transfers, protective orders and, at the very least, a re-assignment so that the victim is not subjected to working with or reporting to the alleged attacker.[41]

Victim advocates, Sexual Assault Response Coordinators, medical personnel, and all other personnel authorized to receive restricted sexual assault reports should be required to inform Service members who have made a sexual assault report, whether restricted or unrestricted, of the right to legal counsel and the right to object to administrative discharge by a staff judge advocate upon being recommended for an administrative discharge.

The military should consider administratively discharging all Service members on active duty who are convicted of sexual offenses and whom it is not punitively discharging.[42]

7.   Data Collection and Research:

DoD should maintain data on Service members who make an unrestricted report of sexual assault for at least two years after the final disposition of the allegations. This would allow the Services to track both any adverse actions taken against the victims, including the initiation of involuntary administrative discharges and other potentially retaliatory actions, and positive professional developments.

---

[41] DoD Directive Type Memorandum 11-063, Subject: Directive-Type Memorandum Expedited Transfer of Military, Service Members Who File Unrestricted Reports of Sexual Assault (Dec. 16, 2011) (Note: Directive-Type Memorandum 11-063 was incorporated into reissued DoDI 6495.02 published on March 28, 2013). The need for an expedited transfer policy was illustrated by the tragic situation of Marine Corps Lance Corporal Maria Lauterbach. Although a verbal protective order was imposed on the Marine whom Lauterbach reported for raping her, Lauterbach was physically attacked, her car was vandalized after she reported, and the Marine she accused of rape ultimately murdered Lauterbach. *See* Inspector General, U.S. Department of Defense, Review of Matters Related to the Sexual Assault of Lance Corporal Maria Lauterbach, U.S. Marine Corps 2-3, 22 (Oct. 18, 2011), *available at* http://www.dodig.mil/Inspections/IPO/reports/LauterbachFR_(redacted).pdf. The need for expedited transfer was also demonstrated by Army Specialist Suzanne Swift who was court-martialed in 2006 for desertion, demoted, and incarcerated for a month for refusing to redeploy under the command of a sergeant whom she had reported for repeatedly raping her. *See* Donna St. George, *From Victim To Accused Army Deserter*, Wash. Post, Sept. 19, 2006, http://www.washingtonpost.com/wp-dyn/content/article/2006/09/18/AR2006091801506.html. Similarly, Marine Corps Corporal Sarah Albertson alleged that her Command forced her to interact repeatedly with her rapist for two years and eventually required her to report to him after his promotion. Cioca v. Rumsfeld, Case No. 1:11cv151 (LO/TCB) (E.D. Va.), Compl. filed Feb. 15, 2011, para. 61-66, *available at* http://www.protectourdefenders.com/appeal-in-cioca-v-rumsfeld/; *See also* One veteran explained that the psychiatrists "basically throw you sleeping pills [and] anti-depressants, and send you back to continue what you were doing." Irina Sadovich Gillett, et al., Female Veterans and Military Sexual Trauma, 3 J. DIVERSE SOCIAL WORK 50 (Spring 2012). Some male victims only had the option for treatment at a women's health clinic. Report of the Defense Task Force on Sexual Assault (2009) at 73; *see also* DEPARTMENT OF VETERANS AFFAIRS, MILITARY SEXUAL TRAUMA/SEXUAL TRAUMA RESIDENTIAL TREATMENT RESOURCES, http://www.ncdsv.org/images/VAMHS_MST-SexualTraumaResidentialTreatmentResources_10-2010.pdf (noting that there is only one all-male facility for military sexual assault victims).

[42] S. 548, Military Sexual Assault Prevention Act of 2013, 113th Congress (2013-2015).

DoD's Sexual Assault Prevention and Response Office (SAPRO) should comprehensively evaluate each Service branch's sexual assault training and response programs and initiatives, and when a particular program or initiative proves to be highly successful, DoD SAPRO should, at a minimum, promote it as a best practice.

DoD should maintain data on whether the accused in each unrestricted sexual assault report has been previously convicted of sexual assault.

IV. Conclusion

In the end, this is really about who we are as a nation. If we cannot, or will not protect our protectors, then we have failed to live up to the ideals upon which our freedom is founded. The military has had much time to remedy this travesty of military sexual assault, and has failed to do so adequately. The military hierarchy must either resolve this crisis immediately, or step aside and let others tend to the victims and prevent the future victimization of our men and women in uniform.

Sexual Assault in the Military

Statement of Vice Chair Abigail Thernstrom

Testimony we received and the military's own reports show the military's prosecution rate for sexual offenses compares favorably with that in the civilian sector.

Political pressure from Congress and advocacy groups has resulted in an increase of charges and prosecutions while doing little to reduce the problem. This has also raised valid concerns that due process for the accused has been compromised.

We know that significant numbers of military women *and* men have reported sexual assaults. But it is not clear that the military was doing a bad job prior to the current political hysteria. For example, sexual harassment training has been part of military culture for many years.

One thing is certain: There is a public relations angle that has been summed up by one military official as follows: "We want [the public and Congress] to see that due process exists. We want to see that victims are happy with the experience of the court-martial, if not the outcome."[43]

A former Army judge advocate put it even more starkly: "In the media and on Capital [sic] Hill, there's this myth that the military doesn't take sexual assault seriously. But the reality is they're charging more and more people with bogus cases just to show that they do take it seriously."[44]

As one panelist at our briefing aptly pointed out, when the military establishes a goal it tends to pursue that goal aggressively, at times with seeming disregard for unintended side effects. This has resulted in charges of undue command influence whereby commanders, military officials, politicians and even the Commander in Chief have made public statements to the effect "We *will* bring more prosecutions, and we *will* convict more offenders." This has resulted in dozens of appeals by accused perpetrators and the departure from the military bench by at least one judge who made inflammatory, prejudicial remarks about "scumbag" defendants.[45]

---

[43] Janet Mansfield, attorney with the Army's Office of the Judge Advocate General, as quoted in McClatchy newspapers, "Military's newly aggressive rape prosecution has pitfalls", Nov. 28, 2011. Available online at http://www.mcclatchydc.com/2011/11/28/131523/militarys-newly-aggressive-rape.html

[44] Michael Waddington, former Army judge advocate, as quoted in McClatchy newspapers, "Military's newly aggressive rape prosecution has pitfalls", Nov. 28, 2011. Available online at http://www.mcclatchydc.com/2011/11/28/131523/militarys-newly-aggressive-rape.html

[45] Michael Doyle, McLatchy Newspapers, "Crackdown on military sexual assault may have unintended consequences", May 9, 2013. Available online at http://www.mcclatchydc.com/2013/05/09/190855/crackdown-on-military-sex-assault.html#.UfmCW6zN6Im

The top down command structure, the loyalty at all costs mentality were bound to result in military judges and prosecutors taking a more aggressive stance, even to the possible detriment of due process. A number of military sexual assault cases are already being appealed based on undue command influence.

Full Integration of Women:

Will the problem of sexual assault against women be reduced once women are fully integrated into the military – whatever "full integration of women" means? We cannot assume it will.

In that context I think it is important to remember that men in the military report a large number of sexual assaults by other men. Obviously, the fuller integration of women would not solve that problem.

Racial Integration Parallel:

It has also been suggested that we use as a model the tremendous, positive effect that the civil rights movement had on the military's efforts to fully integrate racial minorities into its ranks. This is a compelling parallel that may have some utility in this debate, but the dynamics of the two movements -- racial integration and gender integration -- are quite different.

Gender Segregation as a Solution:

One question I explored during our briefing was whether gender segregated military units would be a possible solution.[46]

For most of its existence the military has been overwhelmingly male and therefore by definition has been gender segregated. Yet even under those conditions men reported sexual assaults by other men.

Available data indicate male-on-male sexual assaults are a significant part of the overall problem.

DoD's 2012 annual report on sexual assault in the military reveals that 12% of assault victims are men while 88% are women. The report also shows that over 90% of the "subjects" (perpetrators) are men and 2% are women.[47]

---

[46] Thernstrom at Transcript pp. 70 - 73

[47] "DoD Annual Report on Sexual Assault in the Military - FY 2012", Volume 1, exhibit 17 at page 81 and exhibit 20 at page 83. Available online at
http://www.sapr.mil/public/docs/reports/FY12_DoD_SAPRO_Annual_Report_on_Sexual_Assault-VOLUME_ONE.pdf

However, the Navy estimated that there were 10,700 male victims of sexual assault and 8,300 female victims. Expressed as percentages, the Navy's data suggest that for the reporting period 55% of sexual assault victims were men and 45% were women.[48]

Prosecutorial Discretion:

There are advocates of aggressive action who believe that the civilian and the military justice systems both under-prosecute sex crimes. These critics decry the plea bargains that are a necessary feature of our criminal justice system.[49] A seasoned prosecutor won't waste the taxpayers' money -- and the victim's emotional well-being in contentious testimony and cross examination in which the most intimate details of his or her life are on public display -- on a case that cannot be proven "beyond a reasonable doubt", the highest level of proof. A good prosecutor may agree to bring fewer charges, or allow the defendant to plead to a lesser charge for which the facts will more likely result in a guilty verdict thus achieving a measure of justice that otherwise would not have occurred.

It is true, as our panelist pointed out, that a victim who is unhappy with the results of the criminal prosecution might have the option of filing a civil lawsuit of their own. But in that case the expense of the trial -- and any required additional investigation, expert witnesses, etc. -- will rest on the victim's shoulders. Unless backed by a well-funded advocacy group many plaintiffs may not be able to afford a civil remedy.

Conclusion:

Various proposals to improve prosecution of sexual assaults in the military include such features as removing the reporting, investigation, prosecution, and adjudication of sexual assaults outside the chain of command and into an independent office with "professional military and civilian oversight".[50]

The commander of a military unit necessarily has authority over every aspect of his unit and its members. This includes decisions regarding sexual assault cases. This regime ensures the discipline, obedience and cohesion of unit personnel. It ensures a mission-ready unit whether that mission is combat or logistics and support. Removing the commander's discretion over

---

[48] Testimony of Brian K. Lewis, former Petty Officer Third Class, U.S. Navy, testifying before the U.S. Senate Armed Services Subcommittee on Personnel, March 2013. Mr. Lewis was citing the Navy Personnel Command's 2012 Sexual Assault Awareness Month Training Guide. Testimony available online at: http://www.armed-services.senate.gov/statemnt/2013/03 March/Lewis 03-13-13.pdf

[49] Natelson testimony at transcript page 67.

[50] See, for example, the testimony of Brian K. Lewis, former Petty Officer Third Class, U.S. Navy, before the U.S. Senate Armed Services Subcommittee on Personnel, March 2013. Testimony available online at: http://www.armed-services.senate.gov/statemnt/2013/03 March/Lewis 03-13-13.pdf.

sexual assault cases would represent a loss, however small, of the commander's authority and her ability to command her personnel.

Certainly improvements can be made, but they should be made in the sober light of day, incrementally and scientifically, without rushing to create a new, ill-considered authority or bureaucracy that will necessarily impede the commander's ability to command his troops.

Statement of Commissioner Todd Gaziano,
Joined by Vice Chair Thernstrom and Commissioner Kirsanow

There are several well-meaning but ill-considered proposals from academics, activists, and other commentators to remove responsibility over common-law crimes, or at least sexual-assault offenses, from the chain of command in the military justice system. To these theorists and activists, it's intellectually intriguing to float such proposals, even if they were not paid to come up with novel ideas like that. And for some it's even more exciting to be involved in sweeping social engineering projects, such as changing military culture. Thus, we should not doubt the sincerity of their convictions regarding such proposals. The actual effects are another matter.

Some of the same incentives apply to Members of Congress when they take up such proposals. They are rewarded with press attention for advancing novel initiatives, and most politicians chose their career with the aim of effecting fundamental change. They do not, in general, lack confidence regarding their own expertise, even if they sometimes should. Once they take a public position on an issue, there is little reason for them to critically examine the evidence opposing that position, absent strong political pressure to do so.

Thus, this Commission that was created to "sift out the truth from the fancies"[51] has an important role to inform Congress (and prevent a herd mentality from forming) when the conventional wisdom on a particular civil rights issue seems to be wildly out of sync with the objective facts. The supposed military sexual assault "crisis" and proposals to "fix" it are prime examples.

The best evidence available indicates there is no such crisis. Though any sexual assault is an individual tragedy, none of the studies available to the Commission suggests that: (1) the level of such assaults in the military is high relative to comparable civilian populations, (2) the rate of such assaults is increasing, (3) the military is deficient in responding to them (especially compared to civilian authorities), or (4) there is any lack of attention or commitment to the issue.

On this last point, all the military services have succeeded in increasing the reporting of sexual assaults in recent years and exerted additional efforts to prosecute such crimes. Some of those efforts are admirable, including initiatives by the service JAG Corps to create career tracks for prosecutors and defense counsel and other steps to increase the professionalism and effectiveness of such military lawyers. Yet other efforts to respond to political pressure and

---

[51] Statement of then Senate Majority Leader Lyndon Johnson on the bill that created the U.S. Commission on Civil Rights. 103 CONG. RECORD 13,897 (1957).

meet artificial targets may be undermining the justice process: the Commission received persuasive testimony and data that the incidence of unfounded sexual assault reports has increased and the civil liberties of the accused are being undermined by commanders responding to political pressure to "do more" to respond to the "crisis." The damage to military morale of such a trend, and its negative effect on the integration of women into the military ranks, should give everyone pause.

The most important point, though, is that the radical change in the military justice system pending in Congress won't fix anything. The damage that could be done to command authority far outweighs any benefit that might accrue, and there is no evidence such proposals would benefit sexual-assault victims anyway.

When Systematic Change is Warranted: Edmund Burke v. Oliver Wendell Holmes

The United States military justice system has evolved over centuries to fit the special needs of the military services and the nation that depends on them. That system of justice is based in part on a form of command authority that is foreign to civilian life, but that we civilians ought to carefully study before we change it in ways that would be hard to reverse and might do lasting damage.

The military justice system of the new American nation itself was almost completely borrowed from Britain, so the basic aspects of that system, including the close congruence with the military command structure, go back many centuries more—and were also common in other European military justice systems.

Yet all justice systems evolve. Only the most hidebound would argue that the modern military justice system of the Uniform Code of Military Justice (UCMJ) is not a humane improvement, fitting modern circumstances, over the Eighteenth Century British Articles of War. The UCMJ's adoption of procedural rules and presumptions analogous to the civilian criminal justice system is fitting, but the UCMJ's continued reliance on the chain of command for certain triggers is so deeply attuned to the needs of the military that it has been largely retained.

What presumptions should we apply to proposals to fundamentally change the military justice system and its reliance on command authority? The cautionary principle surely directs that the presumption must be against fundamental change. How strong should that presumption be? What objective factors should we apply to calibrate the presumption? What new conditions and what level of evidence should be required to overcome that presumption? How should concerns about unintended, negative consequences be factored into the above equations?

History, political theory, and common experience provide some useful guidelines.

Proposals for significant change to any system that has evolved to meet the particular needs of a nation for centuries should not be taken up lightly. As Edmund Burke cautioned:

> When ancient opinions and rules of life are taken away, the loss cannot possibly be estimated. From that moment we have no compass to govern us; nor can we know distinctly to what port we steer... . We are but too apt to consider things in the state in which we find them, without sufficiently adverting to the causes by which they have been produced, and possibly may be upheld.[52]

Yet no system should remain immune from change simply because it has been in place for a long time. The history of most landmark civil rights legislation is the story of transformative movements that were long overdue in fulfilling the aspirations of the Declaration of Independence and the founding theory of our nation. Other worthwhile change need not be so compelling or obviously necessary. In another context, Oliver Wendell Holmes quipped in *The Path of The Law*:

> It is revolting to have no better reason for a rule of law than that so it was laid down in the time of Henry IV. It is still more revolting if the grounds upon which it was laid down have vanished long since, and the rule simply persists from blind imitation of the past.[53]

Wisdom then is correctly discerning whether: (a) the reasons for change outweigh the underlying grounds for the existing system, and more importantly, (b) whether the intended and unintended effects of any change will do more good than harm.

As any casual observer of the American political order knows, our system of government was designed to make sudden changes in policy difficult, and for good reason. The Framers distrusted momentary popular opinion, and thought our liberties were best protected when power was properly divided and legislation required the concurrence of three entities with different constituencies and tenures in office.

Progressives from Woodrow Wilson to the present day have expressed frustration with our constitutional design in which it may take a crisis to generate the political momentum for significant legislative change. Modern progressives have learned, however, that if no real crisis exists, the perception of one can be just as useful. Thus, it is the job of the activists to create the perception of a crisis if none really exists, which seems to explain the multi-year goal to convince opinion leaders and policymakers that there is a "sexual assault crisis" in the military.

A few years ago, Rahm Emanuel added a corollary to the activist playbook when he forthrightly stated that "You never want a serious crisis go to waste." So whether the crisis is real or not, progressives like Mr. Emanuel will try to exploit it to advance a long-term agenda

---

[52] EDMUND BURKE, REFLECTIONS ON THE REVOLUTION IN FRANCE ¶¶ 132-33 (New York: P.F. Collier & Son Co. 1909) (1790).

[53] Oliver Wendell Holmes, Jr., *The Path of the Law*, 10 HARV. L. REV. 457 (1897).

item that might have no clear connection to the problem (or supposed problem) as long as it can be sold as one of several activist responses to it. As Mr. Emanuel elaborated: "The crisis provides the opportunity for us to do things ['that were long-term'] that you could not do before."[54]

Undermining command authority in the military and inserting civilian control, not just at the top where it properly belongs but at every level of the military, is one of those long-term goals of the political left since the Vietnam War era. Any crisis, real or imagined, may present a good opportunity to undermine the traditional command authority, which brings us full circle to the analytical approach we should apply to the question at hand:

- Do the reasons for change outweigh the underlying grounds for the existing system?
- Will the intended and unintended effects of any change do more good than harm?

To the second and more important question we should factor in a healthy dose of skepticism about our ability to predict and gauge unintended effects (even though they may be unintended, some close observers might be able to predict some of them), apply the cautionary principle in which unknown risks can be guarded against by a presumption against change (perhaps a strong presumption when it is an institution as important as the military), and insist on both clear and convincing evidence to overcome the presumption.

Facts v. Anecdotes in Evaluating the Claimed "Crisis"

Commissioner Heriot's statement challenges the growing chorus of activists and press reports claiming there is a sexual assault crisis in the military. The truth is that sexual assault rates are comparable to similar civilian populations, and that prosecution rates in the military are comparable if not higher than in the civilian criminal justice system. The need for radically changing the military justice system has simply not been demonstrated. And as discussed in the next two sections of this statement, there are serious risks attendant to decoupling the system from the chain of command.

Although Commissioner Heriot's statement is more thorough in debunking the crisis myth, the facts I set forth below have independent significance because four commissioners voted to include them as official Commission findings in this Report. They were blocked from inclusion as official findings by four other commissioners who support the counterfactual crisis narrative. Whether they were blocked for that reason or not (see footnote 5 below), they are inconvenient truths to those who support the "crisis" point of view.

---

[54] Gerald F. Seib, *In Crisis, Opportunity for Obama*, WALL ST. J., Nov. 21, 2008 (quoting Emanuel).

At a public meeting, I proposed that the following list of facts be included in the Report as official Commission "findings of fact" since they are central to the investigation the Commission was conducting. As the Report citation at the end of each proposed finding of fact showed (when proposed and below), they all are based on information in the body of the Report. The four commissioners who voted to include them were Vice Chair Thernstrom, Commissioners Heriot and Kirsanow, and me. They were blocked as official "findings of facts" by four commissioners appointed or nominated by Democratic Party leaders (in the White House and Congress) even though all of those commissioners voted to approve the body of the Report from which they were taken. Readers can verify for themselves that the facts are accurately drawn from the Report, and further, the accuracy of the original source material that the Commission staff and witnesses relied upon.[55]

1. Based on DoD surveys of active duty service members, DoD concluded there was no statistically significant difference in the number of women reporting being the victim of unwanted sexual contact between the 2006 and 2012 surveys (6.8% vs. 6.1%). There was also no statistically significant difference for men in the same surveys (1.8% vs. 1.2%). [Report at 6.]

2. According to DoD's 2012 Workplace and Gender Relations survey, of the 67 percent of female Service members who did not report unwanted sexual contact they said they experienced to military authorities, 48 percent indicated that they did not report the unwanted sexual contact because the incidents were not serious enough to report. [Report at 19.]

3. After General Amos, Commandant of the Marine Corps, demanded tougher punishment for those accused of sexual misconduct in public speeches, some military judges concluded that his statements presented the appearance of unlawful command influence against accused Marines. [Report at 69.]

4. Military counsel presented credible testimony to the Commission that political pressure to increase the number of sexual assault cases referred to court martial and to increase

---

[55] It should be noted here that Commissioners Thernstrom, Heriot, Kirsanow and I did not vote for any of the findings of fact or recommendations proposed by the other four commissioners. I thought some of them were not true, some were more disputed opinion statements than fact, some were misleadingly or vaguely worded, and still others were irrelevant (e.g., why does it matter that there are minor differences in the way the various services select sexual assault response coordinators and victim advocates; isn't it a good thing that the services act as laboratories of democracy and each benefits from the best practices and innovations of the others, including a career track for JAG trial lawyers?). Perhaps the other four commissioners voted against my proposed findings for similar reasons. That is why the citations to the Report in my proposed findings are important. Readers and policymakers can evaluate their accuracy on their own. Beyond that, it is noteworthy that the Commission was split so sharply on this topic. Such division does not help overcome the burden that the proponents of change should have to meet.

conviction rates prejudices the military justice system against some accused service members, causes over-prosecution, and diminishes counsel's ability to mount an adequate defense. [Report at 69-72.]

5. The military usually does what it takes to achieve its mission, even if collateral damage is high. The Commission received credible testimony that the military's effort to achieve its "strategic goal" of increasing sexual assault reports has increased such reports, but may also have increased the percentage of unfounded reports as a percentage of all reports. [Report at 70 (quoting statement of Bridget Wilson).]

6. Like any other large organizational change, the military's efforts to achieve its "strategic goal" of increasing sexual assault reports has both intended and unintended consequences, all of which merit careful study. Whether related to this "strategic goal" or not, the percentage of sexual assault reports determined by a Military Criminal Investigative Organization to be unfounded has risen from 5.2% in fiscal year 2009 to 10.7% in fiscal year 2010, 11.9% in fiscal year 2011, and 13.6% in fiscal year 2012. [Report at 71 n.87.]

7. Civilian and military prosecution rates for penetration offenses are similar, but the military's use of nonjudicial punishments and adverse administrative actions may increase the number of military offenders who receive some form of punishment for unwanted sexual contact. [Report at 78.]

8. In the civilian criminal justice system, it has been estimated that 14% to 18% of all reported sexual assaults are prosecuted. [Report at 52 n.154 (citing various studies).]

9. Of the 1518 Service members investigated for penetration offenses, unwanted sexual contact, and unwanted attempted sexual contact in fiscal year 2011, 488 (32%) were referred to court-martial, 187 (12%) received nonjudicial punishments, 48 (3%) were administratively discharged, and 67 (4%) received adverse administrative action. [Report at 50-51 & Table 5.1.]

Regarding the first proposed finding, there simply has been no increase in sexual assaults against women from 2006 to 2012, at least according to DOD's surveys. The dip in the percentage in the 2010 survey and partial bounce-back in 2012 has been opportunistically used to proclaim a crisis, ignoring the small decline from 2006 to 2012 as well as previous surveys. *See* Commissioner Heriot's statement at [*7-13].

Findings three through six would have highlighted evidence that enormous pressure has already been placed on commanders to increase the number of sexual assault reports and prosecutions, so much so that the scales of justice already have been unfairly tipped against some accused service members. Not surprisingly, the percentage of unfounded sexual assault reports increased dramatically from 2009 to 2012.

Findings seven through nine would have emphasized the information in the Report showing that commanders and military prosecutors are as aggressive as civilian prosecutors, if not more so, in bringing and prosecuting sexual assault charges. Commanders also have the flexibility to discipline accused service members short of criminal prosecution, unlike a civilian prosecutor who has to choose between prosecution and taking no action.

The above facts alone seriously undermine the narrative that: there is a military sexual assault crisis, the problem is getting worse, and the military is not taking sexual assaults seriously. Indeed, there is convincing evidence that commanders have been overly aggressive at times, which is a concern that the military should also be particularly attentive to address. If it does not do so, the developing political "witch hunt" for sexual assault predators could substantially undermine the rights of accused service members, lead to fundamentally unfair trials, and have a corrosive effect on military morale and cohesiveness among service members.

The Danger of Undermining Command Authority in the Military Services

Since time immemorial, officers in the military have been directly responsible for maintaining the good order and discipline of the service members under their command. They will be relieved of command, and can be held criminally liable under the UCMJ, if they fail in this duty.[56] Under current law, officers have various tools to enforce good order and discipline, including an important role in originating criminal charges against service members under their command.

To remove one of the most important tools (the role in bringing criminal charges) but leave the responsibility, including criminal liability, for failure to keep good order and discipline is a dangerous mix. One of the witnesses before the Commission noted that commanding officers were subject to criminal liability *only* if they were "negligent or culpably inefficient," and urged a tougher standard of criminal liability.

While I am highly skeptical of such change, it is remarkable that either negligence or inefficiency can alone be the basis for a military court martial of an officer involving the actions of others under his or her command. In the civilian employment context, negligence is rarely a ground for even tort liability when the acts complained of are criminal acts by a non-supervisory employee, except in a negligent hiring situation. And absent a conspiracy, there is no criminal liability for the civilian plant manager for assaults by one employee against another, because that is understood to be outside the course and scope of employment.

---

[56] "Any person subject to this chapter who . . . is derelict in the performance of his duties... shall be punished as a court-martial may direct." UCMJ Art. 92, 10 U.S.C. § 892.

Only with some of these comparisons can we begin to comprehend the differences in responsibility a commander has for the actions of those under his command compared to that of an ordinary civilian employer or supervisor. And we also should be mindful that the nation's very existence may depend on good order and discipline in the military services. This is why Congress should be extremely careful when considering changes that may undermine commanding officers' responsibility for, and ability to maintain, good order and discipline.

The military is a unique, hierarchical institution. The Supreme Court has observed that "the military is, by necessity, a specialized society separate from civilian society."[57] It "must insist upon a respect for duty and a discipline without counterpart in civilian life. . . in order to prepare for and perform its vital role."[58] To "accomplish its mission the military must foster instinctive obedience, unity, commitment, and esprit de corps."[59] Courts, the Supreme Court noted, are "ill-equipped to determine the impact upon discipline that any intrusion upon military authority might have."[60]

Moreover, the American military justice system has served the country well since before the founding of the Republic. Col. Dwight Sullivan, a lecturer at the George Washington University Law School, testified before the Commission that removing sexual assault offenses from the chain of command "would be inconsistent with the manner in which the United States' military justice system has operated since General George Washington used it to maintain discipline in the Continental Army." "Caution," Sullivan continued, "should be exercised before adopting such a radical departure from the American system of military justice." Sullivan Statement at 5.

The Report at Chapter 6.C.2 mentions (although all too briefly) some of the arguments made by witnesses in favor of keeping criminal justice within the chain of command, which are worth exploring at greater length. Lt. Gen. Dana K. Chipman, U.S. Army Judge Advocate General, explained that the military justice system is separate from the civilian "because of the worldwide deployment of military personnel, the need for a system that can be responsive to the unique nature of military life and the combat environment, and the need to maintain discipline in the force." Chipman Statement at 1-2. He then discussed why commanders must oversee discipline, among other duties:

Ultimate authority in our system is vested in the commander for very important reasons. The commander is responsible for all that goes on in a unit – health, welfare, safety, morale,

---

[57] Goldman v. Weinberger, 475 U.S. 503, 506 (1986) (quotation marks omitted).

[58] *Id.* at 507 (citations and quotation marks omitted).

[59] *Id.* at 507.

[60] *Id.* at 507 (quotation marks omitted).

discipline, training, and readiness to execute the mission. The commander's ability to punish quickly, visibly, and locally is essential to maintaining discipline in units. The Uniform Code of Military Justice ensures that commanders can maintain good order and discipline in the force. *Id.* at 2.

Maj. Gen. Vaughn A. Ary, Staff Judge Advocate to the Commandant of the Marine Corps, made a similar point, observing: "Commanders have always been responsible for readiness, unit cohesion, and morale.... [C]ommanders are responsible for the safety of all Marines, victim care and services, and ensuring the fair trial of an accused." Ary Statement at 1.

Maj. Gen. Gary S. Patton agreed that authority over criminal justice is necessary if commanders are to be accountable for good order and discipline:

> Suggestions to remove Commanders from the administration of military justice undercut good order and discipline. Commanders are accountable for the good order and discipline of the forces assigned under them and are responsible for what their units do or fail to do. Removing a commander from the administration of justice among his or her troops would undercut a commander's authority, especially in combat, where the [UCMJ] is most tested by the stresses of war. Patton Statement at 4-5.

Gen. Patton expanded on this idea in his oral testimony to the Commission, observing that commanders "are responsible for the health and welfare, accomplishing the mission, the readiness of their unit." He argued that "we . . . owe [commanders] the tools to do the job. One of those tools is training. Another one of those tools is the military justice system" that allows commanders to put standards in place and then enforce those standards against those who choose not to comply. Tr. at 206.

Lt. Gen. Richard C. Harding, The Judge Advocate General of the Air Force, in his oral testimony listed reasons the American military wins the wars it fights. The military brings "four things to every fight: the best equipment; the best people; the best training, those are three legs of a four-legged table; the fourth leg is discipline." The "ability to hold members accountable is important for command and control. This is the art of military science now. So if you start to pull at that thread, the second, third and fourth order effects [are] awfully important... ." Tr. at 209. When you take away authority over discipline, "the second, third and fourth order effects are ugly." Tr. at 208.

And perhaps equally as important for those who may be inclined to embrace change for change's sake alone (may Edmund Burke rest in peace), the Report does not point to any evidence that removing commanders from the prosecutorial function will help victims, reduce sexual assaults, or lead to more convictions of the guilty, except for the thoroughly discredited assertions by some activists and academics that the military is not currently taking sexual assaults seriously.[61] Before adopting a new system of military criminal law, with its obvious negative externalities and added unintended consequences, its proponents ought to have clear and convincing evidence it will do some actual good— apart from casting aspersions on the military as sexist and uncaring.

Lessons from Australia: The Remedy May Not Only Be Worse Than the Disease, It May Be Flatly Unconstitutional

One of the leading bills in Congress that would substitute civilian officials in certain prosecutorial settings in the military appears to be unconstitutional because it violates the Appointments Clause, art. II, § 2, cl. 2, and possibly violates other Separation of Powers principles. *See* Sexual Assault Training Oversight and Prevention Act, H.R. 3435, 112th Cong. (2011). That does not mean that the bill could not be fixed, but this is a very tricky area of constitutional law.

A few decades ago, an Appointments Clause challenge to one UCMJ provision almost rendered the entire military justice system unconstitutional. Instead, the Supreme Court held that since all military officers retained the historic authority to discipline those under their command, any of them could be constitutionally detailed to serve as a military trial judge (without a new appointment distinct from their original appointment as military officers). *See Weiss v. United States*, 510 U.S. 163 (1994). Yet that Supreme Court holding would obviously not save the proposed bill that removes much of that historic command authority.

Australia's unhappy experience changing its military justice system is a cautionary tale for those who propose radical changes to the American military. As two panelists noted in their testimony to the Commission, the High Court of Australia in 2009 held that Australia's new military justice system was unconstitutional, which seriously disrupted the Australian military, putting hundreds of convictions in doubt.[62] The "reform" legislation (progressives label any change they support as a positive "reform") in Australia was similar to H.R. 3435, and the ground for ruling the Australian plan unconstitutional was similar (at least in some respects) to

---

[61] The facts in the previous section and the persuasive testimony of the two and three-star flag officer witnesses who testified before the Commission are hard to ignore, unless the conclusion is reached without a serious examination of the relevant evidence, and instead, anecdotes are substituted for objective data. Although it is not easy to compare the military and civilian justice systems, the best evidence available is that the military already prosecutes sexual assault cases at a higher rate. *See, e.g.*, Commissioner Heriot's Statement at [*13-20].

[62] Briefing Transcript at 123, 128-29 (Professor Elizabeth Hillman testimony); *id.* at 124-25 (Col. Dwight Sullivan testimony); Report at 66 n.61; *Australia military court ruled unconstitutional*, L.A. TIMES, Aug. 27, 2009 (AMC had ruled on 127 military discipline cases, which were under review because of the High Court's decision).

the Appointments Clause and separation of powers problems with H.R. 3435 and similar proposals here.

In 2006, Australia created the Australian Military Court (AMC) to adjudicate cases independent of the chain of command, not subject to review or confirmation by a commanding officer. Previously, the Australian system was similar to the current American military justice system, with decisions of guilt and punishment by courts-martial subject to review within the chain of command.

The High Court held the AMC to be invalid because it "exercise[d] the judicial power of the Commonwealth"—unlike courts-martial, it made binding and authoritative decisions about guilt and punishment with no review within the chain of command—but did not otherwise conform with the Constitution's requirements for exercising this power.[63] For example, the AMC was not "comprised of Justices who are appointed by the Governor-General in Council and with the tenure provided by s 72 of the Constitution."[64] The AMC thus violated an appointments provision in the Australian Constitution and did not provide AMC judges the same tenure as other federal judges.

The Court criticized the Australian Parliament's attempt to create a court that was partly in the military and yet partly, as we might say, in the judicial branch. "There was an attempt by the Parliament," the Court wrote, "to borrow for the AMC the reputation of the judicial branch of government for impartiality and non-partisanship, upon which its legitimacy has been said, in this Court, ultimately to depend, and to thereby apply 'the neutral colours of judicial action' to the work of the AMC."[65]

As a young Department of Justice lawyer in the Office of Legal Counsel in 1992-95, it was my great privilege to serve on the legal team that saved the military justice system from a serious Appointments Clause challenge mentioned above (*see Weiss* v. *United States, infra*), but that was by reinforcing the notion that duly appointed military officers were still in charge of the military justice system. Few lawyers understand this area of law (it is certainly the case that very few lawyers outside the Office of Legal Counsel regularly practice in this area of law), and many who claim to have expertise don't know what they don't know. I fear for the quality of advice rendered in the halls of Congress on this subject.

---

[63] Lane v. Morrison [2009] HCA 29, ¶¶ 9, 97-98.

[64] *Id.* ¶ 9. Further, the High Court held that "the AMC is not supported by s 122 [of the Constitution] as a law with respect to the government of any territory." *Id.* In addition, decisions of the AMC were subject to appeal to the Defense Force Discipline Appeal Tribunal on grounds that were not questions of law. The right to appeal from a federal court, "were the AMC to have that character, to an administrative body such as the Appeal Tribunal, would be repugnant to Ch III of the Constitution." *Id.* ¶ 35.

[65] *Id.* ¶ 11.

The Members of the Australian Parliament were warned that the change faced constitutional problems,[66] but that advice was probably trumped by enthusiasm for the novel proposal at issue. Crisis or no crisis, this is a complicated area to get right, and I don't have a lot of confidence that Congress has the patience to make a careful and constitutional determination. Perhaps ironically, it was a sexual assault prosecution in Australia that was overturned when the High Court held that the new military justice system was unconstitutional.[67] If we want sexual offenders to be punished, we shouldn't risk having all their courts martial or analogous convictions overturned.

Conclusion

Although the number of military sexual assault stories in the press has increased in the past year, they are analogous in one respect to the periodic increase in coverage of shark attacks. Although there is no congruence between a shark's mental state and the personal agency of a sexual assailant, the fluctuating press coverage of shark attacks and "Shark Week" programming on the Discovery Channel have a bigger role in fueling the perception that such attacks are increasing than the relevant data. The truth is that the number of shark attacks is constant or declining relative to the number of people enjoying a swim, regardless of the false impressions caused by press coverage fluctuations.

The American military has approximately 1.4 million service members, most of whom are in the age group that is most likely to engage in misconduct and assaults. Given the increased separation from civilian family life, we might expect a higher rate of assaults from this cohort than is actually present. That does not excuse any criminal or offensive conduct, but anecdotes generally only tell the story that journalists or activists want to relate, and may contain inaccuracies even then.

Radical policy changes should not be based on a press-generated, shark attack mentality. The best available data indicates that there is no sexual assault crisis in the military, nor a lack of attention paid to sexual assaults by military leaders. To the extent the military can do a better job (and who can't do a better job?), the military is, for example, improving the professionalism and career tracks of both JAG prosecutors and defense counsel.

Congress should not rush to make fundamental changes to the military justice system without carefully considering all the facts in the proper context. Nevertheless, the burden on those who

---

[66] *See* Michael Pelly, *Military court is declared 'illegal,'* AUSTRALIAN, Aug. 27, 2009 ("The verdict on the court represents an amazing bungle by the previous government, which ignored advice by a Senate committee to create a body under Chapter III of the Constitution.").

[67] The High Court dismissed charges against Lane, formerly a service member in the Royal Australian Navy, for "'an act of indecency without consent.'" Lane ¶¶ 2, 64.

support radical change simply has not been, and cannot be, met based on the public record to date. In fact, the evidence suggests that inappropriate political pressure on the military may be doing more harm than good.

Statement and Rebuttal of Commissioner Gail Heriot, Joined By Vice Chair Thernstrom and Commissioner Gaziano

The topic of sexual assault in the military has long been an attention-grabber. Congress and the media have given it considerable attention in the past two decades.[1] Nevertheless, when the U.S. Commission on Civil Rights undertook this project, it had not been in the headlines for a while. That changed this spring with the publication of the *2012 Workplace and Gender Relations Survey of Active Duty Members* ("*2012 Survey*"), which purported to show a large uptick in "unwanted sexual contact." Since then, the topic has been widely aired.[2]

When "sexy" topics find their way into newspaper editorials and Congressional hearings, the result is usually unfortunate. Policy mistakes will almost surely be made unless all concerned can be persuaded to stop and take a deep breath before proceeding with great caution.

Everyone agrees that the military must do its level best to prevent forcible rape and other sexual assaults. At the same time, however, I believe the June 4th hearing of the Senate Armed Services Committee at which some of the military's highest ranking officers were berated about the results of the *2012 Survey* was a regrettable spectacle—especially since the survey results were probably faulty.[3] A supplicating Army Chief of Staff Gen. Raymond T. Odierno attempted to reassure the panel by testifying, "Two weeks ago, I told my commanders that combating sexual assault and sexual harassment within the ranks is our No. 1 priority." It was

---

[1] Congressional hearings on the topic include the following: Oversight: Pending Legislation Regarding Sexual Assaults in the Military, U.S. Senate Armed Services, 113th Cong. (2013); Oversight, Sexual Assault in the Military, U.S. Senate Armed Services Committee, 113th Cong. (2013); Preventing and Responding to Incidents, U.S. Senate Armed Services Committee, 109th Cong. (2004); Allegations of Sexual Assault at the U.S. Military Academy, U.S. Senate Armed Services Committee, 108th Cong. (2003); U.S. Air Force Investigation, U.S. Senate Armed Services Committee, 108th Cong. (2003); A Review of Sexual Misconduct at Lackland Air Force Base, House of Representatives Armed Services Committee, 113th Cong. (2013); Sexual Assault in the Military, House of Representatives Armed Services Committee, 111th Cong. (2011); Hearings into Gender Discrimination in the Military, House of Representatives Armed Services Subcommittee on Personnel and Readiness, 102nd Cong. (1992); Women and the Military: The Problem of the Tailhook Affair and Sexual Harassment, House of Representatives Armed Services Committee, 102nd Cong. (1992); Honor Systems and Sexual Assault at the Service Academies, Senate Armed Services Committee, 103rd Cong. (1994); Sexual Harassment of Military Women and Improving the Military Complaint System, House of Representatives Armed Services Committee, 103rd Cong. (1994).

[2] See, e.g., infra at notes 14 & 20.

[3] See infra at (B).

difficult to avoid the conclusion that our leaders—both political and military—were losing perspective.[4]

The military is a large and complex institution with many priorities. But only one can be No. 1. If dealing with sexual assault and sexual harassment is the military's No. 1 priority, that means defending the nation from foreign aggression is not. General Odierno's statement was unfortunate.

It is my hope that some of the information contained in this report—including the accompanying Commissioner statements—will help put the problem of military sexual assault back in perspective. Among the most basic, preliminary questions that need to be considered are whether sexual assault rates are high in the military relative to comparable institutions, like colleges and universities; whether the military is lax in prosecuting sexual assault relative to other jurisdictions, and whether the military has been generally improving its record on sexual assault.

Before I can try to deal with those questions, however, a few words of caution about vocabulary are in order. Note, for example, that in the third paragraph of this introduction, I separated the more specific term "forcible rape" from the more general term "sexual assault." Many members of the public are unaware when they hear purported statistics on "sexual assault" (the media's preferred term) that these numbers include more than just rape. They include conduct that ranges from forcible rape to sexually provocative pats on the bottom.

---

[4] Written Testimony of General Raymond T. Odierno, Chief of Staff of the Army, before the Senate Committee on Armed Services, Hearing on Pending Legislation Regarding Sexual Assaults in the Military, June 4, 2013, at 1.

On June 12, 2013, the *Washington Times* reported that an unnamed "senior Army officer" had recently undergone command training and had been told there that "'stopping sexual assaults is THE primary mission of the Army.'" According to the course instructor, this was contained in a "mission statement" released by Army Chief of Staff Gen. Raymond T. Odierno. See Bill Gertz, Inside the Ring, Wash. Times (June 12, 2013)(capital letters in original). I cannot say for sure, of course, but it seems likely to me that the "mission statement" actually used Gen. Odierno's "No. 1 priority" terminology and not the terminology quoted in the *Times* report. It would be utterly fatuous to state that stopping sexual assaults is "THE primary mission of the Army," although Odierno's "No. 1 priority" terminology is not far off from that. What is significant is that the report strongly suggests Gen. Odierno's statement to the Senate Armed Services Committee was not made off-handedly. It does indeed purport to represent Army policy.

People aren't inspired to join the military because they want to help combat any supposed rampant sexual harassment or even sexual assault. They are drawn to the military primarily because they want to be a part of a just and noble cause—the defense of their country from foreign aggression. I can only imagine what my attitude would be if the president of my university were to pronounce that combating sexual assault and harassment (or combatting any other kind of crime or injustice) was our No. 1 priority without any proof that the university's record was worse than that of similar institutions. I would know that the university has lost its bearings, lost its will to carry out its actual mission: to expand human knowledge in the arts, humanities and sciences as well as in business and the law and to impart that knowledge to the next generation. I would know that it is time to seek a job at a college or university where the primary mission of higher education is taken more seriously.

Even more significantly, they are often unaware that the *2012 Survey* doesn't even ask Service men and women about their experiences with "sexual assault." The term used in the survey is blander—"unwanted sexual contact." Such a term can be easily misunderstood by survey respondents to include "contact" that is not physical at all, like unwanted attention from a would-be suitor. All this can lead to a host of misunderstandings about the nature and scope of the problem.

Note also that even the term "rape" is sometimes used to describe very different kinds of conduct. At one end of the spectrum, it can be used to describe cases of forcible, unconsented-to penile penetration. At the other end, it may describe penile penetration in which both parties have appeared to consent, but both are intoxicated and hence the female (but evidently not the male) is deemed incapable of legally sufficient consent.[5] The distance between these two clear wrongs can lead to cynicism. As one female Navy prosecutor put it, "There is a pressure to prosecute, prosecute, prosecute. When you get [a rape case] that's actually real, there's a lot of skepticism. You hear it routinely: 'Is this a rape case or is this a Navy rape case?'"[6]

I wish I could say that all of this confusion over vocabulary is a matter of miscommunication. But some of it is deliberately calculated to deceive low-information readers and listeners.

A. Does the Military Have a Higher Rate of Sexual Assault (Both Rape and Lesser Offenses) than Other Institutions that are Dominated by Young Adults?

To me, the most striking thing about the subject matter of this report is how little we actually know about it. For example, I have found no evidence so far that sexual assault (no matter how it is defined) is more common in the military than it is at other institutions that house large numbers of young adults. Yet many who write about the issue seem to treat this as given.[7]

---

[5] While the term "rape" gets used in informal settings to refer to penetration to which one party does not consent, the Uniform Code of Military Justice uses the term "aggravated sexual assault" to refer to what informally is called "rape" and also to a broader range of sexual misconduct involving penetration. See 10 U.S.C. 920 and also the discussion of this statute in the body of this report in Chapter 1, Section C. See also notes 37 and 40 and accompanying text.

[6] Marisa Taylor & Chris Adams, Military's Newly-Aggressive Rape Prosecution Has Pitfalls, McClatchy Newspapers (Nov. 28, 2011).

[7] Unfortunately, some of my fellow commissioners have included similarly overblown rhetoric in their statements. E.g.: "In the end, this is really about who we are as a nation. If we cannot, or will not protect our protectors, then we have failed to live up to the ideals upon which our freedom is founded. The military has had much time to remedy this travesty of military sexual assault, and has failed to do so adequately. The military hierarchy must either resolve this crisis immediately, or step aside and let others tend to the victims and prevent the future victimization of our men and women in uniform." Draft Democratic Caucus Joint Statement at 22. For a different view, see Thomas Donnelly, The Military Epidemics that Aren't: A Wildly Off-Base Trend is Medicalizing the Armed Forces as a Group of Victims, Patients, and Predators, Wall St. J. (Aug. 15, 2013)(criticizing the misplaced tendency to see members of the armed forces as victims in need of therapy and the political lobby that benefits from the "hundreds of millions if not billions of health-care dollars per year at stake").

Indeed, the earliest draft of this report contained a lengthy screed blaming "military culture" for its sexual assault problem. At the request of several Commission members and the Commission's newly installed Staff Director, it was deleted.

But consider *The Sexual Victimization of College Women,* a research report funded by the National Institute of Justice and the Bureau of Statistics at the U.S. Department of Justice.[8] The authors of that report surveyed 4,446 women who were attending a two- or four-year college or university, both graduate and undergraduate students, in the autumn of 1996. The survey was undertaken between February and May of 1997, so that the women surveyed were being asked about a period of time that was considerably less than a year. According to the report, the average length of time reported on was 6.91 months, which for the sake of simplicity I will round to 7 months. About 2.8% of these women responded that they had been the victim of rape (1.7%) or attempted rape (1.1%) since school had begun in the fall of 1996.[9]

---

[8] Bonnie S. Fisher, Francis T. Cullen & Michael G. Turner, The Sexual Victimization of College Women, Research Report of the National Institute of Justice & the Bureau of Statistics, U.S. Dep't of Justice (Dec. 2000).

[9] *Id.* at 11, Ex. 3. There was apparently no overlap in the 74 individuals who reported completed rape and the 49 individuals who reported attempted rape, although some individuals reported more than one completed rape or more than one attempted rape. The total number of victims was 123. "Completed rape" was defined as "Unwanted completed penetration by force or the threat of force. Penetration includes: penile-vaginal, mouth on your genitals, mouth on someone else's genitals, penile-anal, digital-vaginal, digital-anal, object-vaginal, and object-anal." "Attempted rape" was defined as "Unwanted attempted penetration by force or the threat of force. Penetration includes: penile-vaginal, mouth on your genitals, mouth on someone else's genitals, penile-anal, digital-vaginal, digital-anal, object-vaginal, and object-anal." *Id.* at 8, Ex. 2. The study also found that the four most prominent risk factors for victimization were: "(1) frequently drinking enough to get drunk, (2) being unmarried, (3) having been a victim of a sexual assault before the start of the current school year, and (4) living on campus (for on-campus victimization only)." *Id.* at 23. Survey respondents were not required to classify their experience as "rape" or "attempted rape" for it to be so classified for the purposes of the study. Indeed, 48.8% of the women whose experience(s) were classified as rape by the study did not consider their reported incident to be "rape." *Id.* at 15.

I find the discussion in the body of this report at Chapter 1(E) comparing this college study to the military studies to be less than useful. The report asserts: "Another difficulty in comparing military sexual assault rates to those researched in other young populations such as colleges or universities, lies in the fact that various available studies use different definitions for the term 'sexual assault' and also implement different study methodologies. [Footnote omitted.] Therefore, available data does not provide a meaningful comparison." This is a self-serving statement. If no meaningful comparisons can be made between the military and other contexts, it is impossible to draw the conclusion that everyone seems bent on arriving at—the military is somehow in the throes of a sexual assault crisis. While it is true that these studies do use different definitions of sexual assault, both reports contain figures regarding the narrower subset of sexual assault incidents comprised of completed and attempted penetration offenses (which I discuss and compare above.) Contrary to the conclusory statement quoted above, it is possible to make some useful comparisons between the two studies.

The body of this report states in the same paragraph, "In addition, the DoD includes a wider range of sexual contact, such as groping, in its definition of sexual assault." If that is true, it cuts in the opposite direction from the one the report and most media reports suggest, since it would cause the military's "unwanted sexual contact" rate to seem higher relative to the college and university rate than it actually is. It should be noted, however, that the National Institute of Justice study did ask college women, "Not counting the types of sexual contact already mentioned, have you experienced any unwanted or uninvited touching of a sexual nature since school began in fall

(cont'd)

It is obviously desirable to compare the results of the military survey, which seeks information about the survey respondent's past 12 months, with figures from the college survey that are also expressed in terms of 12 months. Once this is done, however, the military looks better than colleges and universities, not worse. The 2.8% figure for rape and attempted rape would annualize to 4.8% (assuming no overlap in victimization). According to the *2012 Survey*, 6.1% of the military women who responded had experienced "unwanted sexual contact" during the preceding 12 months. But less than 3.5% responded that they had experienced attempted and completed sexual intercourse, anal or oral sex.[10] The rest reported non-penetration sexual contact. The rates on penetration offenses and attempted penetration offenses are thus roughly comparable, with the military coming off as somewhat better.

Similarly, the college study found a rate of completed non-penetration unwanted sexual contact (with or without force or threat of force) that appears to be at least comparable to the rates of unwanted non-penetration sexual contact in the *2012 Survey* and quite possibly higher. In *The Sexual Victimization of College Women*, 1.7% of women respondents reported that they had

---

(cont'd from previous page)

1996? This includes forced kissing, touching of private parts, grabbing, fondling, and rubbing up against you in a sexual way, even if it is over your clothes." Although the question does not use the word grope, the conduct being described in it is roughly comparable, making the sentence from the body of our report somewhat misleading. In any event, however, I have chosen to focus this section of my statement on comparisons between rates of the more serious offenses described in both studies, since they are the ones they are most troubling.

Commissioner Todd Gaziano proposed edits at the July 12, 2013 Commission business meeting intended to improve this section of the report dealing with colleges and universities. To my disappointment, they were voted down on a 4-4 vote.

I should note also that another well-known study of campus rape and sexual assault made famous by *Ms.* Magazine came up with even higher numbers than the National Institute of Justice study—although the methodology of this study may have been designed to produce numbers that high. See Mary P. Koss, Christine A. Gidycz & Nadine Wisniewski, The Scope of Rape: Incidence and Prevalence of Sexual Aggression and Victimization in a National Sample of Higher Education Students, 55 J. Consulting & Clinical Psych. 162, 168-170 (1987). The Koss study found in a national sample of students in higher education that 27.5% of women had been victims of completed rape (15.4%) or uncompleted attempted rape (12.1%) an average of two times between the ages of 14 and 21. It further found that during a 12-month period, 16.6% of all college women were victims of rape or attempted rape.

The 1987 Koss study has been strongly criticized for many reasons, including the fact that 73% of the women it designates as rape victims did not agree that they had been raped. Neil Gilbert, Realities and Mythologies of Rape, Society (May-June 1992). Thus inflated, however, the study makes the military seem like a Junior League garden party.

The high numbers produced in the Koss study were not confined to non-elite colleges and universities. According to an unpublished study reported in the *Daily Princetonian*, "[m]ore than 15 percent of female undergraduates reported experiencing non-consensual vaginal penetration during their time at the University." Sohee Khim, Survey Quantified Sexual Assault (Mar. 4, 2013). The survey questions in the Princeton study were modeled after the "Sexual Experience Survey" developed by Dr. Koss in 2007.

[10] For the precise question asked in the *2012 Survey*, see infra at note 31 and accompanying text.

been the victim of "completed [non-penetration] sexual coercion," 1.9% reported being the victim of "completed [non-penetration] sexual contact with force or threat of force," and 1.8% reported being the victim of "completed [non-penetration] sexual contact without force."[11] These figures annualize to 2.91%, 3.26% and 3.09% respectively.[12]

Meanwhile, the rate of completed non-penetration unwanted sexual contact for military respondents in the *2012 Survey* is somewhere between 1.95% and 6.1%. The range is broad only because it is unclear from the record how many Service women reported both a completed or attempted penetration offense *and* a non-penetration offense. Of the 6.1% of women who reported one or more incidents of unwanted sexual contact, 32% (or 1.95% of all respondents to the survey) reported that the most serious unwanted sexual contact they experienced was [non-penetration] touching. The rest reported either attempted or completed sexual intercourse, anal sex or oral sex. Since some of those who reported attempted or completed sexual intercourse, anal sex or oral sex might on a different occasion also have experienced non-penetration touching, the rate of unwanted non-penetration touching could go high as 6.1% (though the high figure would be unlikely). Even if it did, however, it is not clear that the military's rate is higher than that of colleges and universities, which could run as high as 9.26% (if we assume no overlap among those who report the three forms of completed non-penetration sexual contact covered in that study).

A more recent project, *The Campus Sexual Assault (CSA) Study*, which was also paid for by the National Institute of Justice of the U.S. Department of Justice, yielded similar results in 2007.[13] Over 6,800 undergraduate students (5,466 women and 1,375 men) responded to the web-based survey used in that research. Approximately 19% of the women reported experiencing completed or attempted "sexual assault" as that term was defined "since entering college." More precisely, 12.6% reported attempted sexual assault and 13.7% reported completed sexual assault (with some reporting both). The survey made a distinction between completed sexual assault by physical force and sexual assault while in an incapacitated state. About 4.7% of

---

[11] The Sexual Victimization of College Women at 16, Ex. 5.

[12] Note that these figures do not include "attempted [non-penetration] sexual coercion," "attempted [non-penetration] sexual contact with force or threat of force," or "attempted [non-penetration] sexual contact without force," which came in at 1.3% (1.73% annualized), 2.0% (2.67% annualized) and 3.0% (4% annualized) respectively. The *2012 Survey* defined "unwanted sexual contact" to include "intentional sexual contacts that were against your will or occurred when you did not or could not consent where someone ... [s]exually touched you (e.g., intentional touching of genitalia, breasts, or buttocks or made you sexually touch them?," but it did not included attempted touching of this kind. By contrast, it included both completed and attempted penetration offenses. In keeping with that definition, the proper comparisons to the statistics in *The Sexual Victimization of College Women* should focus on completed non-penetration offenses and not attempted ones.

[13] Christopher P. Krebs, Christine H. Lindquist, Tara D. Warner, Bonnie S. Fisher & Sandra L. Martin, The Campus Sexual Assault (CSA) Study: Final Report, National Institute of Justice, U.S. Department of Justice xiii, Figure 1 (Oct. 2007).

women respondents reported they had experienced the former and 11.1% reported the latter (again with some reporting both). For rape in particular, the figures were 3.4% (physical force) and 8.5% (incapacitated state). There were no figures for attempted rape in particular.

Since the survey questions asked about events that occurred since the respondent had entered college and the *2012 Survey* asked only about the past 12 months, the results would not be directly comparable even if the questions had been otherwise identical. A senior taking the college survey would be responding for an almost four-year period and not for 12 months. Even so, a rough, back-of-the-envelope calculation demonstrates that, if anything, it is college and universities that look bad in comparison, not the military. The women who responded to the college survey were roughly equally distributed among the freshman, sophomore, junior and senior classes, and the survey was administered in the winter. The average respondent had thus been in college approximately two years (with summer vacations presumably off). Yet the differences in reported rates of completed rape, attempted rape, sexual assault and attempted sexual assault were much too large to be explained solely by the difference in time periods covered. While the comparison is imperfect, the military comes off looking somewhat better— and certainly no worse—than colleges and universities.

So why did *The New York Times* recently call sexual assault in the military "rampant" and attribute it to "the military's entrenched culture of sexual violence"?[14] Why did lawmakers on Capitol Hill hurl "hours of uncomfortable, sometimes withering questions" to the uniformed chiefs of the Services "about the epidemic of sexual assaults?"[15] And why did one member of the Senate "nearly shout" as she addressed the Secretary of the Air Force, telling him that the problem was "undermining the credibility of the greatest military force in the world"?[16]

Well, relative to the population at large, it may be fair to call the military's rate of sexual assault high. Relative to the rates of sexual assault in nursing homes, it is almost certainly extremely high. But the proper comparison is to institutions with disproportionately large numbers of

---

[14] See Editorial, The Military's Sexual Assault Crisis, N. Y. Times (May 7, 2013). See also Editorial, Military Sexual Assault Epidemic Calls for Major Reforms, San Jose Mercury News (June 6, 2013)(accusing military leaders of "archaic ignorance" and demanding "zero tolerance" of unwanted sexual contact); Editorial, Next Steps on Military Sexual Assaults, N. Y. Times (April 28, 2013)(stating that "the Pentagon has nothing less than a sexual assault crisis on its hands"); Editorial, The Military's Approach to Sexual Assault Has to Change, Wash. Post (May 9, 2013)(alleging that "a culture of impunity" exists in the military with regard to sexual assault).

[15] Craig Whitlock, Lawmakers Demand Crackdown on Sex Assault in the U.S. Military, Wash. Post (June 5, 2013).

[16] Jennifer Steinhauer, Sexual Assaults in Military Raise Alarm in Washington, N. Y. Times (May 7, 2013)("The report quickly caught fire on Capitol Hill, where women on the Senate Armed Services Committee expressed outrage at two Air Force officers who suggested that they were making progress in ending the problem in their branch.").

young adults, and when that comparison is made, the *Times'* indictment and Congressional criticisms seem quite unfair.

To be sure, the comparison between colleges and universities and the military cannot be made with precision. The median Service member is somewhat older than the median college or university student. The surveys were administered in different ways and at different times. The questions asked were also different. Although all the surveys seemed designed to yield high sexual assault rates (or "unwanted sexual contact" in the case of the military survey), the two reports funded by the National Institute for Justice were not done in ways that would create a systematic bias toward inflating the college and university numbers relative to the military numbers. With all those caveats, the assumption that the military is a uniquely dangerous place for sexual assault victims is at the very least subject to the Scottish verdict: *Not proven*. Indeed, what little evidence there is suggests that it is colleges and universities that are worse and not the military.[17]

For what it is worth, in 2002, Service women and men seemed to agree that the military is not worse than the rest of American society on this broad issue—although the specific question referred to "sexual harassment" rather than "sexual assault." Survey respondents were asked, "Do you think sexual harassment is more of a problem *inside* the military or more of a problem *outside* the military?"[18] The proportion who considered sexual harassment to be worse inside the military was really quite small for both women and men. For men, 52% said it is more of a problem outside, 10% inside and 39% same. For women, 28% said more of a problem outside, 17% inside, and 54% same.[19] All of this makes it very difficult to explain the overwhelming

---

[17] The notion that the military's entrenched culture of sexual violence" plays a special role in the military's rates of "unwanted sexual contact" was dealt another blow when the records of the military service academies were compared to those of colleges and universities more generally. Sarah Jane Brubaker, Sexual Assault Prevalence, Reporting and Policies: Comparing College and University Campuses and Military Service Academies, 22 Security J. 56, 70 (2009)("Overall, it seems that the prevalence of sexual assault, barriers and necessary improvements to policies and training around prevention and response are more similar than different at military service academies and on college and university campuses.").

[18] See Armed Forces 2002 Sexual Harassment Survey at Appendix A-16 (Question 84).

[19] Armed Forces 2002 Sexual Harassment Survey at 72, Table 7.7. It should be noted, however, that when looking at junior enlisted (E1 - E4) women in particular, the belief that sexual harassment is worse in the military rises to 23%.

The body of this report notes that "According to [the *2012 Survey*], of the 67 percent of female service members who did not report unwanted sexual contact they said they experienced to military authorities, 48 percent indicated that they did not report the unwanted sexual contact because the incidents were not serious enough to report." My colleague Commissioner Kladney argues that this sentence is misleading because the study it cites uses the word "important" instead of "serious." Draft Statement of Commissioner Kladney at 3-4. I have no objection to changing "serious" to "important," nor to (as my colleague proposes) also citing other reasons women gave to researchers for not reporting assaults. But I am baffled by his claim that the report's paraphrase is misleading. I am

(cont'd)

tendency of the media to describe the situation in the military as a unique problem. For reasons that are not explained in the later surveys, this question was later dropped.

Of course, the fact that the military's record on sexual assault may be better than that of colleges and universities is not an endorsement. It means neither that there was never a problem nor that the problem is now being adequately addressed. Further, it does not mean that members of the military should not be held to a higher standard. The comparison to colleges and universities is intended simply to give the reader a sense of proportion as well as a sense of the role that age demographics may play in the situation.

B.   Is the Military's Sexual Assault Rate Increasing?

The common assumption behind the publicity surrounding this issue is that the *2012 Survey* proves that rates of sexual assault have skyrocketed over the last few years.[20] This is also a highly dubious assumption. Nothing in the last few years would account for such a change. If the military has an "entrenched culture of sexual violence" as *the New York Times* has alleged, it must have had that culture in 2010 too. That is why they call it "entrenched." The size of the military is roughly comparable to what it was in 2010. Any changes in the way it deals with

---

(cont'd from previous page)

hard-pressed to think of a case of sexual assault that would ordinarily be classified as important but not serious or vice versa.

One point that needs to be made is that the answers to the survey question about why a female service member did not report an incident must be read together, not in isolation. For example, 50% answered that they "did not think anything would be done" if they reported a particular incident. Read in isolation, this sounds very troubling—and it might well be very troubling. But since survey respondents were permitted to check multiple answers, presumably there was overlap between the 48% who thought their incident "was not important enough to report" and the 50% who "did not think anything would be done." In these cases the female service member may well have agreed that nothing should be done (and if we knew the facts we might agree too). The number who "did not think anything would be done" and thought something *should* be done could be as low as 2%. Similarly, many of those who responded that they thought they "would be labeled as a troublemaker" presumably also responded that their incident "was not important enough to report." Labeling a female Service member "a troublemaker" when she reports an incident that she herself regards as "not important enough to report" is quite a lot different from labeling her "a troublemaker" for reporting an incident that she does regard as "important enough to report." These incidents can range from forcible rape to a well-meaning, but oafish pat on the bottom. When the same Service men who was risking his life to protect yours on a Monday oafishly pats you on the bottom after he's had a beer on a Tuesday, the better response may be a stern look (or to let it go entirely) rather than file a formal complaint to one's commanding officer, who is busy trying ensure everyone's survival. Service women know this. We all know this with regard to the little transgressions that befall us in the course of life. But it doesn't always come through clearly in surveys.

[20] See, e.g., Patrick J. Murphy, Why Senator Gillibrand Is Right About Military Sexual Assault, msnbc.com (June 17, 2013)(calling the sexual assault problem "a cancer on the military" and reporting a 34% increase in assaults from 2010); Associated Press, Sexual Assault a Growing Epidemic in the U.S. Military, Pentagon Documents Show, N.Y. Daily News (May 7, 2013)("Sexual assaults in the military are a growing epidemic across the services and thousands of victims are still unwilling to come forward despite a slew of new oversight and assistance programs, according to Pentagon documents.").

sexual assault are in the direction of getting tougher and providing more training. But even there, the changes are merely in degree. The military has been moving towards tougher and tougher policies on sexual assault for the past two decades.

But let's begin where the evidence is clearest. Judged over the last 25 years rather than the last few years, the military has definitely (although given the exigencies of war not always consistently) improved its record on sexual assault.

In 1988, the Department of Defense conducted the survey that produced the first baseline data on sexual assault. On that occasion, Service members were asked whether they have "ever" experienced various sorts of uninvited and unwanted sexual attention from someone at work while serving in the active-duty military. Among the kinds of attention inquired into were the categories of "Actual or attempted rape or sexual assault" and "Unwanted, uninvited touching, leaning over, cornering, pinching or brushing against of a deliberately sexual nature." Neither category was defined further.

Seven years later, in 1995, a survey asking these identical questions (among others) was undertaken.[21] The results showed a substantial decline in the problem from 1988 to 1995:

	1988	1995
"Actual or attempted rape or Sexual Assault"		
Women	5	4
Men	<0.5	<0.5
"Unwanted, uninvited toughing, leaning over, cornering, pinching or brushing against of a deliberately sexual nature"		
Women	38	29
Men	9	6

At the same time as this 1995 survey (1995 Form A), the Department of Defense introduced a second 133-question survey question (1995 Form B), which was somewhat more elaborate and administered to a different sample of active-duty Service members. Among other things, it asked whether anyone in the last 12 months "Had sex with you without your consent or against your will" or "Attempted to have sex with you without your consent or against your will, but was unsuccessful" whether on or off duty. These two questions were combined into one category entitled "Sexual Assault." In addition, survey respondents were asked whether they had experienced in the last 12 months on or off duty "unwanted sexual attention." Such

---

[21] The 56-question 1995 survey was sent to 30,756 persons and generated a 46% response rate. See Appendix A: Form A Questionnaire, DoD, 1995 Sexual Harassment Survey, DMDC Report No. 96-014 (Dec. 1996).

attention consists of situations in which the wrongdoer "Touched you in a way that made you feel uncomfortable," "made unwanted attempts to stroke, fondle, or kiss you," "Made unwanted attempt to establish a romantic relationship with you despite your efforts to discourage it," and "Continued to ask you for dates, drinks, dinner, etc., even though you said 'No.'"[22]

Note that in the category of "unwanted sexual attention" there will be considerable activity that is beyond the scope of this report because it does not involve physical contact. But it does not include whistling or leering, which were included in a different category. Note also that in the category of "sexual assault" as used in this 1995 survey (unlike the *2012 Survey's* use of the term "unwanted sexual contact") there was apparently the intent to include only penetration and attempted penetration offenses.

An identical set of questions were included in a 90-question survey conducted in connection with the *Armed Forces 2002 Sexual Harassment Survey* ("2002 Survey").[23] A comparison between the 1995 and the 2002 results again shows substantial improvement.

	1995	2002	2006
"Sexual Assault"[24]			
Women	6.2	2.7	5.1
Men	1.2	0.6	2.2
"Unwanted Sexual Attention"[25]			
Women	42	27	n/a
Men	8	5	n/a

None of this should be surprising. During the years between 1988 and 2002, crime rates were declining generally nationwide.[26] In addition, the issue of sexual assault and sexual harassment received massive attention in the media and elsewhere. The military conducted training programs on the issue. If rates of sexual assault and sexual harassment had not declined, it would have been remarkable.[27] While the plasticity of human conduct is sometimes overestimated, it is a mistake to underestimate it too.

---

[22] 1995 Sexual Harassment Survey at Appendix B (Form B Question 71 j, n, q, r, w, & x).

[23] See Appendix A, Form 2002GB, Armed Forces 2002 Sexual Harassment Survey, DMDC Rep. No. 2003-026 (November 2003).

[24] See 2006 Gender Relations Survey of Active Duty Members at 16, Figure 2.

[25] See *2002 Survey* at 12, Figure 3.2 (includes Coast Guard).

[26] Part of the reason for this decline is probably the nation's increasing median age of Americans. On the other hand, the military's median age may not have not changed as fast as the country's; indeed it is likely that it did not. It is thus unclear whether one should have expected criminal misconduct to fall in the military as quickly or at all.

[27] It would have been remarkable, but not impossible. For example, when a difficult-to-define variety of misconduct becomes the subject of considerable attention, reported rates of misconduct may climb even though

(cont'd)

The *2006 Gender Relations Survey of Active Duty Members* ("*2006 Study*") was reconfigured substantially, but for continuity's sake, questions about situations in which individuals "attempted to have sex with [the respondent] without [his or her] consent or against [his or her] will], but were not successful" or "had sex with [the respondent] without [his or her] consent or against [his or her] consent" were still included. The results showed a statistically significant uptick in the proportion of women who reported such incidents—5.1%. This was still lower than the 1995 rate (6.2%), which was itself a substantial improvement over 1988 survey responses. It also showed an increase in the rate for men (2.2%) over both the 2002 rate and the 1995 rate.

It should be noted that the *2002 Survey* was undertaken prior to the Iraq War, while the *2006 Survey* was undertaken during the height of the insurgency. There is therefore a plausible story that might (or might not) explain the difference in survey results.[28] But it should also be noted that women respondents in both 2002 and 2006 identified their attackers as being a civilian only in 4% of cases, so the difference cannot be attributed to sexual assaults by non-Service members in a tumultuous war zone.[29] If sexual assault on Service women increased between 2002 and 2006, it is largely because of increases in attacks by fellow Service members.

In addition, the *2006 Survey* introduced the new category of "unwanted sexual contact," intended to be more consistent with the Uniform Code of Military Justice definition.[30] This question was re-administered in 2010 and again in 2012, so there is an opportunity for comparison. The question read:

> In the past 12 months, have you experienced any of the following sexual contacts that were against your will or occurred when you did not or could not consent where someone ...

_____

(cont'd from previous page)

actual misconduct has declined, because victims may not have thought of their experiences as examples of this misconduct in the past. See infra at note 49 and accompanying text.

[28] My point is not that the military was or was not justified in giving sexual assault lower priority in 2006 relative to 2002. It is simply that unlike in 2012 there is at least a plausible explanation for why the rate of sexual assault might have increased. A more plausible explanation for the survey results in 2012 may be simply the random variation one has to expect with survey results.

[29] 2006 Gender Relations Survey of Active Duty Members at 92 (Figure 53).

[30] It was not fully consistent. The definition of "sexual contact" given at Article 120 reads in full: "touching, or causing another person to touch, either directly or through the clothing, the genitalia, anus, groin, breast, inner thigh, or buttocks of any person, with an intent to abuse, humiliate, or degrade any person; or (B) any touching, or causing another person to touch, either directly or through the clothing, any body part of any person, if done with an intent to arouse or gratify the sexual desire of any person." The survey question does not ask whether the person doing the sexual touching had an intent to "abuse, humiliate or degrade any person" or to "arouse or gratify the sexual desire of any person."

- Sexually touched you (e.g. intentional touching of genitalia, breasts, or buttocks) or made you sexually touch them?

- Attempted to make you have sexual intercourse, but was not successful?

- Made you have sexual intercourse?

- Attempted to make you perform of receive oral sex, anal sex, or penetration by a finger or object, but was not successful?

- Made you perform or receive oral sex, anal sex, or penetration by a finger or object?[31]

In 2010, when the question was first re-administered so as to allow comparisons, the rates dropped dramatically for both men and women. The rate of unwanted sexual contact for women victims dropped by an impressive 35%. For men, it dropped by an astonishing 50%. Interestingly, there was no media frenzy when the *2010 Workplace and Gender Relations Survey of Active Duty Members* was released in March of 2011.[32] Good news—especially on a topic like sexual assault in the military—is boring.

Two years later, however, the rate of sexual assault ticked upwards again—from 4.4 to 6.1 for women—but remained more than 10% below the levels in the 2006 administration of the survey. With confidence intervals of plus or minus 0.6%, this increase was statistically significant. The rate for men also increased, but remained 33% below the 2006 rates. This

---

[31] Although the unwanted sexual touching category is arguably rather broad, only 32% of those women who responded positively in 2012 to this question (i.e. 1.95% of total female respondents) answered that the most serious conduct they experienced was unwanted touching only. The rest of those who responded positively reported that they experienced attempted sex or completed sex. This suggested that unwanted sexual touching may be underreported in the survey. It is possible that some women reading the survey questions do not understand the question or do not regard such activity as important enough to report.

On the other hand, the potential for over-reporting also exists and may help explain the data. The category for unwanted attempted sexual intercourse is troubling and can easily be misconstrued by the survey respondent. The world is full of situations in which one individual would like to have sexual intercourse, but the object of his or her desire is unenthusiastic about this idea. Because the question does not make clear that "sexual contact" means actual physical contact, it is possible that some respondents have interpreted it to include cases in which an individual asked them on a date with the obvious intent that this would (one day perhaps) lead to sexual intercourse. One can see how this could be seen as a case in which the hapless individual "attempted to have sexual intercourse, but was not successful." Given that (1) the rate of positive answers to this question is in the single digits, and (2) the rejected suitor scenario is quite common, misinterpretations of this kind would not need to be common to have a substantial effect on the results of the survey. And it might help explain the otherwise difficult-to-explain high ratio of sexual intercourse/attempted sexual intercourse to sexual touching of a lesser nature.

[32] My special assistant ran a Nexis database search for any evidence of media coverage when the 2010 survey was released in 2011. She found nothing.

increase, however, was not statistically significant, and therefore can be left aside until further evidence is gathered.

	2006	2010	2012
Unwanted Sexual Contact			
Women	6.8	4.4	6.1
Men	1.8	0.9	1.2

The reaction to *2012 Survey* results was stronger than the evidence justified. The military hadn't changed in any way that would make it likely that sexual assault would increase between 2010 and 2012. To the contrary, it had continued to expand its sexual assault training programs. In 2012, 96% of women and 97% of men reported that they had received sexual assault training in the last 12 months. For women, that was 7 percentage points higher than 2006 and 3 percentage points higher than 2010. For men, that was 8 percentage points higher than 2006 and 4 percentage points higher than 2010. Unless these training programs were actually encouraging sexual assault, which doesn't seem likely, it makes sense to look for problems in data gathering and processing before one jumps to the conclusion that sexual assault rates are getting worse.

One possibility is that sexual assault training is having an effect on how survey respondents conceptualize conduct rather than on the conduct itself. For example, at our briefing, at least one witness testified that service members reported to her that they had been told in sexual assault training that a female service member is incapable of consenting to sexual intercourse after having only one drink. If true and if it is only recently that this kind of statement became common in sexual assault training, that might motivate survey respondents to identify conduct that they previously would not have identified as sexual intercourse to which the respondent "could not consent." I am not convinced that this factor alone has had a large effect on the *2012 Survey* results, but there is evidence that it could have had a small one.[33]

Another possibility is that the response rate to the *2012 Survey* was the lowest among surveys for which I found data. The 2012 weighted response rate was only 24%. In contrast, past surveys had a 31% (excluding Coast Guard 2010), a 32% (including Coast Guard 2010), a 30% (2006), a 36% (2002), a 46% (1995 Form A), and a 58% (1995 Form B) weighted response rate.[34] Surveys of this kind depend for their accuracy upon the respondents being a random

---

[33] If one in a hundred female survey respondents changed her response on account of this training, it would have a profound effect on the survey results. Even one in a thousand would have a noticeable effect. For an example of an individual who claimed to have recognized that she had been the victim of aggravated sexual assault only after she received training, see infra at note 49 and accompanying text.

[34] A hypothetical may help to make it clear why this matters. Suppose you have a hundred persons in a target population, three of whom have been assaulted. All are given the opportunity to participate in a survey about assault, and, not surprisingly, the three victims are especially willing to take part, since they know from experience that the problem of assault is serious. If 33% of the target population responds, including the three victims, it will

(cont'd)

sample of the target population. But they seldom actually are, since (among other things) the individuals who take the time to respond to a voluntary survey often do so because they find the survey's subject matter more interesting than the individuals who did not take the time. Even so, so long as the response rates are stable across different administrations of the survey, useful comparisons can be made.[35] Here, however, the response rate was not stable. Rather, they are declining over time. It is entirely possible that some of the seeming increase in the sexual assault rate came from the fact that members of the target population who did not experience sexual assault were less likely to participate in 2012.

A third possibility is simple bad luck in sampling. Bear in mind that even expertly crafted surveys with a genuinely random sample may produce inaccurate results about 5% of the time. The 2010 results may well have been too good to be true—indeed my guess is that they were. If the 2010 result was somewhat off the mark, it was all but inevitable that the results in 2012 would look bad in comparison—even though the 2012 results were still a 10% improvement over the results of the next previous survey in 2006. Alternatively the *2012 Survey* results may have overstated the current level of unwanted sexual contact. The confidence intervals for the 6.1% result tell us that there is no particular reason that 6.1% should be regarded as the precise rate of sexual assault; it could just as easily be anywhere between 5.5% and 6.7 %. But those intervals are calculated to the standard 95% level of confidence. What about the other 5%? If the results are off 5% of the time (or 1 time in 20), this may be one of those times.[36]

No careful statistician would regard the 2012 uptick as a reason to hit the panic button especially in the absence of any evidence that the military took sexual assault less seriously in 2012 than it did in 2010.

(cont'd from previous page)

appear as if 9% of the target population has been sexually assaulted. If the next year nothing has changed, but 25% of the target population responds, including the three victims, it will appear as if 12% of the target population has been assaulted. It will thus seem as if there has been a 33% increase in sexual assaults. In fact, however, the rate of victimization will have been 3% the whole time.

[35] Commentators have assumed that the results of these surveys can generally be extrapolated to determine the overall number of unwanted sexual contacts in the military (and hence the proportion of unwanted sexual contacts that get reported to the authorities). This is a highly dubious assumption. Those who have been victimized by unwanted sexual contact are probably more likely to respond to such a survey. See supra note 32.

[36] The margin of error for the 2010 rate of sexual assault among women respondents appears to be at least 0.3%. See 2010 Survey at 10. Figure 2 on page 10 of the 2010 survey states, "Margins of error range from + or – 0.3 to + or – 1.0." The specific margin of error for the rate of unwanted sexual assault is illustrated in the graph and appears to be at or near the lowest end of that range.

C. Does the Military Justice System Have a Lower Rate of Sexual Assault Prosecution than Civilian Systems?

The answer to this question is that we don't know for sure, but insofar as we have evidence, it appears that the military's rates of prosecution for rape and aggravated sexual assault are higher than those of civilian jurisdictions, not lower, maybe even much higher. This is, of course, precisely the opposite of what those connected with the current frenzy over this issue seem to be assuming. But that is often what happens during frenzies: Actual evidence gets disregarded.

It would be nice to have precise data on this. But it is very hard to make comparisons; the two criminal justice systems are very different. In the military, the commanding officer is in some ways the "work supervisor" to his or her subordinates. But the commanding officer is also central to the criminal justice system. That makes a military complaint over unwanted sexual contact a curious hybrid between a workplace complaint and a criminal complaint. The investigative procedures are different from the criminal justice system outside the military. Just about everything is different. And even if they were the same, data on prosecution rates in civilian jurisdictions are very hard to come by.

As Lt. Gen. Dana Chipman, Judge Advocate General of the Army, put it to the Commission in his testimony:

> There is no comparable civilian data on overall prosecution rates for sexual assaults. The military justice system, through the Annual Report to Congress, is simply the most transparent and scrutinized system in the country. Civilian jurisdictions are not required to report on the circumstances, demographic data and disposition of every report of sexual assault. Some members of the public and media have confused reported "clearance rates" for civilian prosecution rates. ... For purposes of the [Uniform Crime Reports], an allegation is considered cleared when there is an arrest and a presentation for charging or when there is probable cause to identify an offender, but no arrest.[37]

Additionally, the FBI has only recently come to define rape as broadly as the military does, making comparisons even more difficult. As Lt. Gen. Chipman wrote, "Prior to 2012, the [Uniform Crime Reports] definition of rape, unchanged since 1927, was narrowly defined as forcible penetration of the vagina by the penis." [or put Id. in footnote]This definition leaves out "rapes where the victim was incapacitated by drugs or alcohol, sleeping victims, male victims or penetration with an object or finger."[38]

---

[37] Written Submission of Lieutenant General Dana K. Chipman, The Judge Advocate General, United States Army, U.S. Commission on Civil Rights 12-13 (January 13, 2013).

[38] *Id.* at 13.

The Commission must rely on a few scraps of hard information that appear to show that the military prosecutes sexual assault *more aggressively* than civilian authorities. One useful comparison supported by data shows that the military is more likely to prosecute rape than civilian authorities. For rape allegations, in cases in which there was a completed disposition and jurisdiction over the offender, the Army had a prosecution rate of 55% in its Fiscal Year 2011 Annual Report to Congress. In contrast, for those rape allegations that occurred off-post in which the civilian jurisdiction chose to take the lead in handling, the prosecution rate was only 11%. Similarly, for "aggravated sexual assault" in the sense of sexual penetration of a sleeping, intoxicated or otherwise incapacitated victim, the Army reported a rate of prosecution of 62% in its Fiscal Year 2011 Annual Report to Congress. The civilian prosecution rate for off-post aggravated sexual assault over which civilian authorities elected to take the lead was 0%.[39]

This is consistent with the finding by the Congressional Defense Task Force on Sexual Assault in the Military, which examined the prosecution of sexual assault allegations and stated as far back as 2009 that "the military services prosecute many types of sexual assault cases that civilian prosecutors choose not to pursue."[40] Nevertheless, Department of Justice figures indicate that military commanders convened about 70% more courts martial for rape or aggravated sexual assault allegations in 2010 than they did in 2009.[41] When Congress and the media demand more prosecutions, they get them.

The 70% increase is extraordinary and lends credence to the considerable anecdotal evidence of over-prosecution that the Commission chose not to pursue. For example, two years ago, in *Military's Newly-Aggressive Rape Prosecution Has Pitfalls*, McClatchy Newspapers interviewed several former and present military attorneys and others involved in the military justice system who voiced the opinion that the military prosecution rates were not just higher than civilian prosecution rates, but that they were unfairly high.[42] Among those who

---

[39] These statistics were drawn to my attention by a letter dated May 9, 2013, from Lt. Gen. Dana K. Chipman to Commissioner Todd Gaziano in response to an inquiry made by Commissioner Gaziano at the briefing.

[40] Department of Defense, Report of the Defense Task Forces on Sexual Assault in the Military Services, Dec. 2009, at 37[???]. Available at http://www.sapr.mil/public/docs/research/DTFSAMS-Rept_Dec09.pdf.

[41] See Michael Doyle & Marisa Taylor, Military Sexual-Assault Case Triggers Political Furor, McClatchy Newspapers (Mar. 8, 2013). The McClatchy review of documents from 68 sexual assault cases at Georgia's Fort Benning, North Carolina's Camp Lejeune, California's Camp Pendleton and several other bases nationwide found commanding officers sometimes using their prosecutorial discretion to proceed with questionable cases. In 30 of the 68 cases reviewed, the defendants were acquitted or were found guilty only of lesser charges. In a number of the acquittals McClatchy reviewed, commanding officers had proceeded with prosecution despite explicit objections or serious questions raised by investigating officers.

[42] Marisa Taylor & Chris Adams, Military's Newly-Aggressive Rape Prosecution Has Pitfalls, McClatchy Newspapers (Nov. 28, 2011).

commented was Michael Waddington, a former member of the Army JAG Corps and then a defense lawyer handling military cases. "In the media and on Capitol Hill, there's this myth that the military doesn't take sexual assault seriously," he stated. "But the reality is they're charging more and more people with bogus cases just to show that they do take it seriously."

According to the sources quoted in the article, the pressure to prosecute comes from the top. Sadly, this is just what one would expect after watching top military brass under fire at the hearing of the Senate Armed Services Committee on June 4, 2013:

> "Most of the rape cases that I've defended in the military system never would have gone to trial in a civilian system because the prosecutor would say, 'There's no way I'm taking that to trial because I'm not going to get a conviction,'" said Charles Feldmann, a former military and civilian prosecutor who's now a defense attorney.

> "But in the military, the decision-maker is an admiral or a general who is not going to put his career at risk on an iffy rape case by not prosecuting it. It's easy for him to say, 'Prosecute it.' If a jury acquits or convicts, then he can say justice was done either way."

> "If a military commander dismisses a case and there's political backlash, he's going to take some real career heat over that dismissal," Feldmann said.[43]

Two high-profile cases in this year alone demonstrate that high-ranking officers do indeed put their careers on the line when they fail to respond aggressively to sexual assault allegations. On February 26, 2013, Air Force Lt. Gen. Craig Franklin, exercising the authority granted to him under the Uniform Code of Military Justice, overturned the conviction of a service member who had been convicted of aggravated sexual assault.[44] Given that it was Lt. Gen. Franklin's conclusion that guilt had not been proven beyond a reasonable doubt, it was his duty to do what he did. Senators Barbara Boxer and Jeanne Shaheen responded by sending a castigating letter to Secretary of Defense Chuck Hagel—an action that Eugene Fidell, who teaches military law at the Yale Law School, labeled "completely inappropriate." Their letter demonstrated their lack of understanding of the differences between military and civilian criminal procedure and the greater responsibility placed on the commanding officer in the military justice system to ensure that justice is done. Lt. Gen. Franklin was not tampering with the military justice system when he acted as he did. As the commanding officer in charge, he *is* the military justice system—or at least an important part of it. Just as a trial judge must sometimes decline to enter judgment on a jury's verdict, a convening authority must sometimes set aside a finding of guilty

---

[43] *Id.*

[44] Michael Doyle & Marisa Taylor, Military Sexual-Assault Case Triggers Political Furor, McClatchy Newspapers (Mar. 8, 2013).

or change a finding of guilty to a lesser included offense. It was the senators who were exercising their authority inappropriately.

If the Franklin case failed to make it clear to military officers that the failure to prosecute can be hazardous to their careers, the case of Lt. Gen. Susan Helms definitely made the point. Helms, a former astronaut, was nominated by President Obama to be vice commander of the Air Force Space Command. But she had earlier made the decision not to approve the recommended sentence for an individual under her command who had been convicted of aggravated sexual assault. Again, under the military justice system it is the duty of the commanding officer to take such a hands-on approach. The evidence as described in the *Wall Street Journal* that the alleged victim in that case consented to sex was extensive.[45] Senator McCaskill nevertheless put the nomination on "permanent hold," arguing that Helms had "'sent a damaging message to survivors of sexual assault who are seeking justice in the military justice system." It is doubtful that ambitious members of the military will fail to take note of Helms' fate.

---

[45] See James Taranto, Gen. Helms and the Senator's "Hold": An Air Force Commander Exercised Her Discretion in a Sexual-Assault Case. Now Her Career is Blocked by Sen. Claire McCaskill, Why?, Wall St. J. (June 17, 2013). The article described the facts of the case thusly:

> The trial was a he-said/she-said dispute between Capt. Herrera and a female second lieutenant about a drunken October 2009 sexual advance in the back seat of a moving car. The accuser testified that she fell asleep, then awoke to find her pants undone and Capt. Herrera touching her genitals. He testified that she was awake, undid her own pants, and responded to his touching by resting her head on his shoulder.

> Two other officers were present—the designated driver and a front-seat passenger, both lieutenants—but neither noticed the hanky-panky. Thus on the central questions of initiation and consent, it was her word against his.

> On several other disputed points, however, the driver, Lt. Michelle Dickinson, corroborated Capt. Herrera's testimony and contradicted his accuser's.

> Capt. Herrera testified that he and the accuser had flirted earlier in the evening; she denied it. Lt. Dickinson agreed with him. The accuser testified that she had told Lt. Dickinson before getting into the car that she found Capt. Herrera 'kind of creepy' and didn't want to share the back seat with him; Lt. Dickinson testified that she had said no such thing. And the accuser denied ever resting her head on Capt. Herrera's shoulder (although she acknowledged putting it in his lap). Lt. Dickinson testified that at one point during the trip, she looked back and saw the accuser asleep with her head on Capt. Herrera's shoulder.

> In addition, the accuser exchanged text messages with Capt. Herrera after the incident. She initially claimed to have done so only a "couple times" but changed her testimony after logs of the text traffic revealed there were 116 messages, 51 of them sent by her.

I cannot say, of course, whether the Taranto's summary of the facts is fair. But the article certainly raises concerns about whether military officers may regard it as risky to their careers to fail to prosecute and convict those accused of sexual misconduct – even in cases where prosecution and conviction is, in their judgment, inappropriate. This is a topic the Commission could have attempted to shed more light on. See infra at Part D.

Those who are critical of the military's aggressive policy towards sexual assault are not limited to attorneys now working for criminal defendants. But current members of the military JAG Corps are not always comfortable speaking out about the problem. One female Navy prosecutor was quoted in *Military's Newly-Aggressive Rape Prosecution Has Pitfalls*:

> "Because there is this spin-up of 'We have to take cases seriously even though they're crap,' it creates a kind of a climate of blasé attitudes," said one Navy prosecutor, who asked to remain anonymous because she feared retaliation for speaking out.[46]

Of course, defense lawyers and anonymous military prosecutors shouldn't be the last word on whether the pendulum has swung toward over-prosecution—even when their concerns are corroborated by clear examples of inappropriate political pressure and by the limited statistical evidence that exists. That is where the Commission could have done useful research that could have confirmed or refuted the concerns of those quoted in the McClatchy article. But despite prodding from me, the Commission (and its staff) declined to act. See infra at Part D.

To be fair, the staff member who was responsible for the report's first draft was willing to invite two defense attorneys as witnesses to our briefing who could share their experiences with the military's sexual assault prosecution record. Those witnesses echoed the concerns of Waddington, Feldmann, and the anonymous Navy prosecutor. They also sounded the alarm that overzealous prosecution may now be affecting military morale (as well as interfering with the military's ability to prosecute core cases of sexual assault.

For example, Bridget J. Wilson, a criminal defense lawyer specializing in military law and former judge advocate with the California Army National Guard, testified that "[w]hat we have all seen are cases being pursued that would not be in a civilian courtroom":

> The good intention of addressing sexual assault in the military is being buried by a campaign that now lacks credibility in the ranks. There is an increasing perception that the deck is stacked against someone accused of an assault. We speak to those who are told in sexual assault training that if a woman has had a single drink she cannot consent to sex. We have seen commands that fear that if they do not forward every allegation, no matter how dubious, for prosecution that will cost them their careers. When one tries to address the huge problem of binge drinking in the military as a contributing factor to sexual assaults, they are accused of trying to blame the victim.[47]

---

[46] Marisa Taylor & Chris Adams, Military's Newly-Aggressive Rape Prosecution Has Pitfalls, McClatchy Newspapers (Nov. 28, 2011). This was the same Navy prosecutor quoted supra at note 6 and supporting text.

[47] Written Testimony of Bridget J. Wilson at 2 (Jan. 11, 2013).

She further stated:

> The prosecution of sexual assault now is privately being dismissed by many in the armed forces as a political witch hunt, something that will damage the cause of protecting victims for years to come. It will damage the status of women in the institution for years to come. It will give rapists a cover for years to come.[48]

Similarly, Philip D. Cave, a retired Navy prosecutor who now defends military criminal cases, testified that "the perception today, if not the reality, is that a sexual assault case is more likely to go to trial despite unfavorable recommendations from an [investigating officer.]":

> Over the last five to seven years it has been increasingly apparent to an accused going into a sexual assault case that he is presumed guilty, that he must prove his innocence, and that background politics may play an important role in how a case is to be resolved. That more guilty people are convicted and punished could in fact be the right and appropriate result. The greatest fear, especially those in leader or supervision roles is that of being falsely accused.

Written Testimony of Philip D. Cave at 1-2 (Jan.- 11, 2013).

In his testimony before the Commission, Philip Cave recounted several anecdotes, which, if true, almost certainly are already having a profound effect on morale. For example:

> In [Staff Sergeant] Walton's case, the accuser initially denied having sex with him when her commander questioned her.

> After Walton confessed to adultery and urged her to tell the truth, she admitted having an affair with him. At that point, she said in a sworn statement that she and Walton had picked up "protection" before heading to a hotel. She denied drinking any alcohol.

> Three months later, she changed her account again, saying Walton had plied her with hard liquor before taking her to the hotel. While they were watching TV on the bed, she said, "he all of a sudden rolled on top of me."

> "I don't think I said anything," she said in a statement. "I just remember my clothes coming off and I accepted it was happening."

> The woman said she realized she'd been raped after attending anti-sexual assault classes. She notified the lawyer who was defending her against adultery charges. The woman also told her estranged husband.

---

[48] *Id.*

> When a military lawyer, known as an investigating officer, reviewed her allegations, he recommended that the Marines drop the aggravated sexual assault charge.
>
> Not only had the accuser's story changed, friends said she'd told them the sex had been consensual and that she would do it again because she thought her husband was cheating on her.
>
> The commander nonetheless rebuffed the lawyers' advice, pursuing nine charges against Walton that ranged from aggravated sexual assault to indecent language. Walton's possible fate changed from expulsion from the military to 30 years in prison. . . .[49]
>
> [Although acquitted of aggravated sexual assault, Walton] thinks that the justice system has tilted unfairly in favor of the accuser.
>
> After a two-year ordeal, the Marines convicted him of adultery and sent him to prison for six months. As soon as she made the rape accusation, the service dropped the adultery charge against his accuser. She was promoted, while he received a bad conduct discharge.
>
> After 13 years in the military, Walton has lost his retirement and veteran's benefits, and the ability to attend college for free. And he worries that even an acquittal will be seen as a mark of guilt.[50]

The Walton case answers a question that many people ask when presented with arguments that not everyone accused of sexual assault is guilty: Why would a victim lie? One possible motivation is that in the military adultery can be a criminal offense. A useful way to avoid being punished is to claim that one was raped rather than a willing participant in the illicit affair. At least if the facts of this case as recounted by Cave are accurate the putative victim had originally been charged along with the defendant with adultery. Claiming sexual assault got her off the hook. Strict rules against "retaliating" against those who report sexual assault got her a promotion.

There are other ways in which the military setting can create an unusual incentive to engage in false accusation. Sexual intercourse on a military installation is an offense. If two consenting service members get caught, a false claim that it was non-consensual can help a Service

---

[49] Marisa Taylor & Chris Adams, Military's Newly Aggressive Rape Prosecution Has Pitfalls, McClatchy Newspapers (Nov. 29. 2011), quoted in part in Written Testimony of Philip Cave at 6-8 (Jan. 11, 2013).

[50] *Id.*

member avoid punishment. Back in the days that the military prohibited relations between same-sex partners, claiming sexual assault could be a way to save one's career.[51]

Well-meaning efforts to ensure that no one is deterred from reporting a sexual assault can also create incentives for false reports. The military requires, for example, that a Service member who reports such an incident and who requests a transfer out of her unit must have that request acted upon within 72 hours. Such requests are almost always granted.[52] It is surely a good thing to try to prevent the victim of a sexual assault from being subjected to further humiliation at the hands of her tormentor. But doing so unavoidably increases the likelihood that false accusations will be made when Service members desire a transfer for reasons that may be entirely unrelated to any allegation of criminal conduct. To my knowledge, those who report being victimized in other ways are not granted similar transfer privileges.

Like Feldmann, Wilson and Cave were particularly concerned about pressure from the top for high prosecution rates. Both referred to a series of speeches intended for every non-commissioned officer and officer by General James Amos, Commandant of the Marines, in the spring of 2012. In these speeches, which were given on various Marine Corps bases, Amos demanded the Marines get tough on the perpetrators of sexual assault. *Id.* at 13-15.

"Why have we become so soft?" General Amos asked in his April 19, 2012 speech at Parris Island, South Carolina. According to a newspaper report quoted by Cave, Amos described himself as "very, very disappointed" in court-martial boards that don't expel those who misbehave sexually, and he denounced as "bullshit" claims that many sexual assault allegations amount to second thoughts from individuals who initially consented.[53]

Amos's comments might have been considered improper even in civilian life. Comments that are construed to apply to a pending criminal case by someone in authority over jurors are rare, but such comments are recognized as a problem when they occur. In the military criminal justice system, "unlawful command influence" is a critical issue, which well-trained military leaders are ever-vigilant to avoid. As Commandant of the Marines, Amos is "the boss" for

---

[51] Written Testimony of Bridget J. Wilson at 2 (Jan. 11, 2013).

[52] In 2012, the only year for which data has been collected, the Army granted 86 requests and denied 3. The other branches granted all such requests. See Chapter 3, Section C of this report at 19-20.

[53] Michael Doyle, Tough Talk by Marine Commandant James Amos Complicates Sexual-Assault Cases, McClatchy Newspaper (Sept. 13, 2012), quoted in Written Testimony of Philip D. Cave at 13-14 (Jan. 11, 2013). Strangely, Amos took the position that 80% of the allegations of sexual assault are true. If so, that means 20% are not—which would be considered an extraordinarily large number, even larger than I would have predicted. It would be nice if victims of all crimes came with little haloes over their heads telling law enforcement authorities, "I am telling the truth." But the real world isn't so simple. Sorting out the true from the untrue is important and difficult work. If, as General Amos suggests, 20% of the allegations are untrue, that means 100% of them must be examined very carefully in order to distinguish the guilty 80% from the innocent 20%.

every Marine Corps member involved in investigating and deciding sexual assault cases. As the U.S. Court of Appeals for the Armed Forces has put it, "Undue and unlawful command influence is the carcinoma of the military justice system, and when found, must be surgically eradicated." United States v. Gore, 60 M.J. 178, 184 (C.A.A.F. 2004).

According to Cave, Amos's conduct resulted in at least 20 unlawful command influence challenges, at least of some which resulted in findings that unlawful command influence had indeed occurred.

General Amos's case is not the highest-level case of alleged unlawful command influence to receive attention in recent times. After the briefing, newspapers reported a somewhat similar controversy surrounding President Obama's statements to military officers on sexual assault:

> "The bottom line is: I have no tolerance for this. ... I expect consequences. ... So I don't just want more speeches or awareness programs or training, but ultimately folks look the other way. If we find out somebody's engaging in this, they've got to be held accountable -- prosecuted, stripped of their positions, court-martialed, fired, dishonorably discharged. Period."[54]

According to the *New York Times*, this statement "had an effect he did not intend: muddying legal cases across the country."[55] The article continued:

> In at least a dozen sexual assault cases since the president's remarks at the White House in May, judges and defense lawyers have said that Mr. Obama's words as commander in chief amounted to 'unlawful command influence,' tainting trials as a result. Military law experts said that those cases were only the beginning and that the president's remarks were certain to complicate almost all prosecutions for sexual assault."

In view of all this, the Commission should have been much more careful to explore the possibility of over-prosecution. To be clear, over-prosecution and under-prosecution are not necessarily mutually exclusive possibilities. Over-prosecution may be the norm in some quarters, while under-prosecution dominates in others. But greater effort should have been made to make a genuine contribution to our stock of knowledge on the possibility of widespread over-prosecution.

One more point is worth making here: Some of the talk in the media has centered on the notion that military conviction rates are lower than civilian conviction rates. Under the circumstances as described by Waddington, Feldmann, Wilson, Cave and the anonymous Navy prosecutor,

---

[54] David Jackson, Military Judge Raps Obama for Sexual Assault Comments, USA Today (Aug. 15, 2013).

[55] Jennifer Steinhauer, Remark by Obama Complicates Military Sexual Assault Trials, N. Y. Times, July 13, 2013.

lower conviction rates should surprise no one. If the military's prosecution rates are higher than the prosecution rates of civilian jurisdictions, as the figures supplied by Lt. Gen. Chipman suggest they are, more of the military's cases will result in acquittals. In general, the higher the prosecution rate, the lower the conviction rate. When a jurisdiction decides to increase the proportion of sexual assault cases it prosecutes, it will be adding cases that are somewhat weaker than the cases that were already being prosecuted.

D. Where Should We Go from Here?

In the very first sentence of the joint statement of my colleagues Chairman Castro and Commissioners Achtenberg, Kladney and Yaki, they state that they recognized the "serious and pervasive nature" of sexual assault in the military even before the research for this report began. Alas, that is part of the problem: My colleagues already knew the conclusion they intended to draw. No wonder they resisted efforts to consider the possibility that the military's sexual assault crisis was more a media phenomenon than a real one. It didn't fit the established narrative.

But our job as commissioners is not to follow the narrative established by the media. As then-Senate Majority Leader Lyndon Johnson put it in 1957 when Congress created the Commission, its task is to "gather facts instead of charges." "[I]t can sift out the truth from the fancies; and it can return with recommendations which will be of assistance to reasonable men."[56] I fear we have done a less-than-commendable job at that. The first draft of this report assumed the current crisis atmosphere was justified and was written to highlight accusations that would support the narrative—sometimes in almost apocalyptic terms. The second draft, which was ultimately adopted by the Commission, was a vast improvement over the first (and mainly written by a different team of staff members). It attempts to be even-handed and in many respects succeeds in doing so. But it came too late to explore issues in a way that could have made a genuine contribution to the controversy. It fails to "sift out the truth from the fancies."[57] It does have the virtue, however, of bringing information on the controversy into a single report.

I believe that, rather than complaining that the college and university surveys on sexual assault and the military surveys on "unwanted sexual contact" are not comparable, see supra at note 9, the Commission could have undertaken to survey college and university students using the questions used in the 2012 Survey. Such an approach would have eliminated concerns over

---

[56] 103 Cong. Rec. 13,897 (1957) (statement of Sen. Lyndon Johnson).

[57] I ultimately voted against this report as did my colleague Commissioner Peter Kirsanow. Commissioner Todd Gaziano abstained and the rest of the members of the Commission voted in favor. U.S. Commission on Civil Rights, Transcript of Business Meeting at 70 (July 12, 2013).

comparability. This is the kind of project our budget is for and we should have used it. Unless the President or members of Congress specifically request us to conduct such a survey now, it is probably too late for the Commission. Perhaps other researchers will exercise more initiative.

On the question of whether the military under- or over-prosecutes sexual assault cases relative to civilian jurisdictions, it would have been useful to assemble a committee of experienced civilian prosecutors and give them the files on a sample of the sexual assault complaints that have been handled over the last few years. Included in the sample would have been a significant number of complaints that were handled by civilian authorities as a control. Files would have been sanitized to the extent possible so that committee members would be able to exercise their judgment without knowing whether the case was initially handled by the military or by civilian authorities or what its disposition had been. These experts could then have told us which of these cases they would have pursued and which they would not have (or ranked them in terms of prosecutorial priority). The perception being fueled by the media is that the military is lax relative to civilian authorities. Someone needs to get to the bottom of that issue, and I am sorry that the Commission decided not to be that someone.[58]

The purpose of this exercise would not have been to suggest that the military should or should not be somewhat more aggressive in prosecuting forcible rape or other sexual assaults than civilian jurisdictions. It would have been to determine whether the military is in fact more aggressive. The current public perception is that the military is less aggressive. Public policy should not be fashioned on myth and false assumption.

A third area the Commission could have helped clarify centers on unlawful command influence and improper political pressure. As discussed in Section C, Feldmann, Wilson and Cave have expressed concern that commanding officers and others involved in the military system of criminal justice are being subjected to inappropriate pressure from higher ups. On this issue it is important to recognize that even the perception that one's career will suffer if one fails to prosecute a flimsy accusation of sexual assault is a problem for the military criminal justice system (just as even the perception that sexual assault is rampant is a problem for recruitment and mission readiness). Confidential surveys could have shed some light on whether officers view themselves as under pressure to refer alleged sexual assault cases for court martial, whether they view the failure to order the prosecution of an alleged sexual assault perpetrator to be risky to their careers and indeed whether they were aware of high-profile cases like General

---

[58] A less ambitious proposal of mine was to conduct a confidential survey of military prosecutors and defense attorneys to find out whether attorneys like Waddington, Feldmann, Wilson, Cave and the anonymous Navy prosecutor quoted in the McClatchy article were representative of JAG Corps sentiment or not. The Commission and its staff were uninterested in this too.

Franklin's and General Helms's. We dropped the ball on this. I hope somebody else picks it up.[59]

One of the most important aspects of the sexual assault issue is the way in which it affects the morale of ordinary service members. On the one hand, it is certainly true that rampant sexual assault (or even the perception of rampant sexual assault) can greatly harm the morale and mission readiness of the military. But the other hand deserves some thought as well: Does a take-no-prisoners war on sexual assault (or even the perception that such a war is taking place) affect morale and mission readiness too? If, as Bridget J. Wilson testified before the Commission, there is "an increasing perception that the deck is stacked against someone accused of an assault," then there is trouble ahead. If joining the military means that an individual might be unfairly punished for a crime he did not commit, recruitment will almost certainly suffer.

Certainly some of the anecdotes recounted to the Commission about individual prosecutions would be enough to dampen the enthusiasm for a military career of a potential recruit. Philip Cave's discussion of Staff Sergeant Walton, supra at Part C, is a good example. After spending two years of his life defending himself against what appears to be an entirely false charge of rape ("aggravated sexual assault" in the military's parlance), serving six months in prison for adultery, being expelled from the army after 13 years of service and losing his retirement and veteran's benefits, Walton's life was devastated. "A lot of people aren't going to like me because I made a stupid decision and I cheated on my wife," he said. "But I don't deserve to be seen as a rapist."[60]

Stories like this get around. The accused's friends and family will know. And their friends and family will know. Walton's story ended up in the newspaper, and so have some others.[61] Somewhere there may be a high school student who is re-considering his ambition to join the Army. Maybe he is thinking that serving one's country is not such a noble thing after all. Maybe he ought to take his Uncle Herbert's advice and become a Certified Public Accountant.

---

[59] To be fair, I failed to propose this particular survey (of commanding officers) in the early stages of the Commission's investigation. I just did not think of it. At the time I was not as familiar as I am now with how the military criminal justice system works. As a part-time federal official, I can't think of everything—or at least I don't. By the time I figured it out, I had become convinced that neither the Commission nor its staff would be receptive to this research proposal.

[60] Marisa Taylor & Chris Adams, Military's Newly Aggressive Rape Prosecution Has Pitfalls, McClatchy Newspapers (Nov. 29, 2011), quoted in part in Written Testimony of Philip Cave at 6-8 (Jan. 11, 2013).

[61] Another recent example of alleged over-prosecution to make the newspapers is the story of Trent Cromartie. James Taranto, A Strange Sort of Justice at West Point: Trent Cromartie was Cleared of Sexual Assault Charges, But the Cadet was Kicked Out of School Anyway, Wall St. J. (July 26, 2013).

After all, accounting pays better. And the kind of mistake made by Staff Sergeant Walton doesn't get a C.P.A. accused of rape or sent to prison for six months.

All this suggests an additional avenue for survey research. Do ordinary Service men and women worry about being falsely accused of sexual misconduct? Have they heard about Walton's case? Have they heard about other cases in which the military has treated someone accused of sexual assault unfairly? Do they believe that they would be treated fairly if they were falsely accused of sexual assault? Do they believe the military's current approach to sexual assault strikes the right balance between the interests of the accuser and the accused?

This would have been a useful project for the Commission.[62] But it is also something the military could do itself—at least if its officers didn't have to fear incurring the wrath of Congress for doing so. The 2012 Survey (as well as its numerous previous sexual assault surveys) asked questions designed to elicit whether the Service members have been victimized by sexual assault. But it did not ask questions designed to elicit whether the campaign to prevent sexual assault "now lacks credibility in the ranks" or whether there is "an increasing perception that the deck is stacked against someone accused of an assault."

The more candid advocates of stricter military enforcement of laws against sexual assault sometimes admit that their project is to hold the military to a higher standard of conduct and not to simply to bring the military up to civilian standards.[63] In the abstract, I have no objection to this (although if that is what is intended here we need to be upfront about that and not deceive others into believing in a dubious sexual assault epidemic or in a supposed failure of military leaders to prosecute sexual misconduct). If men and women wish to don the uniform of the United States Army, Navy, Air Force or Marines, they must understand that more will be expected of them than from civilians.

Of course, in some ways the military has long held its members to a higher standard of sexual conduct than civilians. For example, Service members can be and sometimes are sent to prison

---

[62] Indeed, I suggested it on several occasions to the Commission staff member originally in charge of the report's first draft. I also pushed my Commission colleagues in business meetings to try to adopt a strategy for uncovering new facts, but was again unsuccessful. See U.S. Commission on Civil Rights, Transcript of Nov. 9, 2012 Business Meeting at 11-16.

[63] My colleague Commissioner Kladney may be among them. In the copy of his Draft Statement provided to me, he did not quibble with my statistical comparisons, but seems inclined to dismiss the comparison as inapt. Perhaps oddly, Commissioner Kladney cites a paragraph of expert testimony presented to the Commission by Dr. David Lisak, which is intended to prove that my comparison is off base: "Every society on this planet has a serious problem with sexual violence, and every major institution within our society has a serious problem. In particular, any community or institution, like the military or any university, that brings together young people in the age range of 18-24, will have an acute problem with sexual violence. That's the age range among adults of maximum risk for sexual assault." I agree with Dr. Lisak's comments. I think that they help illuminate why my chosen comparison is useful and why comparisons to older populations might be less useful.

for adultery under Article 134 of the Uniform Code of Military Justice, which prohibits conduct that brings discredit on the armed services and conduct that is prejudicial to good order and discipline. See Manual for Courts-Martial Part IV, ¶ 62.c.(2). Article 134 also criminalizes officers' fraternizing with one or more enlisted persons in violation of the custom that officers shall not fraternize with enlisted members on terms of military equality.

If advocates seek to raise the bar still further, that proposal should be scrutinized carefully before action is taken. Such action may have upsides, but it will almost certainly have downsides too. Not everybody will wish to affiliate himself or herself with a military where ordinary interactions between the sexes are fraught with the potential for disastrous misunderstandings. Moreover, we shouldn't be surprised that we are viewed with suspicion by potential recruits when we praise Service members as heroes out of one side of our mouths and then insist that they be held to a higher standard of morality out of the other.

Finally, it is important to add that it is not just issues that don't fit the sexual assault epidemic narrative that the Commission neglected to pursue. Consider, for example, the incendiary claim that rather than prosecute sexual malefactors the military discharges their victims with trumped-up psychiatric diagnoses. The Commission never got to the bottom of this claim. It didn't try. My colleagues assert that there were "credible allegations of institutional retribution and retaliation against [Military Sexual Trauma] victims who report assaults" and that these include allegations that "the military initiates mental health evaluations of [Military Sexual Assault] victims that lead to the misapplication of personality disorder and adjustment disorder diagnoses."[64] But these colleagues—like the media report that was prominently cited in the initial proposal for this project—seem to assume that the allegations must be true and that there is thus no need for further analysis.[65] This is not what Lyndon Johnson had in mind when he said our job is to "gather facts instead of charges" and to "sift out the truth from the fancies."[66] While it is not always possible to conclusively prove or disprove allegations, we ought to have been able to at least make progress.

A finding by the military that a particular person has a personality disorder or an adjustment disorder is not self-refuting. With a military of over a million, some members really will have psychiatric or other problems that prevent them from effectively carrying out their responsibilities. The military has an obligation to discharge such persons rather than allow them to compromise its mission. The fact that a person so discharged might disagree that they in fact have a personality disorder or adjustment disorder is not evidence one way or another of the

---

[64] Draft Democratic Caucus Statement at 4, 10.

[65] David S. Martin, Rape Victims Say Military Labels Them Crazy, CNN, April 14, 2012, available at http://www.cnn.com/2012/04/14/health/military-sexual-assaults-personality-disorder/index.html.

[66] See supra at note 55 and accompanying text.

correctness of the military's action. One would have to expect such a reaction from both those who have been fairly diagnosed and those who have been unfairly diagnosed.

The one item of evidence that initially impressed me was that women are apparently disproportionately likely to be discharged for personality or adjustment disorders. Upon investigating further, however, I learned that women are disproportionately likely to be hospitalized for many of these disorders in civilian life too—most likely because they are more likely to have them. At a minimum, if there is a problem with over-diagnosing personality or adjustment disorders in women, it is not unique to the military.[67] When I brought this information to the attention of the Commission's staff members, to their credit they incorporated it into the report.[68]

The trickiest part of the this aspect of the controversy over sexual assault in the military is that many of the women who argue that they were wrongfully discharged from the military as having a personality disorder or adjustment disorder do in fact claim to suffer from post-traumatic stress disorder today. Put differently, they agree that they have problems, but disagree as to how the problem came about. Their advocates argue that their disorder is the direct result of the sexual assault, rather than the allegation of the sexual assault being the direct result of preexisting psychiatric issues. Suffice it to say these matters are not easily sorted out after the fact. I therefore have more sympathy for the difficulties faced by the Commission in investigating this aspect of the general controversy than I do for the previously discussed aspects.

E. Should Congress Legislate in this Area?

Here's one that I think I can at least partially answer. As every member of the Services knows, when in doubt, hold your fire. Congress should heed that advice in connection with the proposed legislation to reform military criminal justice. Some of these bills are narrowly focused on sexual assault; others sweep more broadly than sexual assault. What they have in

---

[67] Women are more likely to be diagnosed with borderline personality disorder and unipolar depression, both of which may result in the need for military discharge. See Office of Women's Health, U. S. Department of Health and Human Services, Borderline Personality Disorder, available at http://www.womenshealth.gov/mental-health/illnesses/borderline-personality-disorder.html; The World Health Organization, "Gender and women's mental health," available at http://www.who.int/mental_health/prevention/genderwomen/en/. Men, on the other hand, are more likely to be diagnosed as sociopaths, a diagnosis more likely to result in a military prison sentence than in discharge. See National Institutes of Health, "Antisocial personality disorder," available at http://www.nlm.nih.gov/medlineplus/ency/article/000921.htm.Under the circumstances, the fact that women are disproportionately likely to be discharged from the military for personality or adjustment disorders is less telling than it might otherwise appear.

[68] See Report at 36.

common is that the rhetoric in their favor hinges on the supposed sexual assault crisis.[69] There is a lot that needs to be understood before significant changes to military criminal justice are undertaken.

Much has been made of late about the differences between civilian criminal justice and military criminal justice. The two systems are indeed profoundly different. There is no counterpart in civilian life to the military's reliance on commanding officer discretion. But it would be surprising if the two systems were not different. Each evolved over time in response to very different circumstances. In an era when a military unit could be deployed to distant places with at best an unreliable courier service to communicate with higher authorities, the maintenance of good order could depend on the commanding officer's ability to act quickly and decisively to punish crime. One of the hallmarks of the military criminal justice system is therefore the authority it confers on commanding officers.

It is entirely possible that as a result of further improvements in telecommunications that military criminal justice is in need of more tinkering if not another complete overhaul. Here I am in no position to judge and must defer to those who are intimately acquainted both with the military generally and with comparative criminal justice systems. It is also possible, however, that the reasons the military's criminal justice system evolved as it did go beyond issues of communications.[70] The military is a unique institution. The need for commanders to maintain

---

[69] One recommendation proposed in the Democratic Joint Caucus statement reads, "DoD should strengthen the Army's policy of encouraging that the performance evaluation process should appraise commanders' achievement of the goals of the Equal Opportunity and Equal Employment Opportunity programs to require such evaluation, and it should make this tool mandatory for all other Service branches." I declined to support this recommendation in part because it lies outside the scope of this report, which deals only with sexual assault in the military and not with equal opportunity employment practices in the military more generally. I would note, however, that the potential for over-reach here, too, is a problem. In the civilian world, employment legislation requiring equal treatment has sometimes been misinterpreted as a call to make sure that opportunities are meted out in precise proportion to the general population.

[70] In his testimony before the Commission, the Judge Advocate General, Lt. Gen. Dana K. Chipman described the system this way:

> Ultimate authority in our system is vested in the commander for very important reasons. The commander is responsible for all that goes on in a unit—health, welfare, safety, morale, discipline, training and readiness to execute the mission. The commander's ability to punish quickly, visibly, and locally is essential to maintaining discipline in units. The Uniform Code of Military Justice ensures that commanders can maintain good order and discipline in the force.

This unique role of the commander has raised questions in two areas: why do we allow a non-lawyer to make disposition decisions in a criminal justice system? And can a commander improperly influence the military justice process? Our system addresses these concerns through training, the role of the Judge Advocate, and other procedural safeguards. First, the commanders who make these dispositions do not go into this process blindly, nor execute their authority in a vacuum. They are trained in their responsibilities under the Uniform Code of Military Justice from the day that they are commissioned and throughout their careers. Second, commanders have at their disposal judge advocates to provide advice and counsel. Judge Advocates are an integral part of the military justice system, and they serve as command legal advisors, prosecutors, defense counsel, and military judges. Judge

(cont'd)

authority over troops has no counterpart in the rest of society. It is obviously true that the authority conferred on commanding officers is capable of being abused (as all power is capable of being abused). But it may also be true that further limits to the discretion of commanding officers to deal with criminal matters will undermine the ability of those officers to lead. Since my understanding of the American military comes from watching McHale's Navy, Gomer Pyle U.S.M.C., and other television sit-coms of the 1960s, I defer.

The one thing I am quite sure of is that if the military's system of criminal justice needs reform, the reform should not be a mere appendage of the emotionally-charged sexual assault issue. Reform in haste, repent at leisure.

F. ADDENDUM: Should All the Services Have the Same Sexual Assault Policies?

Here is a relatively minor issue that I should nevertheless comment on: Some of my colleagues have made much of my declining to support findings that the services have "inconsistent" policies or "lack uniformity" regarding sexual assault and corresponding recommendations that the services should adopt "consistent" or "uniform" policies.[71] These recommendations called for greater uniformity in policies concerning recruits with past histories of sexual assault; in selection of sexual assault response coordinators and victim advocates; and for a civilian task force to perform an audit that would look for consistency in the disposition and sentencing of cases between services.[72] I voted against all these findings and recommendations as did Vice Chair Thernstrom, Commissioner Kirsanow and Commissioner Gaziano. As a result, they did not pass.

(cont'd from previous page)

advocates are trained to analyze evidence to determine if there are sufficient facts to support allegations, and to make recommendations to commanders on disposition. Third, there are a variety of procedural safeguards that ensure commanders make evidence-based disposition decisions particularly in regard to sexual assault allegations. These include the ability of senior commanders to pull an allegation from a subordinate and the monitoring agencies at each installation such as the Sexual Assault Review Board . The ultimate procedural safeguards are written into the UCMJ in Article 37, which prohibits unlawful command influence, and the oversight authority vested in the civilian judges of the Court of Appeals of the Armed Forces.

[71] See Draft Statement of Commissioner Kladney at 1-2; Draft Democratic Caucus Statement at 9-10, 18; see also Draft Statement of Commissioner Yaki at 1: "It begs the question of whether they also believe that the adjudication of all civil rights in this country should differ on the cultural and geographic differences, or perhaps even state boundaries, where a violation occurred."

Commissioner Yaki's formulation is particularly odd. Laws prohibiting rape and sexual assault do vary from state to state. They don't vary fundamentally, but they do in some of the details. Indeed, no two states have precisely the same criminal code. Even more so, no two police departments have precisely the same procedures for conducting investigations of sexual assault cases. Of course, there are certain commonalities, some of which are mandated in the Constitution and some of which are not. But none of the findings and recommendations that the four conservative members of the Commission voted against had anything remotely to do with ensuring that the military is in compliance with the Constitution.

[72] See Draft of Democratic Caucus Statement at 18.

Perhaps this is a fundamental difference between the political orientations of Chairman Castro and Commissioners Yaki, Achtenberg and Kladney on the one hand and Vice Chair Thernstrom and Commissioners Kirsanow, Gaziano and me on the other. I believe I speak for the four of us when I say that we do not favor uniformity for the sake of uniformity—even for the Uniformed Services. Uniformity reduces productive experimentation; it also ignores genuine differences among the Services. Sometimes a case for uniformity can be convincingly made. But no such case had been made on behalf of our colleagues' findings and recommendations: They were simply a case of uniformity for its own sake.

Allowing the different branches of the military to have different approaches to dealing with the problem of sexual assault will in the long run help all of them to hit the sweet spot. Sometimes, policymakers err on the side of creating policies that are too harsh; sometimes they go wrong by being too lenient. Policies vary along many different axes. In the military sexual assault context, there are some policies that all Americans would find overly draconian or overly permissive. But those are not the policies that are at issue here. A substantial middle ground exists and letting each branch decide how to approach sexual assault within that middle ground makes sense. The branches can then learn from each other which approaches work best.

Moreover, it is hardly obvious that the best approach for one branch is necessarily the best approach for another. Each of the armed services has its own history, traditions, and customs. The Marines, for example, take pride in being the "elite of the elite." The Air Force is the youngest of all the service branches and has a reputation for being "more about brains than about brawn."[73]

These differences in history and culture have historically led each branch to approach recruiting differently. While the Marines used to advertise that they "are looking for a few good men," the Army had a somewhat more approachable slogan—"Today's Army wants to join you." Under the circumstances, the Marines might well want to have tougher recruiting you." Under the circumstances, the Marines might well want to have tougher recruiting standards, perhaps excluding recruits who had been accused of any kind of sexual impropriety in the past. Likewise, services that view themselves as having particularly rigorous disciplinary procedures might wish to punish sexual assault (as well as other offenses) more harshly than those services that have historically been more permissive.

As a civilian law professor, it is difficult for me to fully understand and appreciate these differences. Nor has the rest of the Commission attempted to engage with this complex history

---

[73] Jeremiah Coble, Discerning Differences Between the Military Branches, available at http://jeremiahcoble.wordpress.com/2009/03/09/discerning-differences-between-military-branches/ (last accessed Aug. 15, 2013.)

and figure out whether a one-size-fits-all approach really makes sense here. Without more fully understanding the ramifications of adopting a uniform service-wide sexual assault policy, I could not vote in favor of the proposed findings and recommendations.

Conclusion: There is sufficient evidence to warrant a serious investigation into whether the military has been overzealous rather than lackadaisical in its prosecution of sexual assault allegations. The world is funny that way. All too often things are the opposite of what they appear to be on television. Real people's lives and well-being depend on getting this right. It is our job to find the truth. Why else have an independent commission?

Statement of Commissioner Dave Kladney

Sexual assault within the military first gained national attention with the Navy's 1991 Tailhook convention at Las Vegas.

It took two Inspector General ("IG") investigations to determine the truth of the occurrence. The first investigation conducted by the Navy's IG and the Naval Investigative Service (NIS) was cursory. Soon after their report was released, criticisms were raised about the thoroughness of the investigations, chiefly that they were narrow in scope and were aimed at lower-ranking officers.

The Department of Defense (DoD) IG was subsequently assigned to do an investigation. The DoD IG's report found the earlier investigators failed to interview high-ranking officers, refused to follow-up on allegations of many offenses, and made demeaning comments about women in the military.[1] In the end, several officers—including a couple of admirals--were forced to resign for their actions at Tailhook or for their handling of the subsequent investigation. Some of these officers were however permitted to retire with full military pensions.[2]

Twenty-two years later, there are those who seek to downplay the problem of sexual assault in the military. They look at the number of assaults as proof there is no crisis. One Republican-appointed Commissioner, for instance, has sought to compare the rates of sexual assault on college campuses to those that occur in the military to support a "no crisis" conclusion.[3] This in spite of the expert testimony of Dr. David Lisak before the Commission:

> "Every society on this planet has a serious problem with sexual violence, and every major institution within our society has a serious problem. In particular, any community or institution, like the military or any university, that brings together young people in the age range of 18-24, will have an acute problem with sexual violence. That's the age range among adults of maximum risk for sexual assault."[4]

---

[1] Rear Adm. Duvall M. Williams, Jr., commander of the NIS and the officer who most directly oversaw the initial investigation, repeatedly expressed a desire to end the probe and on one occasion he told Assistant Secretary of the Navy, Barbara S. Pope, words to the effect that "a lot of female Navy pilots are go-go dancers, topless dancers or hookers." Melissa Healy, *Pentagon Blasts Tailhook Probe, Two Admirals Resign,* L.A. TIMES, Sept. 25, 1992

[2] Id.; John Cushman, *Adm. Frank B. Kelso Dies at 79; Tied To Tailhook Scandal,* N.Y. TIMES, June 28, 2013.

[3] Gail Heriot, *Harassing The Military; There Is No Sexual Assault Crisis,* THE WEEKLY STANDARD, July 8, 2013. If Commissioner Heriot would like to have the Commission on Civil Rights take a look at the situation with respect to sexual assault on campuses I would certainly support such an investigation. I hope she does.

[4] Testimony of Dr. David Lisak before the USCCR on January 11, 2013, Transcript p.102; l.14-22.

Perhaps, some believe there is an acceptable number of sexual assaults in any given group until a "crisis" is reached. This Commissioner does not believe that; nor do I believe the current criminal procedures used by the military offer adequate protection for the accused, for the alleged victims, or for the military itself.

The reason a crisis does exist is that sexual assault is not an arm's-length criminal transaction. It is up close, personal with devastating results for each individual occurrence.

Commissioner Heriot also objected to a proposed finding of fact which simply (and accurately) noted that DoD has not issued a uniform standard of proof to the Service Branches for the imposition of non-judicial (Article 15) punishments.

The proposed finding read:

> The DoD has not issued a uniform standard of proof to all of the Services regarding the imposition of non-judicial punishment in sexual assault cases.[5]

Commissioner Heriot, objected to this proposed finding. She stated :

> ...that's one of the main problems that reports of this have. They like to go into the question of whether something is consistent. We have several Services in the military for a reason. We don't want them to be consistent. We want them to have different approaches.[6]

Commissioner Yaki then interjected:

> "So what you're saying is because someone goes by water, and someone goes by air, and someone goes on the ground, that somehow that has a difference in how they should deal with sexual harassment? That's ridiculous."[7]

To which Commissioner Gaziano, responded:

> "We refer to them as "laboratories of democracy," Commissioner Yaki. That improves our democracy."[8]

Of course the UCMJ and its procedures are the stated law of all the Service Branches.

---

[5] "The DoD has not issued a uniform standard of proof to all of the Services regarding the imposition of non-judicial punishment in sexual assault cases." Unedited Transcript of Meeting of U.S. Commission on Civil Rights, no pages provided in draft, dated July 21, 2013. (p.20 l. 20-22)

[6] Ibid. (p.22 l.6-13)

[7] Ibid. (p.22 l.9-23)

[8] Ibid. p. 22-23 l.24-1)

I support a standardized burden of proof for all non-judicial Article 15 offenses, not just sexual assault. This gives the officer imposing the disciplinary penalty a guideline and gives notice to servicemembers what standard of conduct is expected of them. This is especially true in joint military units where soldiers and sailors or any other combination of servicemembers may find themselves working together under one command.

I believe equal application of the law is a good thing for democracy. A neutral standardized burden of proof, whether for felonies, gross misdemeanors or misdemeanors, not just sexual crimes, is the democratic way. It retains freedom throughout the Service Branches by giving notice to all members of the Armed Forces what standard is required of them. It does not further democracy to have one burden of proof in one Branch and different burden of proof in another. Another rationale for this point of view is in many cases the several Service Branches work in an integrated fashion across Branch-lines. They also work together when coordinating their approach to military problems, such as a unified attack on a target. Standardization, where possible and where best practices can occur, works to the benefit of all. Of course, if one approach is successful in one Branch and fails in another, rational beings would expect the Branch instituting the unsuccessful policy to discontinue it and continue to develop its own successful policy. Demonstration projects exist to try out policy initiatives.

"Later on, after his misuse of Justice Brandeis,[9] Commissioner Gaziano proposed a factual finding which downplayed sexual assault by misstating the evidence gathered by the Commission staff from the DoD. The proposed finding read:

> "According to DoD's 2012 Workplace and Gender Relations survey, of the 67 percent of female servicemembers who did not report unwanted sexual contact they said they experienced to military authorities, 48 percent indicated that they did not report the unwanted sexual contact because the incidents were not serious enough to report."[10]

The statistics in the proposed finding are accurate, but misleading—as is the paraphrase that makes up the rest of the proposed finding. The 2012 Workplace and Gender Relations Survey provided respondents many possible reasons to choose among to explain their decision not to report an incident of unwanted sexual contact to military authorities. "Not serious enough" however was not one of the options provided.

---

[9] *New State Ice Co. v. Liebmann*, 285 U.S. 262, 311, (1932)(Brandeis, J., dissenting).

[10] Findings and Recommendations submitted and voted upon at the USCCR meeting held July 21, 2013.

The full results of the pertinent section of the survey are as follows:

Of the 67% of women who did not report to a military authority, the reasons for not reporting were:

- 70% did not want anyone to know
- 66% felt uncomfortable making a report
- 51% did not think their report would be kept confidential
- 50% did not think anything would be done
- 48% thought it was not important enough to report
- 47% thought they would be labeled a troublemaker
- 47% were afraid of retaliation/reprisals from the person(s) who did it or from their friends
- 43% heard about negative experiences other victims went through who reported their situation
- 43% thought they would not be believed
- 35% thought reporting would take too much time and effort
- 28% thought their performance evaluation or chance for promotion would suffer
- 23% feared they or others would be punished for infractions/violations, such as underage drinking
- 23% were afraid of being assaulted again by the offender
- 16% another reason
- 15% thought they might lose their security clearance/personnel reliability certification
- 14% did not know how to report[11]

I list all of these responses to provide a more accurate and truthful context for the "48% thought it was not important enough to report" statistic. My colleague's paraphrase, "not serious enough to report", standing by itself, gives the false impression that half of the non-reports were due to victims considering the incidents to be trivial.

As the full survey results reveal, most servicemembers experiencing unwanted sexual contact have multiple reasons for choosing not to report. Many undoubtedly believe that the unwanted contact was serious, but that reporting the contact was not as important to them as avoiding reprisals, damaging their career opportunities, or other negative experiences they believed would result from their reporting. This would especially be the case for the 50% of non-reporting servicemembers who also believed that no disciplinary actions against their abusers would result from a report to military authorities. Why would you put yourself through all the

---

[11] 2012 Workplace and Gender Relations Survey of Active Duty Members p. 106

real and perceived difficulties associated with reporting a sexual assault if you thought that, at the end of the day, your assailant would not be held accountable?

Comparing sexual assault numbers with other populations is not very meaningful. The crisis is not simply percentages or numbers. Rather the crisis arises from a combination of the assaults themselves, the procedures the military uses to respond to them, and the effects they have on the alleged victim, the accused, the chain of command, the Service Branches and, more broadly, the public's confidence in and respect for the military. Efforts to downplay the extent of the problem that the military has with sexual assault demean the brave men and women who serve in the Armed Forces. This subject deserves an honest appraisal, not misdirection or hackneyed—and inapt—slogans.

Statistics, the UCMJ and Military Procedure

The military, in a good faith attempt to address sexual assault, has made changes to: the investigative process, the Uniform Code of Military Justice (UCMJ) and its procedure in handling sexual assault cases. (6.1% of women and 1.2% of men have reported unwanted sexual contact).[12]

The military considers many different acts to constitute "sexual assault." (To be clear, the 26,000 reported sexual assaults from the military survey did not mean 26,000 acts of intercourse itself.) The Commission staff asked DoD for statistics showing the breakdown of the different types of offenses DoD considered sexual assault and the numbers associated with each offense reported in the survey. DoD could not provide these figures as they do not breakout the different sexual offenses. Rather, they lump them all together from sexual harassment to rape terming these acts as Unwanted Sexual Contact.[13]

Clearly, statistics need to be kept on the individual offenses.

---

[12] As a function of the more than 5:1 male to female ratio among servicemembers, more men report sexual assaults in absolute numbers then women; however, proportionally, more women report sexual assault the men.

[13] "In 2012, the *WGRA* (Workplace and Gender Relations Survey of Active Duty Members) showed that 6.1 percent of Active Duty women and 1.2 percent of Active Duty men experienced an incident of USC in the 12 months prior to the survey. USC is the survey term for the range of contact sexual crimes between adults prohibited by military law, ranging from abusive sexual contact to rape.   DEPARTMENT OF DEFENSE, DEPARTMENT OF DEFENSE FISCAL YEAR 2012 ANNUAL REPORT ON SEXUAL ASSAULT IN THE MILITARY 11-13 (2013), AVAILABLE AT:. *HTTP://WWW.SAPR.MIL/PUBLIC/DOCS/REPORTS/FY12_DOD_SAPRO_ANNUAL_REPORT_ON_SEXUAL_ASSAULT-VOLUME_ONE.PDF*

Although pertinent sections of the UCMJ have been re-written, more improvements are needed..[14] It must spell out specific crimes with specific elements. The elements of those crimes need to be clear. Punishments need to have minimum and maximum penalties associated with each offense.[15] The accused need to know what they face. The judge, not the jury,[16] needs to impose the punishments. Judges are the people in the process that see the criminal offenses everyday. They are in the best position to consider whether the particular criminal act deserves severe or lenient punishment. Military jurors who do not deal with offenses on a regular basis do not have the context within which to appraise the severity of the criminal offense.

Most controversial is the issue of whether command should retain the authority to refer soldiers, sailors, marines and airmen to courts martial or merely administer Article 15 discipline. Here there is a clear split of opinion, with the Generals and Admirals coming down of the side of keeping the command structure intimately involved, from making the initial referral of charges to having the final say when it comes to sentencing after a court martial has found guilt. Advocacy groups and many members of Congress believe a separate civilian system or a special military prosecutor and defense should be established, taking all decision-making out of the chain of command.[17]

I believe a compromise is necessary to create a more effective prosecutorial, defense, appellate and appeal of last resort (pardon) system.

I would propose that a separate prosecutor's office should be created in DoD, made up of civilian and military lawyers and investigators. This office should decide, after its investigative

---

[14] See, Jim Clark, *Analysis of Crimes and Defenses 2012 UCMJ Article 120, effective 28 June 2012*, LEXISNEXIS LEGAL NEWSROOM, June 15, 2012, available at . Clark quotes the Hon. John Maksym, judge of the Navy-Marine Corps Court of Appeal, who described the statute as a "poorly written, confusing and arguably absurdly structured and articulated act of Congress." United States v. Medina, 68 M.J. 587, 595 (N-M.C.C.A. 2009). Clark went on to add, "Congress' inclusion of defenses of consent and mistake of fact as to consent in the revised law created an unconstitutional conflict in the law, and also returned the victim to the center of many prosecutions."

[15] The range of offenses captured in Article 120 of the UCMJ includes conduct such as rape, sexual assault though the sexual act of penetration by any object, of oral sex, and unwanted sexual contact through touching of private parts in Article 120(a); child sexual abuse offenses in Article 120(b); and finally other sexual misconduct like indecent viewing of private parts, prostitution, or indecent exposure are included in Article 120(c). It is fair to say there is some division within Article 120 of these very different groups of sexual offenses. The one of most concern to this report would be Article 120(a). It is important to note that in Article 120(a) rape and sexual assault offenses are separated, as well as, aggravated sexual contact and abusive sexual contact. However, it does not spell out minimum and maximum penalties for each offense.

[16] Or "panel" to use the UCMJ term of art for "jury"

[17] The various proposals to set up a new system to deal with crimes committed by servicemembers also differ on whether the jurisdiction for these new systems should cover all or most serious crimes, or whether it should be limited to sexual assaults only.

staff has examined an incident, whether to bring charges and, if charges are brought, whether they will be at a court martial or an Article 15. They will act as the prosecutors for any trial. At trial, the panel will decide guilt or innocence. Where the trier of fact finds guilt, the judge shall issue all sentences within the minimum and maximum allowable as set forth in the UCMJ. Appeals will be heard as they are now. The determination of the court martial and the appeals court shall be widely disseminated at the duty station where the offense occurred, by reading the result of each at unit formations and posting on company and squadron bulletin boards. The Commanding General/Admiral over the duty station where the offense occurred shall retain final authority over the case to change the sentence after the entire legal process has run its course. Should they change any disposition, they shall provide specific reasons therefore in a letter and transmit the letter to the President, the Secretary of Defense, and the Joint Chiefs of Staff, and circulate its contents, as set forth above, to those at the duty station where the offense occurred for publication to all servicemembers at that duty station.[18]

Finally, a separate defense office should also be created with civilian and military lawyers, as well as investigators who specialize in sexual assault crimes. This unit must be afforded the same resources and assets as the prosecutors' office.

The current system is fraught with traps for all involved.

The officer deciding whether to bring charges is not specifically trained in the law. With the UCMJ considered unclear on the issue of sexual assault,[19] this puts the determining officer at a disadvantage. As hard as they might try not to, the officer will almost inevitably consider conflicts that arise above and/or below their rank in the chain of command. Whether those below them will consider their determination fair and bolster the esprit de corps or seen as unfair and demoralizing. Or, whether those above them will second guess their decision as right or wrong, either furthering or damaging their careers; or even cause the superior officers to perceive the incident as exposing the referring officer to a charge of inadequately training and controlling the personnel in their command.

---

[18] The cases involving unexplained dismissal of sexual assault convictions by Lt. Gen. Susan J. Helms, USAF, (General's promotion blocked over her dismissal of sex-assault verdict, Washington Post, (May 6, 2013)) and Lt. Gen. Craig Franklin, USAF, (Convicted of sex assault - then cleared - fighter pilot sparks protest at Tucson base), U.S. News/NBCnews.com, (Apr. 25, 2013)) are the reason this recommendation is made. Unexplained pardons of criminal conduct do not enhance the military criminal justice system. It could easily lead to allegations of favoritism.

[19] See Clark, supra note 14.

At the time of the USCCR briefing, commanding officers were empowered to change a guilty disposition to not guilty without explanation. This is the equivalent to the unfettered pardon power vested in the President of the United States. Standing alone, it is unacceptable.[20]

Prior Victims of Military Sexual Trauma

Testimony before the Commission clearly indicated many prior servicemembers feel their administrative and personality disorder discharges where the result of Military Sexual Trauma suffered while in service.[21] These former members of the Armed Forces should be given the opportunity to file appeals and given the opportunity to be heard at before a neutral panel at a hearing on whether to upgrade their discharges. I would recommend that upon the filing of the appeal, the former servicemembers should be given immediate access to health care through the Veteran's Administration and they should be afforded counsel and the costs necessary to pursue their claim. If they prevail, no cost of counsel or costs shall be required; however, upon loss, they should be required to pay their own costs.

I will leave it to others to setup the process for such claims.

Consideration of Character and Prior Military Service

Several witnesses took issue with the military's use of the accused's character and prior military service being used as a rationale to significantly reduce or dismiss the dispositions at the court martial. I understand this concern. This practice should be prohibited, unless meaningful minimum and maximum penalties are set forth in the UCMJ. If the UCMJ is so amended, consideration, by the trial Judge only, should be allowed of character only--as is allowed in the civilian courts. Prior military service, on the other hand, should not be used as a mitigating circumstance toward a sentence. Character should mediate toward either the maximum or minimum sentence of the convicted person. However, under no condition should this factor be allowed to reduce a sentence below the minimum or beyond the maximum sentence set forth in the UCMJ.

The convicted person's character should also not be available to the commanding General/Admiral of the duty station as justification for changing the disposition of a court martial.

---

[20] See footnote 18 supra.

[21] A discharge for administrative, personality disorder, and similar categories deny the servicemember certain benefits upon separation. One of these benefits is medical care.

Military Dependents and Civilians

Military dependents and civilians assaulted by military personnel should be allowed to make restricted and unrestricted reports to military personnel authorized to take reports of unwanted sexual contact.

Training and Sexual Assault Personnel

The different Branches should continue to work to develop the best training programs for servicemembers about sexual crimes in the military. The results of each program should be shared between the Services and implemented when possible. However, the Branches must recognize that using many different approaches are important as there are many different ways people learn the same material. DoD must use the best methods to choose and train those who are designated to accept information and assist victims on sexual assault at each duty station.

Conclusion

There are many other improvements that can be instituted to deal with the problem of sexual assault in the military, such as better background investigations of potential recruits or notifying persons reporting sexual assault of the right to a JAG officer to assist them through the process.

These proposed changes and other necessary changes are a tall order for the military. However, they are essential for the good order and morale of the armed forces. The Commander-in-Chief, Congress and those commanders responsible for their charges should not shirk from their responsibility to put in place the best judicial and medical care system possible to protect the rights of everyone who is involved in these most difficult and personal of cases.

Statement of Commissioner Michael Yaki

I join with my Democratic colleagues on the Commission in calling for serious, substantial reform of the system of military justice that has failed the victims of sexual assault in the military, a failure so profound and so deep that its ability to deter – much less punish -- is, quite frankly, questionable at best, and an affront to victims and survivors in particular.

But as I pointed out in the debate on this Report[1], this is not an issue that is partisan in nature. No one is sexually assaulted in the military because of their party affiliation. No victim of sexual assault is denied justice or given an unwarranted discharge or lacking in post-traumatic treatment because they are Democrats or Republicans. But denied and discharged they are, and the lack of available, reliable avenues of redress and justice is made all too evident in the record.

Yet, somehow, several of my colleagues on this Commission have chosen to ignore the simple truth that there is a severe problem in our military branches. They warn of the perils of "political pressure" on an adjudication process that is inconsistent, haphazard, and arbitrary in the administration of justice. Indeed, they believe that such inconsistency is a good thing because, after all, the military services are "different."[2] It begs the question of whether they also believe that the adjudication of all civil rights in this country should differ on the cultural and geographic differences, or perhaps even state boundaries, where a violation occurred.

I hardly think the crime of rape is different because of the color of one's uniform. I hardly think that the wheels of justice should spin differently depending on whether one is a marine, sailor, airman, or soldier. And I sincerely doubt that the Secretary of Defense would tolerate differential treatment of sexual assault based upon the service branch in which it was committed. It strains credulity, much less constitutional principles, to think otherwise.

This is, pure and simple, an issue of justice, and as an issue of justice it is one where it is a shame that the United States Commission on Civil Rights cannot find bipartisan agreement on a civil rights issue that violates the trust of young women and men in uniform and undermines confidence in our armed services.[3] If we are to truly have equality, it cannot be that those who

---

[1] Transcript of USCCR Commission Meeting, July 21, 2013, pp. 32-34

[2] Transcript of USCCR Commission Meeting, July 21, 2013, pp.22-23

[3] Commissioner Heriot blithely dismisses reform efforts because there is "no evidence . . that sexual assault . . . is more common in the military than it is at other institutions that house large numbers of young adults." Indeed she goes on to bludgeon her thesis further by stating that it is "not proven" that the military "is a uniquely dangerous place for sexual assault victims." Notwithstanding the fact that the Report clearly states:

(cont'd)

are willing to risk their lives on behalf of our nation have to face a "reality" that their own personal safety is in jeopardy from their own brothers in arms, that sexual assault by fellow soldiers, sailors, and airmen is prevalent and the likelihood of justice is arbitrary and capricious.[4] As a deterrent to recruitment for an all-volunteer army, it affects force levels and troop readiness for our country. As a civil rights matter, it is simply intolerable.

We need look no further than a body that is seen by many in the public as overly partisan, the United States Congress, to understand that bipartisanship is achievable in ending the scourge of sexual assault in our armed forces. Remedies similar to the ones proposed by myself and my Democratic colleagues, based on testimony and findings that echo what we heard in our hearing, find members reaching across the aisle to join forces on this important issue.[5]

To illustrate and underscore this point I have, below, attached pertinent examples of legislation and statements that have the support of both Republicans and Democrats[6]. It should serve as a model for how this address must be addressed going forward, and as a reminder to our conservative colleagues on the Commission that pushing past the blinders of party is not only possible, but a reality, and needed more than ever on this important and urgent issue.

(cont'd from previous page)

> The military environment is unlike college/university settings and even other civilian settings for a variety of reasons. For example, Service members tend to live in an insular military environment which fosters an expectation of group cohesion and loyalty. As a result, these expectations and cultural norms can hamper the ability of military personnel to transfer out of their unit if they are feeling harassed or if they have been victims of assault. In contrast, college students may have greater ability to remove themselves from their environment, either temporarily or permanently. Also for Service members, attempts to transfer out of their unit may be denied. Leaving their military unit without permission may lead to criminal penalties for being absent without leave (AWOL) or for insubordination. (Report, page 8)

So Commissioner Heriot believes that erroneous statistical comparisons can somehow alleviate the military chain of command from responsibility for protecting its soldiers. What is even worse is that she chooses to reduce the issue to a series of comparisons that either minimize the issue or maximize her concerns. What is baldly lacking is any sense of concern, much less compassion, for the victims of sexual assault.

[4] Commissioner Gaziano shrugs off concerns as a "supposed . . . crisis" and mocks the press coverage of hearings and testimony as analogous to television "Shark Week" promotions – that the very act of coverage itself fuels a problem that does not exist. Commissioner Gaziano's "shark" comparison would be best served if he read a statement made by Army Chief of Staff General Ray Odierno, who said "There's a predator problem in almost every unit of some size, and so everybody has to work our way through this," he told Army Times. http://www.militarytimes.com/article/20130616/NEWS06/306160006/Leaders-renew-resolve-stop-sex-assault

[5] My colleague Commissioner Gaziano attempts to paint reform attempts as the work of "modern progressives" and the "political left." I am sure that my colleague would agree that some of the Senators and Congresspersons mentioned in this Statement would be surprised, and perhaps angered, to find themselves so characterized.

[6] The list of sponsors and cosponsors are taken from the official government website that tracks current legislation, Thomas (cite). If there are additional sponsors and cosponsors added since the publication of this statement, Thomas will provide the most up-to-date list. Additionally, some of the legislative summary language has been drawn from the Thomas page.

Senate

S.967

Military Justice Improvement Act of 2013

Sponsor: <u>Sen Gillibrand, Kirsten E.</u> [NY] (introduced 5/16/2013)   <u>Cosponsors</u> (38)

This bi-partisan bill would remove the decision-making authority for prosecuting serious crimes (including rape and sexual assault) from the accused's chain of command, and place it in the hands of trained military prosecutors. It would also prohibit a service member's military service record from being used as evidence to prove reasonable doubt when deciding whether a case has enough merit to proceed to trial. This legislation is strongly backed by advocates of reform, which, they argue, would make the judicial process more objective and remove any bias that may exist between a commander and his troops. {summary description from policymic.com)

COSPONSORS(38), ALPHABETICAL (note that Republicans are in italics)

Sen Baldwin, Tammy [WI] - 6/10/2013
Sen Begich, Mark [AK] - 5/16/2013
Sen Bennet, Michael F. [CO] - 7/24/2013
Sen Blumenthal, Richard [CT] - 5/16/2013
Sen Boxer, Barbara [CA] - 5/16/2013
Sen Cantwell, Maria [WA] - 6/18/2013
Sen Cardin, Benjamin L. [MD] - 6/11/2013
Sen Carper, Thomas R. [DE] - 6/3/2013
Sen Casey, Robert P., Jr. [PA] - 6/4/2013
Sen Collins, Susan M. [ME] - 5/16/2013
Sen Coons, Christopher A. [DE] - 5/16/2013
Sen Cowan, William M. [MA] - 6/18/2013
Sen Feinstein, Dianne [CA] - 5/16/2013
Sen Franken, Al [MN] - 5/16/2013
Sen Grassley, Chuck [IA] - 5/16/2013
Sen Harkin, Tom [IA] - 6/20/2013
Sen Heinrich, Martin [NM] - 6/10/2013
Sen Heitkamp, Heidi [ND] - 6/6/2013
Sen Hirono, Mazie K. [HI] - 5/16/2013
Sen Johanns, Mike [NE] - 5/16/2013
Sen Johnson, Tim [SD] - 6/3/2013
Sen Kirk, Mark Steven [IL] - 7/24/2013
Sen Leahy, Patrick J. [VT] - 6/11/2013

Sen Markey, Edward J. [MA] - 7/16/2013
Sen Menendez, Robert [NJ] - 6/11/2013
Sen Merkley, Jeff [OR] - 6/4/2013
Sen Mikulski, Barbara A. [MD] - 5/16/2013
Sen Murkowski, Lisa [AK] - 5/22/2013
Sen Pryor, Mark L. [AR] - 5/16/2013
Sen Rockefeller, John D., IV [WV] - 5/16/2013
Sen Sanders, Bernard [VT] - 6/19/2013
Sen Schatz, Brian [HI] - 5/16/2013
Sen Schumer, Charles E. [NY] - 6/11/2013
Sen Shaheen, Jeanne [NH] - 5/16/2013
Sen Udall, Tom [NM] - 7/16/2013
Sen Vitter, David [LA] - 7/18/2013
Sen Warren, Elizabeth [MA] - 5/22/2013
Sen Wyden, Ron [OR] - 6/17/2013

Although this is the official list, it has recently been announced that Senators Rand Paul and Ted Cruz will also support the legislation.

House
H.R.2016
Military Justice Improvement Act of 2013 (echoing the Senate bill)

Sponsor: <u>Rep Benishek, Dan</u> [MI-1] (introduced 5/16/2013)   <u>Cosponsors</u> (48)

COSPONSORS(48), ALPHABETICAL (Republicans are in italics)

Rep Amash, Justin [MI-3] - 7/18/2013
Rep Bachmann, Michele [MN-6] - 7/18/2013
Rep Beatty, Joyce [OH-3] - 7/8/2013
Rep Bentivolio, Kerry L. [MI-11] - 7/17/2013
Rep Bishop, Timothy H. [NY-1] - 5/20/2013
Rep Bonamici, Suzanne [OR-1] - 7/16/2013
Rep Camp, Dave [MI-4] - 7/19/2013
Rep Carson, Andre [IN-7] - 7/30/2013
Rep Cole, Tom [OK-4] - 6/17/2013
Rep Crowley, Joseph [NY-14] - 6/26/2013
Rep DeLauro, Rosa L. [CT-3] - 7/8/2013
Rep Esty, Elizabeth H. [CT-5] - 7/8/2013
Rep Flores, Bill [TX-17] - 7/17/2013
Rep Gabbard, Tulsi [HI-2] - 5/16/2013
Rep Hanabusa, Colleen W. [HI-1] - 5/20/2013

Rep Hanna, Richard L. [NY-22] - 5/16/2013

Rep Huizenga, Bill [MI-2] - 7/18/2013

Rep Jackson Lee, Sheila [TX-18] - 6/27/2013

Rep Jenkins, Lynn [KS-2] - 6/12/2013

Rep Kildee, Daniel T [MI-5] - 6/3/2013

Rep Kuster, Ann M. [NH-2] - 5/21/2013

Rep Latham, Tom [IA-3] - 6/5/2013

Rep Loebsack, David [IA-2] - 5/20/2013

Rep Lofgren, Zoe [CA-19] - 6/24/2013

Rep Lowenthal, Alan S. [CA-47] - 6/11/2013

Rep Lowey, Nita M. [NY-17] - 5/20/2013

Rep Maloney, Carolyn B. [NY-12] - 6/27/2013

Rep Markey, Edward J. [MA-5] - 6/

Rep McCollum, Betty [MN-4] - 5/21/2013

Rep McGovern, James P. [MA-2] - 7/10/2013

Rep Miller, Candice S. [MI-10] - 6/18/2013

Rep Neugebauer, Randy [TX-19] - 7/17/2013

Rep Norton, Eleanor Holmes [DC] - 6/28/2013

Rep O'Rourke, Beto [TX-16] - 6/6/2013

Rep Pingree, Chellie [ME-1] - 7/16/2013

Rep Posey, Bill [FL-8] - 6/19/2013

Rep Ros-Lehtinen, Ileana [FL-27] - 6/5/2013 19/2013

Rep Schakowsky, Janice D. [IL-9] - 7/8/2013

Rep Sensenbrenner, F. James, Jr. [WI-5] - 6/28/2013

Rep Sinema, Kyrsten [AZ-9] - 5/16/2013

Rep Smith, Christopher H. [NJ-4] - 6/19/2013

Rep Stivers, Steve [OH-15] - 6/6/2013

Rep Tipton, Scott R. [CO-3] - 7/30/2013

Rep Upton, Fred [MI-6] - 6/14/2013

Rep Veasey, Marc A. [TX-33] - 6/13/2013

Rep Walberg, Tim [MI-7] - 7/17/2013

Rep Wasserman Schultz, Debbie [FL-23] - 6/19/2013

Rep Young, Don [AK] - 6/18/2013

Some Republicans offered strong statements supporting sexual assault legislation. The following are statements from the websites of several Republicans offering support for the Military Justice Improvement and several other bipartisan sexual assault-related bills:

Senator Murkowski (R-Alaska)

Senator Murkowski is encouraged that the Secretary of Defense has admitted the Pentagon needs a cultural change when it comes to sexual misconduct among our men and women in uniform, but believes it is critical that Congress do all it can to promote the protection of those who protect our freedoms. The Senator is pleased that everyone is talking about the issue now and some positive steps are being made on the legislative level, but continues to look for a thorough response.

Sexual Assault in the Military

Sexual Assault within the military is occurring at frightening levels, with a six percent increase reported in the last year. Too often, cases of sexual assault go unreported out of fear of retribution or that nothing will be done. According to the Department of Defense, an estimated 26,000 cases of sexual assault occurred in 2012, with only 3,374 cases being reported. That means thousands of military sexual assault victims are left to face the aftermath of their assault alone, while their attackers may never face justice.

Though the issue has drawn the attention of millions of Americans recently, Senator Lisa Murkowski has been raising this issue for years. In a 2009 Senate Defense Appropriations Subcommittee hearing, Murkowski asked military medical officials if they believed they were "doing enough" in terms of building awareness of this issue among the ranks.

Senator Murkowski believes the present rates of sexual assault among the military men and women are a shame to the nation's defense – made worse by the fact that the reports of sexual assault are likely a fraction of the actual number of offenses. A factor to this troubling rate of underreporting is the fact that victims are frequently concerned about internal retaliation - such as promotions not received or additional duties added. To address this problem, the Senator has co-sponsored five separate bills to crack down on this crisis.

Senator Murkowski has co-sponsored the:

Combating Sexual Assault Act of 2013 to provide victims of sexual assault with Special Victims' Counsel – a military lawyer who will assist sexual assault victims throughout the process. The Army already provides this Counsel, and the SVC would be an effective and essential ally for all victims. The Senator was pleased that provisions from this legislation were considered in the National Defense Authorization Act (NDAA) considered by the Senate Armed Services Committee.

Military Sexual Assault Prevention Act of 2013 to prevent sexual offenders from serving in the military, improve tracking and review of sexual assault claims in the military, and help ensure victims can get the justice they deserve.

Coast Guard STRONG Act of 2013. The Coast Guard is in the jurisdiction of the Department of Homeland Security, not the Pentagon – so there are different protocols. This bill will extend protections given to members of the armed services to our guardians.

Military Justice Improvement Act of 2013. In the case of offenses which have a sentence of confinement for more than one year, the military judge advocate (in pay grade of O-6 or higher) has the authority to decide whether the case goes to trial or not. The bill carves out a category of exceptions for offenses that are unique to the military and allows commanders to decide whether the case should proceed to trial or not.

S. 1092. This bill would increase protections from retaliatory actions for victims who report violations. This legislation would require an investigation by the IG when there are allegations of retaliatory personnel actions taken in response to reporting a sexual assault and expands the IG investigations to reports of rape, sexual assault, or other sexual misconduct.

National Defense Authorization Act (NDAA). Within the NDAA, Senator Murkowski secured the inclusion of language to provide victims of sexual assault in all military branches access to Special Victims' Counsel (SVC), a trained military lawyer to assist the victim throughout the legal process.

Fort Greely Investigation

Additionally, Senator Murkowski is closely following an investigation into recent allegations that sexual affairs were condoned at Fort Greely, the nation's main missile-defense base in Alaska. Murkowski believes the allegations coming out of the investigation at Fort Greely are deeply upsetting and further evidence that we must see a drastic change made to a military culture that has seemingly turned its eyes away from facing critical, systemic problems and addressing them. The Senator will demand to see the results of the Greely investigation lead to a true zero-tolerance policy for all sexual misconduct in the military.

Senator Paul (R-Kentucky)

Jul 16, 2013

WASHINGTON, D.C. - Sen. Rand Paul this morning joined Sens. Kristen Gillibrand (D-N.Y.), Ted Cruz (R-Texas), Chuck Grassley (R-Iowa), Barbara Boxer (D-Calif.), Mazie Hirono (D-Hawaii), and Richard Blumenthal (D-Conn.) at a press conference in the U.S. Capitol to discuss the Military Justice Improvement Act, to combat sexual assault in the military. Below is video of Sen. Paul's remarks:

TRANSCRIPT:

I try not to look at issues from a partisan point of view. I'm sure I do sometimes, but I try not to. As a physician, I look at problems and try to find solutions.

I'm concerned about justice and I want it to occur in the military for victims as well as for those who are potentially accused. Justice is very important to me. Both justice for the accused and for the victim. I am concerned that victims of assault may be deterred from reporting assault if they have to report it to their boss.

I am also concerned about interposing too many lawyers into military life and having lawyers get in the way of the military mission. The vast majority of our soldiers are honorable and upstanding individuals. We're talking about a very small percentage but if they commit crimes, they should be punished. In finding justice for victims, we must make sure that we have due process for all.

Some say we have no bipartisan cooperation around here. I disagree. I think this is a great example of how people from both sides come together to work on a problem and look honestly at what a problem is. So when I heard about this, my first impression was a positive one. As I looked at the bill, Senator Gillibrand came by to talk to me about it and I thought there were one or two things that were included in this that we should exclude. She was very open to the discussion and it makes my support even stronger for this.

There were a couple of things that were removed that weren't sexual assault, that weren't murder, these were disobeying orders and some other things and we said you know what we will keep that in the line of command. We want to keep serious crimes, murder, rape, sexual assault in here. And I think it's made the bill even stronger. I always thought the motive for the bill was good but now I think the bill is even stronger and I see no reason why conservatives shouldn't support this.

The only thing I think standing in the way is just sort of the status quo. Senator Boxer was right. Everyone says they are against sexual assault, and if it appears that there is some sort of deterrence from victims reporting the crime, why don't we fix it? I don't see why we wouldn't fix it and I am happy to be a part of the process.

Senator Collins (R- Maine)

Senator Collins Leads Bipartisan, Bicameral Effort to Reform Military Justice System to Address Sexual Assaults

Senate-House Bill Would Create Transformational Change Needed for Real Accountability In Military Justice System by Removing the Chain of Command From Decision Making Over Whether Serious Crimes Are Prosecuted, Also Reforms Article 60 so Commanders Cannot Overturn Jury Verdicts for Serious Crimes

According to DOD Estimates, More Than 26,000 Incidents of Sexual Assault or Unwanted Sexual Contact occurred in 2012; Overall Reports Increased 37%; Sexual Assault Crimes Increased 6% to 3,374 Reports; Only 238 Convictions

Washington D.C. - During a news conference today, U.S. Senators Susan Collins and Kirsten Gillibrand (D-NY), along with a bipartisan group of their colleagues in the Senate and House, announced new legislation that would reform the military justice system by removing the prosecution of all crimes punishable by one year or more in confinement from the chain of command, except crimes that are uniquely military in nature, such as disobeying orders or going Absent Without Leave. Senators Collins and Gillibrand were joined by survivors of sexual assault in the military, including Jennifer Norris of Rumford, and by representatives from organizations who assist victims of Military Sexual Trauma.

According to the FY2012 SAPRO report released last week by the Defense Department, an estimated 26,000 cases of sexual assault occurred in FY2012, a 37% increase from FY2011. Another report released by the Defense Department late last month showed that more than 1 in 5 female service members reported experiencing unwanted sexual contact while serving in the military. The Military Justice Improvement Act would for the first time remove the decision whether to take a case to special or general court-martial completely out of the chain of command and give that discretion to experienced military prosecutors for all crimes punishable by one year or more in confinement, except crimes that are uniquely military in nature, such as disobeying orders or going AWOL.

Many of our allied modern militaries have reporting outside of the chain of command, such as Britain, Canada, Israel, Germany, Norway and Australia. For example, the British military has prosecutors making trial decisions for all crimes through the Service Prosecuting Authority (SPA) within Britain's Ministry of Defense.

The Military Justice Improvement Act would also:

- Codify Secretary Hagel's proposed changes to the UCMJ's Article 60 so that the convening authority may not (a) set aside a guilty finding or (b) change a finding of guilty to a lesser included offense. The legislation further alters Article 60 to require the convening authority to prepare a written justification for any changes made to court-martial sentences.

- Provide the offices of the military chiefs of staff with the authority and discretion to establish courts, empanel juries and choose judges to hear cases (i.e. convening authority).

- This legislation would not amend Article 15. Commanding officers would still be able to order non-judicial punishment for offenses not directed to trial by the prosecutors.

"To be sure, the vast, overwhelming majority of our military personnel are honorable, conscientious, and respectful individuals, not rapists or harassers. It is for their sake that the pattern of covering up, blaming the victim, and failing to provide even the most basic protections that has been all too common for far too long must end," said Senator Collins.

"What does it say about us as a people, as the nation, as the foremost military in the world when some of our service members have more to fear from their fellow soldiers than from the enemy? This epidemic of sexual abuse cannot stand. We must ensure that justice is swift and certain to the criminals who have perpetuated these crimes."

Senator Collins spoke about a 2004 Senate Armed Services Subcommittee on Personnel hearing during which she questioned military leaders about sexual assault in the military and strongly urged that more must be done to address this crisis. She said while she believes current military leaders are committed to solving the problem, legislation is clearly needed, and this bill is a step in the right direction.

"America is home to the world's best and brightest, brave men and women who join the armed services for all the right reasons - to serve our country, defend all that we hold sacred, and make America's military the best the world has ever known," Senator Gillibrand said. "But too often, these brave men and women find themselves in the fight of their lives not off on some far-away battlefield, but right here on our own soil, within their own ranks and commanding officers, as victims of horrific acts of sexual violence. Our bipartisan bill takes this issue head on by removing decision-making from the chain of command, and giving that discretion to experienced trial counsel with prosecutorial experience where it belongs. That's how we will achieve accountability, justice and fairness."

According to the FY2012 SAPRO report released last week by the Defense Department, an estimated 26,000 cases of sexual assault or unwanted sexual contact occurred in FY2012, a 37% increase from FY2011. Meanwhile, overall rates of reporting dropped from 13.5% in 2011 to 9.8% in 2012. In 2011, victims reported 3,192 out of 19,000 incidents, compared to 2012, where victims reported just 3,374 out of 26,000 incidents. While the number of perpetrators convicted of committing a sexual assault increased from 191 in 2011 to 238 in 2012, the conviction rate dropped from 1% in 2011 to 0.9% in 2012.

Of the 3,374 total reports in 2012, 2,558 reports were unrestricted, which means they were actionable. Of those unrestricted reports, 27 percent were for rape, 35 percent were for abusive and wrongful sexual contact, and 28 percent were for aggravated sexual assault and sexual assault. The remaining cases were for aggravated sexual contact, nonconsensual sodomy, indecent assault and attempts to commit those offenses.

According to the FY2012 SAPRO report released last week by the Defense Department, an estimated 26,000 cases of sexual assault or unwanted sexual contact occurred in FY2012, a 37% increase from FY2011. Meanwhile, overall rates of reporting dropped from 13.5% in 2011 to 9.8% in 2012. In 2011, victims reported 3,192 out of 19,000 incidents, compared to 2012, where victims reported just 3,374 out of 26,000 incidents. While the number of perpetrators convicted of committing a sexual assault increased from 191 in 2011 to 238 in 2012, the conviction rate dropped from 1% in 2011 to 0.9% in 2012.

Of the 3,374 total reports in 2012, 2,558 reports were unrestricted, which means they were actionable. Of those unrestricted reports, 27 percent were for rape, 35 percent were for abusive and wrongful sexual contact, and 28 percent were for aggravated sexual assault and sexual assault. The remaining cases were for aggravated sexual contact, nonconsensual sodomy, indecent assault and attempts to commit those offenses.

Also according to the FY2012 SAPRO report, across the Services, 74% of females and 60% of males perceived one or more barriers to reporting sexual assault. 62% of victims who reported a sexual assault indicated they perceived some form of professional, social, and/or administrative retaliation.

In a separate report released late last month by the Department of Defense, the Health-Related Behaviors Survey of Active Duty Military Personnel for 2011 showed that more than 1 in 5 female service members reported experiencing unwanted sexual contact while serving in the military.

Senator Johanns (R-Nebraska)

Johanns Sponsors Bipartisan Bills Addressing Military Sexual Assault Cases

The Department of Defense estimates more than 26,000 incidents of sexual assault in 2012, yet only 238 convictions.

WASHINGTON – U.S. Sen. Mike Johanns (R-NE) today sponsored three bipartisan pieces of legislation to address cases of sexual assault.

"Our brave men and women who put on a uniform already take enough risks on the battlefield without having to worry about sexual assault," Johanns said. "It's up to Congress to enact any reforms to the Uniform Code of Military Justice, which outlines how these cases are handled. The bipartisan legislation I'm sponsoring helps our military better address these crimes to ensure harsh penalties for convicted offenders."

A recent Department of Defense report estimates that there were approximately 26,000 cases of sexual assault or unwanted sexual contact within the military during fiscal year 2012 alone. That's an average of 71 per day.

The Combatting Military Sexual Assault Act was introduced by Sens. Kelly Ayotte (R-N.H.) and Patty Murray (D-Wash.).

- S. 871 would establish a Special Victims' Counsel for each branch of service. This individual would provide legal advice and assistance to sexual assault victims. The legislation also increases the responsibilities and authority of the DOD's Sexual Assault Prevention and Response Office to strengthen oversight of development, implementation, and accountability policies for sexual assault prevention and response.

The Military Justice Improvement Act was introduced by Sen. Kirsten Gillibrand (D-N.Y.).

- This legislation would give military prosecutors, who are not in the accused individual's chain of command, the authority to determine if a case goes to a special or general court-martial. It also establishes a 90 day deadline for military judges to call general and special-courts martial into session and prohibits commanders from overturning convictions.

The Coast Guard Sexual Trauma Response Oversight and Good Governance Act (STRONG Act), which will be introduced next week, is authored by Sens. Susan Collins (R-Maine) and Claire McCaskill (D-Mo.).

- The STRONG Act, which passed in 2011, requires the military services to put in place protections for victims of sexual assault, including the right to legal assistance and the right for a victim to request a transfer away from the geographic location of his or her attacker. This legislation would also apply these provisions to the Coast Guard. Currently, many STRONG ACT provisions do not apply to the Coast Guard because of its unique status as a component of Department of Homeland Security.

Senator Grassley (R-Iowa)

Tuesday, July 16, 2013

RAND PAUL AND TED CRUZ JOIN GILLIBRAND, BOXER, GRASSLEY EFFORT TO CREATE INDEPENDENT, NON-BIASED MILITARY JUSTICE SYSTEM FOR VICTIMS OF SEXUAL ASSAULT WHEN DEFENSE BILL COMES TO SENATE FLOOR THIS MONTH

Growing Bipartisan Momentum for Measure Supported by Major Victims' Advocacy Groups and Former JAG Officers Creating Real Reform and Accountability in Military Justice System by Having Trained, Independent Military Prosecutors Make Decisions Over Whether Serious Crimes Go to Trial -- Military Justice Improvement Act to be Offered as Amendment to Annual Defense Bill, Could Be Debated on Senate Floor As Soon As This Month

According to Pentagon Estimates, 25% of Women and 27% of Men Who Received Unwanted Sexual Contact Indicated the Offender Was Someone in Their Military Chain of Command -- More Than 26,000 Incidents of Sexual Assault or Unwanted Sexual Contact Occurred in 2012

Washington D.C. – U.S. Senators Rand Paul (R-KY) and Ted Cruz (R-TX) joined Kirsten Gillibrand (D-NY), Barbara Boxer (D-CA), Charles Grassley (R-IA), Mazie Hirono (D-HI), Richard Blumenthal (D-CT), Susan Collins (R-ME), Lisa Murkowski (R-AK) and Jeanne Shaheen (D-NH) today to announce their full support of a proposal offered by a bipartisan coalition of 33 Senators that seeks to reverse the systemic fear that numerous victims of military sexual assault have described in deciding whether to report the crimes committed against them due to the clear bias and inherent conflicts of interest posed by the military chain of command's current sole decision-making power over whether cases move forward to a trial.

The carefully crafted Military Justice Improvement Act moves the decision whether to prosecute any crime punishable by one year or more in confinement to independent, trained, professional military prosecutors, with the exception of crimes that are uniquely military in nature, such as disobeying orders or going Absent Without Leave. The decision whether to prosecute 37 serious crimes uniquely military in nature plus all crimes punishable by less than one year of confinement would remain within the chain of command. The Military Justice Improvement Act will be offered as an amendment when the annual National Defense Authorization Act (NDAA) is debated on the full Senate floor, which is expected as early as the last two weeks of July. Similar legislation was stripped out of the underlying NDAA bill by the full Senate Armed Services Committee this past June.

According to the FY2012 SAPRO report released earlier this year by the Defense Department, an estimated 26,000 cases of unwanted sexual contact and sexual assaults occurred in FY2012, a 37% increase from FY2011. Another report released by the Defense Department this year showed that more than 1 in 5 female servicemembers reported experiencing unwanted sexual contact while serving in the military. Also according to the FY2012 SAPRO Report, 25% of women and 27% of men who received unwanted sexual contact indicated the offender was someone in their military chain of command. Further, 50% of female victims stated they did not report the crime because they believed that nothing would be done with their report. Even the current top military leadership admits the current system "has failed" and as Commandant of the Marine Corps General James F. Amos stated this year, victims do not come forward because "they don't trust the chain of command."

"What our strong and growing bipartisan coalition has shown is that ending sexual assaults in the military by creating an independent and accountable military justice system is not a partisan or ideological issue. Our carefully crafted common sense proposal written in direct response to the experiences of those who have gone through a system rife with bias and conflict of interest is not a Democratic or Republican idea – it is just the right idea," said Senator Gillibrand.

"It's time to reboot the U.S. military's approach towards sexual violence by reforming the military justice system, preventing sexual violence, empowering victims to come forward and prosecuting sex crimes. Failing to crack down on a corrosive culture or on individuals who use sexual violence as a means of power will create lingering institutional problems that jeopardize morale and impact recruitment and retention of troops," Senator Grassley said. "The bipartisan Military Justice Improvement Act would give members of the Armed Forces more confidence in the military system of justice, including protection from sexual violence and prosecution for those who violate the rule of law."

"For the last two decades, every Secretary of Defense has promised a zero tolerance policy for sexual assault," Senator Boxer said. "We need to reform our military justice system so that survivors of sexual assault will finally feel confident reporting these heinous crimes knowing that justice will be served."

"The vast majority of our service members are honorable and upstanding individuals. In the instance when one is accused of a serious crime, especially one of harassment or assault, the allegation needs to be taken seriously and conflicts of interest should not impact whether a crime is prosecuted properly," said Senator Paul.

"Sexual abuse in the military is a grave violation of trust and the duty we owe to protect our men and women in uniform," said Senator Cruz. "Despite good-faith efforts from the chain of command, sexual assault remains a persistent problem. We must act to ensure that assaults are prevented and victims of assault are able to report any crimes that occur. Senator Gillibrand should be commended for her leadership working to modernize our military justice system to protect our men and women from sexual assault, and this amendment makes real progress in that regard. Several of our strongest allies such as Israel, the United Kingdom, and Germany have made similar reforms to their military justice systems, and seen marked improvement. I support this amendment and believe it will improve readiness and capability so that the United States military remains the greatest fighting force in the world."

"Our service members deserve the opportunity to report assaults without fear of retaliation and to face a fair military justice system. I am pleased this bipartisan group of my colleagues are rallying behind these changes to fight sexual assaults in the military," said Senator Hirono.

"Recent incidents involving alleged sexual assault by military personnel assigned to stop them, dramatize the urgent need to give this problem greatly heightened priority," Senator Blumenthal said. "We must have action now, not merely plans or promises. When sexual assault protectors become perpetrators military order and discipline become a mockery. For victims already afraid to come forward before these incidents, the chilling effect is incalculable. Sexual assault is a vicious, predatory crime that must be vigorously investigated and punished in the military so that more survivors will be encouraged to report it and more perpetrators will be deterred from committing it. We have the best and strongest military force in the history of the nation and the world, and our men and women in uniform deserve a military justice system worthy of their excellence."

"To be sure, the vast, overwhelming majority of our military personnel are honorable, conscientious, and respectful individuals, not rapists or harassers. It is for their sake that the pattern of covering up, blaming the victim, and failing to provide even the most basic protections that has been all too common for far too long must end," said Senator Collins. "What does it say about us as a people, as the nation, as the foremost military in the world when some of our service members have more to fear from their fellow soldiers than from the enemy? This epidemic of sexual abuse cannot stand. We must ensure that justice is swift and certain to the criminals who have perpetuated these crimes."

"I've just heard too much from Alaskans, I've read too much of cases nationwide, to say, 'Well, maybe we just need to nibble around the edges here on this,'" Senator Murkowski said. "There is consensus from the Pentagon to the bottom of the chain of command that the current system has not been working. The number of victims we see coming forward is evidence that it is not working. And so if we need to reform the military-justice system in this way, I'm prepared to take that step."

"Protecting our men and women in uniform is one of our most important responsibilities but sadly, the Pentagon has failed to reduce incidents of sexual assault in the military. Removing responsibility for investigation and prosecution of these crimes from the chain of command will eliminate conflicts of interest, improve the professionalism of the handling of these crimes, and most importantly send a message to victims that the status quo will no longer be tolerated," said Senator Shaheen.

The problem of sexual assault in the military is not new, neither are the pledges of "zero tolerance" from commanders, which date all the way back to then-Secretary of Defense Dick Cheney in 1992. The Military Justice Improvement Act would for the first time remove the decision whether to take a case to special or general court-martial completely out of the chain of command and give that discretion to experienced military prosecutors for all crimes punishable by one year or more in confinement, except crimes that are uniquely military in nature, such as disobeying orders or going AWOL.

Many of our allied modern militaries have reporting outside of the chain of command, such as Britain, Canada, Israel, Germany, Norway and Australia. For example, the British military has prosecutors making trial decisions for all crimes through the Service Prosecuting Authority (SPA) within Britain's Ministry of Defense.

The Military Justice Improvement Act also:

- Provides the offices of the military chiefs of staff with the authority and discretion to establish courts, empanel juries and choose judges to hear cases (i.e. convening authority).

- This legislation does not amend Article 15. Commanding officers will still be able to order non-judicial punishment for lesser offenses not directed to trial by the prosecutors.

According to the FY2012 SAPRO report released earlier this year by the Defense Department, an estimated 26,000 cases of sexual assault or unwanted sexual contact occurred in FY2012, a 37% increase from FY2011. This number does not include incidents of sexual harassment. The Pentagon defines unwanted sexual contact as: "…intentional sexual contact that was against a person's will or occurred when the person did not or could not consent. The term describes completed and attempted oral, anal, and vaginal penetration with any body part or object, and the unwanted touching of genitalia and other sexually related areas of the body."

Meanwhile, overall rates of reporting dropped from 13.5% in 2011 to 9.8% in 2012. In 2011, victims reported 3,192 out of 19,000 incidents, compared to 2012, where victims reported just 3,374 out of 26,000 incidents. While the number of perpetrators convicted of committing a sexual assault increased from 191 in 2011 to 238 in 2012, the conviction rate dropped from 1% in 2011 to 0.9% in 2012.

Of the 3,374 total reports in 2012, 2,558 reports were unrestricted, which means they were actionable. Of those unrestricted reports, 27 percent were for rape, 35 percent were for abusive and wrongful sexual contact, and 28 percent were for aggravated sexual assault and sexual assault. The remaining cases were for aggravated sexual contact, nonconsensual sodomy, indecent assault and attempts to commit those offenses.

Also according to the FY2012 SAPRO report, across the Services, 74% of females and 60% of males perceived one or more barriers to reporting sexual assault. 62% of victims who reported a sexual assault indicated they perceived some form of professional, social, and/or administrative retaliation.

The Military Justice Improvement Act is cosponsored by a bipartisan coalition of 33 Senators: Mark Begich (D-AK), Richard Blumenthal (D-CT), Barbara Boxer (D-CA), Susan Collins (R-ME), Chris Coons (D-DE), Dianne Feinstein (D-CA), Al Franken (D-MN), Chuck Grassley (R-IA), Mazie Hirono (D-HI), Mike Johanns (R-NE), Barbara Mikulski (D-MD), Mark Pryor (D-AR), Jay Rockefeller (D-WV), Brian Schatz (D-HI), Jeanne Shaheen (D-NH), Elizabeth Warren (D-MA), Lisa Murkowski (R-AK), Tim Johnson (D-SD), Tom Carper (D-DE), Robert Casey (D-PA), Jeff Merkley (D-OR), Heidi Heitkamp (D-ND), Martin Heinrich (D-NM), Tammy Baldwin (D- WI), Charles E. Schumer (D-NY), Patrick Leahy (D-VT), Robert Menendez (D-NJ), Ben Cardin (D-MD), Ron Wyden (D-OR), Maria Cantwell (D-WA), Bernie Sanders (I-VT), and Tom Harkin (D-IA).

The Military Justice Improvement Act is supported by the International Federation of Professional & Technical Engineers (IFPTE), CLC, AFL-CIO and all the leading victim's advocates groups, including but not limited to, Service Women's Action Network (SWAN), Protect Our Defenders (POD), Iraq and Afghanistan Veterans of America (IAVA), and the National Women's Law Center and Vietnam Veterans of America.

.

There are of course numerous other bills related to sexual assault and the military, and they, too demonstrate bipartisan support. Several of them are listed here.

S871

Combating Military Sexual Assault Act of 2013

A Senate bill, co-sponsored by Republican Senator Ayotte and Democratic Senators Patty Murray of Washington and Richard Blumenthal of Connecticut, that would create a special counsel for victims of sexual assault committed by a member of the armed forces

Sponsor: <u>Sen Murray, Patty</u> [WA] (introduced 5/7/2013)   <u>Cosponsors</u> (38) (again, Republicans are in italics)

Sen Ayotte, Kelly [NH] - 5/7/2013
Sen Begich, Mark [AK] - 6/3/2013
Sen Bennet, Michael F. [CO] - 5/14/2013
Sen Blumenthal, Richard [CT] - 5/7/2013
Sen Brown, Sherrod [OH] - 5/23/2013
Sen Burr, Richard [NC] - 5/21/2013
Sen Cantwell, Maria [WA] - 5/13/2013
Sen Cardin, Benjamin L. [MD] - 5/13/2013
Sen Casey, Robert P., Jr. [PA] - 6/4/2013
Sen Chambliss, Saxby [GA] - 5/8/2013
Sen Coons, Christopher A. [DE] - 5/9/2013
Sen Cornyn, John [TX] - 5/15/2013
Sen Durbin, Richard [IL] - 5/15/2013
Sen Feinstein, Dianne [CA] - 5/14/2013
Sen Hagan, Kay [NC] - 6/3/2013
Sen Harkin, Tom [IA] - 5/15/2013
Sen Heitkamp, Heidi [ND] - 5/20/2013
Sen Heller, Dean [NV] - 6/3/2013
Sen Hirono, Mazie K. [HI] - 5/15/2013
Sen Hoeven, John [ND] - 7/10/2013
Sen Isakson, Johnny [GA] - 5/16/2013
Sen Johanns, Mike [NE] - 5/16/2013
Sen Johnson, Tim [SD] - 6/3/2013
Sen King, Angus S. Jr. [ME] - 5/16/2013 (independent)
Sen Klobuchar, Amy [MN] - 5/20/2013
Sen Landrieu, Mary L. [LA] - 5/21/2013
Sen McCain, John [AZ] - 5/13/2013
Sen Merkley, Jeff [OR] - 6/4/2013
Sen Murkowski, Lisa [AK] - 5/8/2013
Sen Portman, Rob [OH] - 5/20/2013
Sen Rockefeller, John D., IV [WV] - 6/3/2013
Sen Schatz, Brian [HI] - 5/16/2013

Sen Shaheen, Jeanne [NH] - 5/9/2013
Sen Tester, Jon [MT] - 5/9/2013
Sen Thune, John [SD] - 6/3/2013
Sen Toomey, Pat [PA] - 5/23/2013
Sen Udall, Mark [CO] - 5/23/2013
Sen Warren, Elizabeth [MA] - 5/22/2013.

.

H.R.430
Protect Our Military Trainees Act

A House bill, co-sponsored by Democratic Rep. Jackie Speier of California and Republican Rep. Joe Heck of Nevada, that would amend the Uniform Code of Military Justice to prohibit sexual acts and sexual contact between military instructors including drill instructors and recruiting commanders and their trainees;

Sponsor: <u>Rep Speier, Jackie</u> [CA-14] (introduced 1/25/2013)   <u>Cosponsors</u> (4)

COSPONSORS(4), ALPHABETICAL

Rep Heck, Joseph J. [NV-3] - 1/25/2013
Rep Johnson, Henry C. "Hank," Jr. [GA-4] - 4/16/2013
Rep Lowey, Nita M. [NY-17] - 5/17/2013
Rep Quigley, Mike [IL-5] - 4/16/2013

.

H.R.1864

To amend title 10, United States Code, to require an Inspector General investigation of allegations of retaliatory personnel actions taken in response to making protected communications regarding sexual assault.

Sponsor: <u>Rep Walorski, Jackie</u> [IN-2] (introduced 5/7/2013)   <u>Cosponsors</u> (112)

Requires the Inspector General of the Department of Defense (DOD), the Department of Homeland Security (DHS) with respect to the Coast Guard, or any of the military departments to investigate allegations of retaliatory personnel actions taken in response to making protected communications to such Inspector General regarding alleged instances of rape, sexual assault, or other forms of sexual misconduct in violation of the Uniform Code of Military Justice.

COSPONSORS(112), ALPHABETICAL (Republicans are in italics)

Rep Amodei, Mark E. [NV-2] - 6/12/2013
Rep Bachmann, Michele [MN-6] - 5/15/2013

Rep Barber, Ron [AZ-2] - 5/17/2013

Rep Beatty, Joyce [OH-3] - 6/3/2013

Rep Bera, Ami [CA-7] - 6/6/2013

Rep Black, Diane [TN-6] - 6/6/2013

Rep Blackburn, Marsha [TN-7] - 5/9/2013

Rep Brady, Robert A. [PA-1] - 5/15/2013

Rep Braley, Bruce L. [IA-1] - 6/26/2013

Rep Bridenstine, Jim [OK-1] - 6/6/2013

Rep Brooks, Susan W. [IN-5] - 5/9/2013

Rep Brownley, Julia [CA-26] - 5/22/2013

Rep Bucshon, Larry [IN-8] - 6/6/2013

Rep Bustos, Cheri [IL-17] - 5/13/2013

Rep Capito, Shelley Moore [WV-2] - 5/9/2013

Rep Carson, Andre [IN-7] - 5/15/2013

Rep Cartwright, Matt [PA-17] - 5/13/2013

Rep Castor, Kathy [FL-14] - 6/6/2013

Rep Castro, Joaquin [TX-20] - 6/13/2013

Rep Coffman, Mike [CO-6] - 5/17/2013

Rep Cook, Paul [CA-8] - 6/6/2013

Rep Cramer, Kevin [ND] - 6/6/2013

Rep Daines, Steve [MT] - 5/9/2013

Rep Davis, Rodney [IL-13] - 5/9/2013

Rep DelBene, Suzan K. [WA-1] - 6/6/2013

Rep Duckworth, Tammy [IL-8] - 6/6/2013

Rep Ellmers, Renee L. [NC-2] - 5/17/2013

Rep Enyart, William L. [IL-12] - 6/6/2013

Rep Eshoo, Anna G. [CA-18] - 6/3/2013

Rep Esty, Elizabeth H. [CT-5] - 6/6/2013

Rep Farenthold, Blake [TX-27] - 5/17/2013

Rep Foxx, Virginia [NC-5] - 5/16/2013

Rep Frankel, Lois [FL-22] - 5/22/2013

Rep Fudge, Marcia L. [OH-11] - 5/16/2013

Rep Gabbard, Tulsi [HI-2] - 5/9/2013

Rep Gallego, Pete P. [TX-23] - 6/3/2013

Rep Gardner, Cory [CO-4] - 6/3/2013

Rep Gibson, Christopher P. [NY-19] - 6/3/2013

Rep Granger, Kay [TX-12] - 6/6/2013

Rep Grijalva, Raul M. [AZ-3] - 6/12/2013

Rep Hartzler, Vicky [MO-4] - 6/6/2013

Rep Heck, Denny [WA-10] - 6/12/2013

Rep Heck, Joseph J. [NV-3] - 6/6/2013

Rep Herrera Beutler, Jaime [WA-3] - 5/22/2013

Rep Horsford, Steven A. [NV-4] - 6/3/2013

Rep Hudson, Richard [NC-8] - 6/3/2013

Rep Hunter, Duncan D. [CA-50] - 6/6/2013

Rep Jeffries, Hakeem S. [NY-8] - 6/6/2013

Rep Jenkins, Lynn [KS-2] - 6/3/2013

Rep Joyce, David P. [OH-14] - 6/6/2013

Rep Keating, William R. [MA-9] - 6/12/2013

Rep Kelly, Robin L. [IL-2] - 6/3/2013

Rep Kennedy, Joseph P. III [MA-4] - 5/9/2013

Rep Kildee, Daniel T [MI-5] - 6/3/2013

Rep Kilmer, Derek [WA-6] - 5/22/2013

Rep Kirkpatrick, Ann [AZ-1] - 6/6/2013

Rep Kline, John [MN-2] - 5/15/2013

Rep Kuster, Ann M. [NH-2] - 5/9/2013

Rep Lamborn, Doug [CO-5] - 6/6/2013

Rep Latham, Tom [IA-3] - 6/3/2013

Rep Latta, Robert E. [OH-5] - 5/15/2013

Rep Lowenthal, Alan S. [CA-47] - 6/6/2013

Rep Lujan Grisham, Michelle [NM-1] - 6/3/2013

Rep Lummis, Cynthia M. [WY] - 6/6/2013

Rep Maffei, Daniel B. [NY-24] - 6/3/2013

Rep Maloney, Sean Patrick [NY-18] - 6/3/2013

Rep McCollum, Betty [MN-4] - 6/26/2013

Rep McMorris Rodgers, Cathy [WA-5] - 5/15/2013

Rep Meng, Grace [NY-6] - 6/3/2013

Rep Messer, Luke [IN-6] - 5/22/2013

Rep Miller, Candice S. [MI-10] - 6/3/2013

Rep Miller, Jeff [FL-1] - 6/3/2013

Rep Murphy, Patrick [FL-18] - 6/3/2013

Rep Nadler, Jerrold [NY-10] - 6/12/2013

Rep Negrete McLeod, Gloria [CA-35] - 6/3/2013

Rep Noem, Kristi L. [SD] - 5/9/2013

Rep Nolan, Richard M. [MN-8] - 6/6/2013

Rep Nugent, Richard B. [FL-11] - 5/13/2013

Rep O'Rourke, Beto [TX-16] - 6/3/2013

Rep Paulsen, Erik [MN-3] - 5/16/2013

Rep Pingree, Chellie [ME-1] - 6/6/2013

Rep Pocan, Mark [WI-2] - 6/3/2013

Rep Reed, Tom [NY-23] - 6/13/2013

Rep Rigell, E. Scott [VA-2] - 5/9/2013

Rep Roby, Martha [AL-2] - 6/3/2013

Rep Roe, David P. [TN-1] - 6/6/2013

Rep Rokita, Todd [IN-4] - 6/6/2013

Rep Ros-Lehtinen, Ileana [FL-27] - 6/3/2013

Rep Roybal-Allard, Lucille [CA-40] - 6/6/2013

Rep Ruiz, Raul [CA-36] - 6/6/2013

Rep Rush, Bobby L. [IL-1] - 6/3/2013

Rep Ryan, Tim [OH-13] - 5/9/2013

Rep Sanchez, Loretta [CA-46] - 5/7/2013

Rep Schwartz, Allyson Y. [PA-13] - 5/22/2013

Rep Scott, Austin [GA-8] - 6/6/2013

Rep Shea-Porter, Carol [NH-1] - 6/3/2013

Rep Shuster, Bill [PA-9] - 6/12/2013

Rep Sinema, Kyrsten [AZ-9] - 6/3/2013

Rep Southerland, Steve II [FL-2] - 6/6/2013

Rep Speier, Jackie [CA-14] - 5/14/2013

Rep Stockman, Steve [TX-36] - 5/13/2013

Rep Stutzman, Marlin A. [IN-3] - 5/15/2013

Rep Swalwell, Eric [CA-15] - 6/3/2013

Rep Tierney, John F. [MA-6] - 6/3/2013

Rep Titus, Dina [NV-1] - 6/6/2013

Rep Tsongas, Niki [MA-3] - 5/15/2013

Rep Turner, Michael R. [OH-10] - 5/15/2013

Rep Vargas, Juan [CA-51] - 6/6/2013

Rep Wagner, Ann [MO-2] - 6/3/2013

Rep Wenstrup, Brad R. [OH-2] - 6/3/2013

Rep Yoho, Ted S. [FL-3] - 5/9/2013

Rep Young, Todd C. [IN-9] - 5/22/2013.

.

S.871
Combating Military Sexual Assault Act of 2013

Sponsor: <u>Sen Murray, Patty</u> [WA] (introduced 5/7/2013)   <u>Cosponsors</u> (38)

Combating Military Sexual Assault Act of 2013 - Directs each military department Secretary to implement a program providing a Special Victims' Counsel (Counsel) to a victim of a sexual assault committed by a member of the Armed Forces (member). Outlines Counsel qualifications and duties, including providing advice and assistance in connection with criminal and civil legal matters related to the assault.

Allows a member or member dependent who is a victim of an assault by another member to receive Counsel assistance.

COSPONSORS(38), ALPHABETICAL (Republicans in italics)

Sen Ayotte, Kelly [NH] - 5/7/2013
Sen Begich, Mark [AK] - 6/3/2013
Sen Bennet, Michael F. [CO] - 5/14/2013
Sen Blumenthal, Richard [CT] - 5/7/2013
Sen Brown, Sherrod [OH] - 5/23/2013
Sen Burr, Richard [NC] - 5/21/2013
Sen Cantwell, Maria [WA] - 5/13/2013
Sen Cardin, Benjamin L. [MD] - 5/13/2013
Sen Casey, Robert P., Jr. [PA] - 6/4/2013
Sen Chambliss, Saxby [GA] - 5/8/2013
Sen Coons, Christopher A. [DE] - 5/9/2013
Sen Cornyn, John [TX] - 5/15/2013
Sen Durbin, Richard [IL] - 5/15/2013
Sen Feinstein, Dianne [CA] - 5/14/2013
Sen Hagan, Kay [NC] - 6/3/2013
Sen Harkin, Tom [IA] - 5/15/2013
Sen Heitkamp, Heidi [ND] - 5/20/2013
Sen Heller, Dean [NV] - 6/3/2013
Sen Hirono, Mazie K. [HI] - 5/15/2013
Sen Hoeven, John [ND] - 7/10/2013
Sen Isakson, Johnny [GA] - 5/16/2013
Sen Johanns, Mike [NE] - 5/16/2013
Sen Johnson, Tim [SD] - 6/3/2013
Sen King, Angus S. Jr. [ME] - 5/16/2013 (independent)
Sen Klobuchar, Amy [MN] - 5/20/2013
Sen Landrieu, Mary L. [LA] - 5/21/2013
Sen McCain, John [AZ] - 5/13/2013
Sen Merkley, Jeff [OR] - 6/4/2013
Sen Murkowski, Lisa [AK] - 5/8/2013
Sen Portman, Rob [OH] - 5/20/2013
Sen Rockefeller, John D., IV [WV] - 6/3/2013
Sen Schatz, Brian [HI] - 5/16/2013
Sen Shaheen, Jeanne [NH] - 5/9/2013
Sen Tester, Jon [MT] - 5/9/2013

Sen Thune, John [SD] - 6/3/2013
Sen Toomey, Pat [PA] - 5/23/2013
Sen Udall, Mark [CO] - 5/23/2013
Sen Warren, Elizabeth [MA] - 5/22/2013.

.

S.548
Military Sexual Assault Prevention Act of 2013

Sponsor: <u>Sen Klobuchar, Amy</u> [MN] (introduced 3/13/2013)   <u>Cosponsors</u> (5)

Prohibits any person convicted under federal or state law of rape, sexual assault, forcible sodomy, or incest from being commissioned or enlisting in the Armed Forces. Requires administrative separation from the Armed Forces, when not punitively discharged, for any member of the Armed Forces (member) on active duty, and any reserve member in an active status, who is convicted of rape, sexual assault, forcible sodomy, or an attempt thereof (covered offenses). Allows the Secretary of the military department concerned to waive such a separation in the interests of national security on a case-by-case basis.

COSPONSORS(5), ALPHABETICAL (Republicans are in italics)

Sen Baldwin, Tammy [WI] - 6/10/2013
Sen Chambliss, Saxby [GA] - 4/9/2013
Sen Durbin, Richard [IL] - 6/24/2013
Sen Harkin, Tom [IA] - 5/8/2013
Sen Murkowski, Lisa [AK] - 3/13/2013

.

H.R.2002
Combating Military Sexual Assault Act of 2013

Sponsor: <u>Rep Ryan, Tim</u> [OH-13] (introduced 5/15/2013)   <u>Cosponsors</u> (31)

Combating Military Sexual Assault Act of 2013 - Directs each military department Secretary to implement a program providing a Special Victims' Counsel (Counsel) to a victim of a sexual assault committed by a member of the Armed Forces (member). Outlines Counsel qualifications and duties, including providing legal representation and assistance in connection with criminal and civil legal matters related to the assault. Provides conditions for legal representation in court, and requires the Manual for Courts-Martial to be revised to allow for such representation.

Allows a member or member dependent who is a victim of a sexual assault by another member to receive Counsel assistance. Requires such victim to be informed of the availability of such assistance at the time the victim originally seeks assistance from a sexual response coordinator or sexual assault victim advocate, a military criminal investigator, a victim/witness liaison, a trial counsel, health care providers, or any other personnel designated by the Secretary concerned. Makes such assistance available regardless of whether the victim elects unrestricted or restricted (confidential) reporting of the incident.

Provides additional duties of the Director of the Sexual Assault Prevention and Response Office within the Department of Defense (DOD), including: (1) providing guidance and assistance for the military departments in addressing matters relating to sexual assault prevention and response, (2) acting as liaison between DOD and other federal and state agencies on sexual assault prevention and response programs, and (3) overseeing development of program guidance and joint planning objectives in support of such program. Requires the Director to also collect, maintain, and disseminate data of the military departments concerning sexual assault prevention and response.

Amends the Uniform Code of Military Justice (UCMJ) to provide for disposition and other requirements in connection with sex-related offenses, and to provide for victims' rights under such actions (including the right to a Counsel).

Requires a convening authority (the official acting on the sentence of a court-martial), when taking any action other than approving a sentence, to prepare a written justification of such action which shall be made part of the record of the court-martial. Prohibits a convening authority from: (1) dismissing or setting aside a finding of guilty, or (2) reducing a finding of guilty to a finding of guilty to a lesser included offense.

Amends the National Defense Authorization Act for Fiscal Year 2012 to require the National Guard of each state and territory to ensure that a sexual assault response coordinator is available at all times to its members.

COSPONSORS(31), ALPHABETICAL (Republicans are in italics)

Rep Bonner, Jo [AL-1] - 5/17/2013
Rep Brownley, Julia [CA-26] - 6/11/2013
Rep Calvert, Ken [CA-42] - 6/3/2013
Rep Cartwright, Matt [PA-17] - 7/25/2013
Rep Cole, Tom [OK-4] - 5/15/2013
Rep Crenshaw, Ander [FL-4] - 5/15/2013
Rep Cummings, Elijah E. [MD-7] - 7/8/2013
Rep DeLauro, Rosa L. [CT-3] - 7/10/2013
Rep DelBene, Suzan K. [WA-1] - 6/5/2013
Rep Frelinghuysen, Rodney P. [NJ-11] - 5/17/2013
Rep Granger, Kay [TX-12] - 5/15/2013
Rep Jones, Walter B., Jr. [NC-3] - 6/27/2013
Rep Kaptur, Marcy [OH-9] - 5/15/2013

Rep Kingston, Jack [GA-1] - 6/11/2013
Rep Kuster, Ann M. [NH-2] - 5/15/2013
Rep Larsen, Rick [WA-2] - 5/21/2013
Rep Lowey, Nita M. [NY-17] - 5/15/2013
Rep McCollum, Betty [MN-4] - 5/15/2013
Rep McGovern, James P. [MA-2] - 7/10/2013
Rep Meeks, Gregory W. [NY-5] - 7/8/2013
Rep Meng, Grace [NY-6] - 6/25/2013
Rep Moran, James P. [VA-8] - 6/3/2013
Rep Nadler, Jerrold [NY-10] - 6/12/2013
Rep Nunnelee, Alan [MS-1] - 5/21/2013
Rep Owens, William L. [NY-21] - 5/17/2013
Rep Pingree, Chellie [ME-1] - 6/14/2013
Rep Rush, Bobby L. [IL-1] - 5/17/2013
Rep Shea-Porter, Carol [NH-1] - 6/25/2013
Rep Sinema, Kyrsten [AZ-9] - 6/6/2013
Rep Visclosky, Peter J. [IN-1] - 6/3/2013
Rep Walz, Timothy J. [MN-1] - 7/10/2013

www.ingramcontent.com/pod-product-compliance
Lightning Source LLC
Chambersburg PA
CBHW080240180526
45167CB00006B/2349